THE
NEW ENGLAND
MILTON

K. P. Van Anglen

THE
NEW ENGLAND
MILTON

Literary Reception and
Cultural Authority
in the
Early Republic

The Pennsylvania State University Press
University Park, Pennsylvania

Library of Congress Cataloging-in-Publication Data

Van Anglen, K. P.
The New England Milton: literary reception and cultural authority in the early
republic / Kevin Van Anglen.
    p.   cm.
Includes bibliographical references and index.
ISBN 0-271-00848-2 (alk. paper)
    1. Milton, John, 1608–1674—Appreciation—New England. 2. American liter-
ature—New England—History and criticism. 3. American literature—English influences. 4. Politics and literature—New England. 5. Milton, John, 1608–1674—Influence. 6. New England—Intellectual life. I. Title.
PR3588.V36 1992
821'.4—dc20   91–41333
                                                                            CIP

It is the policy of The Pennsylvania State University Press to use acid-free paper for
the first printing of all clothbound books. Publications on uncoated stock satisfy the
minimum requirements of American National Standard for Information Sciences—
Permanence of Paper for Printed Library Materials, ANSI Z39.48–1984.

CONTENTS

PREFACE

John Milton's influence has long been a subject of critical inquiry. Even before R. D. Havens, some seventy years ago, wrote his pioneering study of the poet's impact on eighteenth and early nineteenth-century British verse, Milton's effect on English literature was well known. Similarly, George Sensabaugh's 1964 account of Milton's place in colonial and postrevolutionary American high culture reinforced earlier impressions of him as a new world figure; and more recently, Harold Bloom and his students have shown—again, not for the first time—how central Milton was both psychologically and intertextually to the Anglo-American romantic and postromantic traditions.[1] Despite this, however, Milton's influence on American romanticism has until now not received full critical treatment (something that is all the more surprising because of his obvious importance to such authors as Emerson, Thoreau, Brockden Brown, Cooper, Stowe, Fuller, Hawthorne, Melville, and Whitman). *The New England Milton* is intended to fill this gap by providing readers with the first extended account of the poet's reception in antebellum America. It will do so by concentrating on Milton's place in

1. In addition to being good examples of the older sort of influence study, R. D. Havens, *The Influence of Milton on English Poetry* (Cambridge, Mass.: Harvard University Press, 1922), and George F. Sensabaugh, *Milton in Early America* (Princeton, N.J.: Princeton University Press, 1964) remain the standard (though now dated) treatments of Milton's influence on English and American literature during the eighteenth and early nineteenth centuries. Harold Bloom's many sustained or incidental treatments of Milton's influence on Anglo-American romanticism are too numerous to mention; but see also Leslie Brisman, *Milton's Poetry of Choice and Its Romantic Heirs* (Ithaca, N.Y.: Cornell University Press, 1973); Julie Ellison, *Emerson's Romantic Style* (Princeton, N.J.: Princeton University Press, 1984); and Robert Weisbuch, *Atlantic Double-Cross: American Literature and British Influence in the Age of Emerson* (Chicago: University of Chicago Press, 1986).

the thought of the Unitarians and Transcendentalists, thus presenting a survey of one regional literary group's response, which is meant to act as the preface to a more general treatment of the poet's influence during the decades before the Civil War in a second, companion volume.[2]

In taking up the subject of Milton's reception in Boston and Concord the present work will, however, adopt a broader cultural historical context than Havens or Sensabaugh or Bloom, by seeing the poet's influence as an example of the ways in which literary influence can indicate those sociopolitical tensions in modernity that manifest themselves in its ongoing crisis of authority. The Introduction to *The New England Milton* will thus survey the structural and discrete tensions within colonial New England that helped create the region's conflicted culture and will enumerate the hegemonic responses of the region's dominant class to the crisis of authority that resulted from those tensions. Chapter 1 will then discuss how this background created the cultural politics out of which Milton rose to prominence as a literary influence during the Revolutionary and Federalist periods. In particular it will show two things: first, that the poet—who was himself a classic example of the conflictions of seventeenth-century bourgeois puritanism—was invoked and imitated by the American elite as part of an ideologically consensualist defense of their privilege and authority; and second, that this effort was in vain, as it only served to underscore the contradictions of this hegemonic attempt to accommodate the paradigmatically Arminian demands of hierarchy and order with the antinomian ones of liberty, equality, and personal autonomy. Chapter 1 will also show how this doomed effort continued in New England in the early nineteenth century in Unitarian circles, and Chapter 2 will show how it even overwhelmed the most original and daring Unitarian of them all: William Ellery Channing, whose 1826 review of Milton's *De Doctrina Christiana* represents the most innovative attempt by any upper-class Bostonian of the postrevolutionary era to find a way out of the cultural contradictions of the age.

However, as Chapter 3 will go on to prove, Ralph Waldo Emerson later used Milton to wrestle more successfully with these matters than did his erstwhile coreligionists. For the first half of his career was, in fact, an evolving meditation on Milton, one in which he moved from a conventionally Unitarian view of the poet to that of the profound, but Janus-faced, Milton of *The Divinity School Address* period, to the Milton of the poem "Uriel," which brilliantly bridges the polarizing structures of feeling in New England cul-

---

2. The second volume (tentatively entitled *Milton and the American Renaissance: The Literary Elite and the Coming of the Civil War*) will treat a wide sampling of the major American novelists, essayists, and poets of the antebellum period.

ture by rewriting part of *Paradise Lost*. Chapter 4 will then illustrate Emerson's quick decline after 1842 from this synthetic high point and show how other Transcendentalists (e.g., Jones Very, Margaret Fuller, and Theodore Parker) also used Milton to address their situation—though mostly by falling back into the contradictions of the Milton of their dominant class predecessors. Finally, Chapter 5 will introduce Thoreau, a Yankee Miltonist who, in *A Week on the Concord and Merrimack Rivers, Walden,* and *The Maine Woods,* effectively followed up on Emerson's use of the poet and his works as a means of synthesizing Anglo-American culture's structures of feeling, thereby creating a rhetoric of authority unlike any seen in the region during the previous two centuries. It was a rhetoric that aimed to empower the American poet to speak directly to the crisis of modern civilization, and in creating it Thoreau at his best set a precedent for the other great Miltonists of his generation, a challenge most ably met (as the second volume will show) by the least elitist of them all: Walt Whitman.

As this may suggest, this volume adopts much of the terminology and shares many of the conclusions about Anglo-American culture of the "new historicism" that informs the most recent (albeit tangential) treatment of Milton's reception in the New World: Keith W. F. Stavely's *Puritan Legacies: "Paradise Lost" and the New England Tradition.* At the same time, however, *The New England Milton* differs in important ways in both focus and methodology from that study and the kind of historiography it practices. For in terms of focus, Stavely, despite the subtitle of his excellent book, is not really interested at all in the historical impact of Milton and his writings on New England culture; rather, he is concerned with exploring Puritanism's bourgeois cultural conflictions and their legacy of false consciousness to the exclusion of such issues as historical impact (which have traditionally been associated with the study of "high culture"). Stavely justifies this emphasis on the basis of his belief that a culture is ultimately constituted by what Raymond Williams calls its "structure of feeling" and that therefore its "high culture" is merely a series of ideological formations linked to strategies of dominant class control that are best understood in terms of "Antonio Gramsci's concept of hegemony." *Puritan Legacies* consequently starts with the assumption that the "structure of feeling" in a culture indicates a level of experience and reality that is deeper and more pervasive than that constituted by "ideology." For whereas

> ideology primarily denotes the "articulate and formal meanings, values and beliefs which a dominant class develops and propagates," hegemony functions in a way that is both socially more pervasive and

psychically deeper. It amounts in effect to "a saturation of the whole
process of living," so much so that "the pressures and limits of what
can ultimately be seen as a specific economic, political, and cultural
system seem to most of us the pressures and limits of simple experience and common sense." So within Williams's overall theoretical
construct, hegemony constitutes his recognition that in any place and
at any time, the structure of feeling is relative to the configurations of
political, social, and cultural power. It is neither spontaneous expression nor imposed indoctrination, but rather a synthesis of the two.[3]

Thus, in Stavely's view, one cannot read a poem like *Paradise Lost* in intertextual isolation (as Bloom does) or with the political naïveté of traditional
literary history; rather, one must read it paradigmatically instead (in the
manner of Christopher Hill) as the "analogue to the history of the [English]
Puritan commonwealth par excellence": as a work that consciously addresses
and yet also manifests the disintegrative bourgeois tendencies at the center of
seventeenth-century English culture. Moreover, because of the priority of
structural feeling over ideology, Stavely seems to argue implicitly that it is
only this paradigmatic dimension of Milton's epic (or any of his other works)
that is of real use to the literary historian. This is certainly the reason why the
poem merits mention in the subtitle of his own study, for he believes that it
is only because "the broad course of modern Anglo-American development . . . was crucially shaped by Puritan ideology and sensibility" (i.e., by
that combination of "spontaneous expression" and "imposed indoctrination" which constituted the Puritan structure of feeling) that one can say that
in *Paradise Lost* the supreme "poet of the Puritans may also have offered in
advance a paradigm for" the cultural contradictions of New England and
America generally, even "down to the verge of our own day."[4]

There is much to be said for this approach, particularly as a way of ana-
lyzing New England culture, since in addition to its powerful theoretical
claims "the new historicism" is (in English-speaking countries at least) itself
also partly an offshoot of the study of Anglo-American Puritanism. Stavely's
rejection of the ideology of the dominant class as his frame of reference (like
his emphasis on the experiential dimension of New England's cultural con-

3. Keith W. F. Stavely, *Puritan Legacies: "Paradise Lost" and the New England Tradition,
1630–1890* (Ithaca, N.Y.: Cornell University Press, 1987), 10–11. Stavely mostly draws upon
material here from Raymond Williams's chapter on "Hegemony" in *Marxism and Literature* (Oxford: Oxford University Press, 1977), 108–14.
4. Stavely, *Puritan Legacies*, 7.

flictions) is therefore quite congenial to the facts at hand. One token of this is that in *Puritan Legacies* he convincingly—indeed, brilliantly—uses a broader survey than usual of the region's textual remains in order to show how the histories of two Massachusetts towns reflect the central fissures in New England culture as they actually spread over a 250-year period through "the practical consciousness" (that "level on which 'meanings and values . . . are actively lived and felt' ") of folk both high and low.[5] Moreover, in doing this, Stavely does what the "new historicism" does at its best: he escapes the constrictions often imposed on literary studies by their deep historical implication in the very system of bourgeois interests and ideology that contributes substantially to what Williams terms the "official consciousness."[6] Stavely is on less solid footing, however, when he agrees with Williams that the reason why "artistic and literary expression" have any "place and function . . . within a given society and culture" at all is that "art and literature" are " 'the articulation (often the only fully available articulation)' . . . of exactly this present, practical consciousness . . . the densely interwoven fabric of past, present, and future, of formal belief and spontaneous impulse and intuition, of sociocultural complexity, contradiction, tension, and resolution."[7] For however praiseworthy the refusal to privilege the interests, values, and expression of the elite that motivates this assertion may be, it tends to deny the validity of studying the ideology of the dominant class itself—and with it, the need to study the ways in which the literary production of that class was constituted so as to serve hegemonic ends.

In the case of Milton and the New England tradition the practical effect of this theoretical decision is that Stavely overlooks the principal means by which both Milton the perceived historical figure and his writings actually became present in the consciousness of eighteenth- and nineteenth-century New Englanders: the evolving ideology that justified elite rule itself.[8] And

5. Ibid., 11; this is once more dependent upon Williams (see *Marxism and Literature*, 128–35). For Stavely's own account of his work vis-à-vis that of Perry Miller and other scholars of New England Puritanism who adopt the ideology of the dominant class as their informing context, see *Puritan Legacies*, 101–8.

6. For the historically bourgeois context of Anglo-American literary studies, see Williams, esp. 11–54, 145–64.

7. Stavely, *Puritan Legacies*, 11.

8. In adopting the literary ramifications of the ideology of the New England dominant class as the focus of this study, I will in a sense be working from both Sacvan Bercovitch's theoretical distinction (which is also indebted to Williams) between "an *ideological* consensus" and "a quantitatively measured 'social reality' " and his use of "the concept of the middle class" largely "for its ideological implications, as a term expressing the norms we have come to associate with the free-enterprise system." For despite my acceptance of the facts of Puritan New England's

so, however salutary his modus operandi may be in enhancing our general understanding of Puritanism and its cultural legacy, its displacement of the "official consciousness" as an object for study tends to efface Milton's actual historical place in the New England tradition as well. This is precisely why, in fact, after an initial diagnostic survey of *Paradise Lost* aimed at establishing its paradigmatic status, *Puritan Legacies* ignores both the poem and its author—with the implication that neither was a historical or textual presence in the lives of the region's inhabitants. Yet as shall be seen, Milton should have much more than merely paradigmatic value for students of New England, especially as one approaches the nineteenth century. For as early as the time of the Revolution his works and personal example had been consciously adopted to serve the needs of the elite as it faced the forces that challenged its authority; and from the 1780s on he and his writings were even more prominently used by the intellectuals of upper-class Boston to help reinforce their latest revision of the moderate, bourgeois ideology by which Americans like them (learned professionals within a local dominant class) had long tried to deal with "the profound ambiguities and instabilities that Puritanism introduced into the traditional relations of superiors and inferiors."[9] Their appropriation of Milton and his poetry and prose for this end is, in fact, an almost classic example of the ways in which the "relatively formal and articulated system of meanings, values and beliefs" that constitute the ideology of such a group are developed and propagated through literary texts in order to combat a felt threat to the group's power.[10] For their Milton was an ideologically useful "sainted spirit" whose historic defense of liberty and literary stature could be invoked—thanks to the contradictory impulses within the New England tradition—as precedent for the central role of the bourgeois man of learning in the affairs of a republic. Indeed, so

---

sociocultural diversity and deep divisions, and despite all the arguments about the atypicality of this region and its first settlers, like Bercovitch I believe that "in America, the foundations of that system" of middle-class dominance "were laid in seventeenth-century New England" and had considerable strength, both there and elsewhere. This was not because "Puritan society was . . . middle class, . . . even in the sense that most of its members had 'middling' incomes. Then as always in this country (through the nineteenth century to our own times) the majority of people were 'lower class' "; but because "what the Puritans instituted in New England"— rather less thoroughly than many would once have imagined, I concede—"was effectually a new hierarchical order, ranging not from peasantry to aristocracy and crown, but from lower to higher levels of a relatively fluid free-enterprise structure," an order that is still effectively with us today. (*The American Jeremiad* [Madison: University of Wisconsin Press, 1978], xii–xiii.)

9. Stavely, *Puritan Legacies*, 7.

10. Williams, 109; for a discussion of ideology, the official consciousness, and the dominant class, see esp. 55–71 of his book.

strongly did this version of the poet seem to speak to the crisis of authority facing such men and women that it later almost naturally came to serve as a major device in the strategy by which the writers of the so-called "American Renaissance" tried to play the game of cultural politics as well. For no less than their Puritan or Unitarian ancestors, they too were ever busy building up breastworks against invasion from without—but whether from Heaven or Hell, they knew not.[11]

Before beginning to explore the New England Milton tradition, I would first like to acknowledge the support I have received over the years from a number of friends, colleagues, and institutions. This book had its origins as a Harvard doctoral dissertation written under the supervision of Professor Joel Porte and the late Professor Herschel C. Baker. My research benefited immensely from their attention and learning, as it did from funds generously provided by a Charles Dexter Traveling Fellowship, a Samuel P. Colehour Fellowship in American Studies, and Graduate School of Arts and Sciences scholarships. Professors Walter Jackson Bate, Jr., James Engell, Gwynne Blakemore Evans, and Alan Heimert also kindly read parts of the dissertation, while Professors Briggs Bailey, James Basker, Andrew Delbanco, John Hildebidle, and Elizabeth McKinsey, and Drs. Paul Erickson, Laura Gordon Fisher, Marten Liander, Janet Rich, and Prudence Steiner aided me by their friendship and advice. Similarly, later, when "I was a Bostonian who sojourned in Philadelphia awhile," I was the beneficiary of funding provided for faculty salaries by the Andrew W. Mellon Foundation and of the counsel of Donald and Elizabeth Fox, Sarah Mace, and Professors John Anderson, Michael Berthold, Hennig Cohen, Peter Conn, Rick Delano, Betsy Erkkila, Alan Filreis, Cynthia Fuchs, Daniel Hoffman, Mark Halliday, Ted Irving, Alice Kelley, Gwynne Kennedy, Paul Korshin, Ann McGuire, James Rosier, Robert Y. Turner, Siegfried Wenzel, and William Werpehowski. During that time my good and (in every sense) gracious friend Professor Rebecca Bushnell also read parts of the manuscript, as did Professor Nicholas von Maltzahn of the University of Ottawa. The Department of English and the Institute for Research in the Humanities at the University of Wisconsin,

11. Please note that in general this volume will only give references to Milton's poetry and prose when they are directly cited or discussed, as the editions of the American authors treated here generally give the Miltonic sources of quotations from and allusions to his works made by them. For Milton's poetry, I will use Douglas Bush, ed., *Milton: Poetical Works* (Oxford: Oxford University Press, 1966); for his prose, I will use the edition cited below, Ch. 2, n. 1, or the relevant nineteenth-century edition.

Madison, in addition granted me a Post-Doctoral Fellowship that was crucial to this book's eventual completion, as was the help of the Institute's then director (Professor Robert Kingdon), its staff (Mrs. Loretta Freiling and Mrs. Sharon Granke), and a number of Institute Fellows and Wisconsin faculty members (including Professors William Andrews, David Bethea, Emmett Bennett, Sargent Bush, Jr., Hal Cook, Suzanne Desan, Bill Eamon, Dena Goodman, Philip Harth, Philip Herring, Lynne Keller, Walter Rideout, the late Merton A. Sealts, Jr., Jeffrey Steele, and Howard Weinbrot). Finally, in the last stages of composition my editor, Mr. Philip Winsor, and my fellow Thoreauvians and friends, Professors Philip Gura and Robert D. Richardson, Jr., gave me the benefit of their wisdom and knowledge; and Ms. Eily Pearl proofread the manuscript.

Both Professor Joel Myerson of the University of South Carolina and the University Press of Virginia have kindly given me permission to reprint parts of Chapters 1 and 2 that in an earlier version appeared in *Studies in the American Renaissance: 1983*. The editors of *ESQ: A Journal of the American Renaissance* and the Washington State University Press have granted similar permission for the republication of that part of Chapter 3 which originally appeared in a different form in that journal. The references in Chapter 3 to Emerson's lecture notes on Milton in the John Gorham Palfrey Papers and the quotations from Jones Very's sermons in Chapter 4 are made with the permission of the Houghton Library at Harvard and with the kind cooperation of the curator of manuscripts there, Rodney G. Dennis; and the passages from Jones Very's undergraduate writings quoted in Chapter 4 are cited by permission of the Harvard University Archives and of its curator, Harley P. Holden. Additionally, I have been privileged to use the resources of the Widener, Houghton, and Child Memorial Libraries at Harvard; the Harvard University Archives; the University and Pembroke College Libraries, Cambridge; the Beinecke and University Libraries at Yale; and the libraries of the Thoreau Lyceum, Princeton University, Villanova University, the University of Pennsylvania, the University of Wisconsin at Madison, Haverford College, Saint Anselm College, and Boston College. To them and to their staffs I owe a great deal.

Three other things are worth mentioning. The first is that this book was largely finished while I was a visiting faculty member at Boston College. For that privilege and for much else I wish to thank my colleagues there, Professors Paul Dougherty, Dayton Haskin, John Mahoney, Alan Richardson, Mary Thomas Crane, Philip O'Leary, Paul Schweitzer, S.J., and Chris Wilson. The second is the abiding love and sometimes bemused support of my parents. They have been my first and most influential teachers and are the ones to whom I owe the greatest debt. The third is the fact that *The New England Milton* was completed during a bleak and bitter winter "up country" in New Hampshire when, to my surprise, I grew in learning as in love, not least from my proximity to Saint Anselm Abbey. To the members of that Benedictine community I therefore owe much more than this mere volume.

Eliot House
Harvard University

INTRODUCTION: PURITAN AND EIGHTEENTH-CENTURY BACKGROUND

The origins of New England's long authority crisis reveal themselves when one remembers that, for all its peculiarities, in the "seventeenth century" the region "was an English province, and many of its features" were thus ones that "had long been part of old England."[1] Chief among these were those class divisions and socioeconomic changes that caused Englishmen to disagree and eventually wage civil war during the very years of the area's first settlement. For these divisions and changes not only divided Churchman from Puritan, and royalist from republican, but divided Puritan from Puritan as well—thereby sowing the seeds of later new world discord.

It is now well established that early seventeenth-century English Puritanism was divided into two camps, each of which was further fragmented into numerous subdivisions. One consisted of those among the merchants and gentry whose opposition to Charles Stuart and the bishops was rooted in the class interests first (and perhaps most famously) described by Max Weber and R. H. Tawney.[2] These Puritans sought not to replace hierarchy as the structuring principle of society but merely to achieve their own empowerment as a new, middle-class elite; and they justified this attempt at securing their hegemony through an ideology characterized by moderate Protestant dissent, bourgeois economic and social values, and political constitutionalism. These moderates eventually triumphed at the Glorious Revolution, an

1. David Cressy, *Coming Over: Migration and Communication between England and New England in the Seventeenth Century* (New York: Cambridge University Press, 1987), 292.
2. Max Weber, *The Protestant Ethic and the Spirit of Capitalism*, trans. Talcott Parsons (1904–5; English trans., New York: Charles Scribner's Sons, 1930), and R. H. Tawney, *Religion and the Rise of Capitalism: A Historical Study* (1926; rpt. Gloucester, Mass.: Peter Smith, 1962).

event which solidified their control because it "established the sacred rights of property (abolition of feudal tenures, no arbitrary taxation), gave political power to the propertied (sovereignty of Parliament and common law, abolition of prerogative courts), and removed all impediments to the triumph of the ideology of the men of property—the protestant ethic."

The moderate Puritan party was not the only one to oppose Stuart absolutism, however. "There were . . . two revolutions in mid-seventeenth-century England," not one. In contrast to the moderate "one which succeeded, . . . there was . . . another revolution which never happened, though from time to time it threatened" to. This was not the revolution of "the gentry and merchants who had supported the Parliamentary cause in the civil war, [and who] expected to reconstruct the institutions of society as they wished, to impose their values" much as they later did after "the political settlement of 1688." It was instead the revolution of those who sought more radical goals than "Parliamentary sovereignty, limited monarchy," a financially beneficial "imperialist foreign policy, [and] a world safe for businessmen to make profits in." It was the revolution of the Levelers, Diggers, and Ranters, the radicals and the unwashed: the revolt of those who, had they succeeded, would have enshrined their own lower-class interests by establishing "communal property, a far wider democracy in political and legal institutions, [and] might have disestablished the state church"—thereby calling not only "the values of the old hierarchical society . . . in question, but also the new [bourgeois] values, the protestant ethic itself."[3]

Partisans of both camps emigrated to the New World, and so at its foundation New England was a battleground between the moderate and radical wings of English Puritanism. Moreover, these same conflicting groups (with their contradictory class interests and views on justice, freedom, authority, and individual rights) laid the groundwork for the social tensions that later afflicted the region—tensions that only got worse as they collided with both historical developments and the ideological contradictions of the dominant moderate group, to produce the context within which several generations of New Englanders lived out their lives (as either defenders of

3. Christopher Hill, *The World Turned Upside Down: Radical Ideas during the English Revolution* (London: Maurice Temple Smith, 1972), 12. Among Hill's many works, the following are particularly useful in describing the history and origins of English Puritan radicalism: *Change and Continuity in Seventeenth-Century England* (Cambridge, Mass.: Harvard University Press, 1975), esp. 3–102 and 181–247; *Society and Puritanism in Pre-Revolutionary England* (New York: Schocken, 1964); and *Puritanism and Revolution: Studies in Interpretation of the English Revolution of the Seventeenth Century* (London: Secker and Warburg, 1958), esp. 3–196.

or dissenters from an emergent, secularizing, Protestant, capitalist, constitutionalist order).[4]

The first constituent element in New England's authority crisis was thus the class divisions of seventeenth-century Anglo-American culture. From the start those in positions of religious, political, and cultural authority (the ministers and magistrates who comprised the New World Puritan establishment) not only had much the same class interests as their English counterparts but were challenged by the same kinds of people who had opposed them in the mother country as well. As a result, their attempt to establish a hegemonic order controlled by an elite of moderate gentlemen, clerics, and wealthy bourgeois flew in the face of the fact that, as in England, *"heterogeneity,* not unanimity, actually characterized" their society.[5] The strong centrifugal forces that had given rise to that heterogeneity in England in the first place were then later encouraged over time by a series of discrete New World social, economic, psychological, political, and geographical factors that transformed the province by the 1690s (thus not only further complicating the leadership task of the dominant elite but also guaranteeing that they would not even have the same measure of success as their Old World contemporaries).

Many examples of this interplay between structural class conflict and events exist. For instance, as Philip Gura has recently demonstrated in new detail, the full range of English Puritan religious dissent was present in the colonies from the beginning. The moderate Puritans thus early on faced the same diverse band of radicals in Massachusetts as they had in London or Lincolnshire: from Separatists and Spiritists to Anabaptists, millenarians, and Quakers. The reasons for this are not hard to find, since the class roots and socioeconomic forces behind Protestant radicalism were the same on both sides of the Atlantic; in much the same way, because the class interests of the colonial Puritan leadership were the same as those of their moderate English contemporaries, they responded in like manner to the radical challenge: working tirelessly from the Antinomian crisis in the 1630s on to establish their hegemony by deflecting, suppressing, and (especially) co-opting the dissidents. Yet as Gura also shows, unlike the English Puritans, the leaders of

4. Good discussions of the causes and patterns of conflict in New England and their persistence in the face of attempts at elite dominance can be found in Kenneth Lockridge, *A New England Town, The First Hundred Years: Dedham, Massachusetts, 1636–1736* (New York: W. W. Norton, 1970), and Philip F. Gura, *A Glimpse of Sion's Glory: Puritan Radicalism in New England, 1620–1660* (Middletown, Conn.: Wesleyan University Press, 1984). For Stavely's two brilliant case studies illustrating these patterns, see *Puritan Legacies,* 101–271.

5. Gura, *Sion's Glory,* 7.

Massachusetts Bay were unsuccessful in their effort; for as early as the Restoration it was clear that though they might banish the likes of Anne Hutchinson and Samuel Gorton to the margins of the English settlements, they could not end the threat these radicals posed to their power.

In part this failure to suppress dissent effectively was due to the staying power of the socioeconomic factors and class divisions that had caused it in the first place. The region's socioeconomic instability was simply too deep-seated to be easily eradicated. But in addition, as Gura documents, by 1660 conditions within the province had changed in ways that were even less conducive to the imposition of spiritual consensus than they had been in the beginning, as internal disagreements within the elite, the evolving facts of life in an immigrant setting, an increase in social and class differences, the frustration of New England's millennial and particularist hopes by events in England, generational and gender-role conflicts, and the peculiar psychological pressures imposed by Puritan spirituality all combined to undermine social cohesion and sap the power of the dominant class.[6]

Significantly, however, a third element lay behind the failure by the first two generations of the New England elite to impose religious conformity (a failure that typifies their inability to impose conformity generally). Like their English fellow moderates they were frustrated by the contradictions of their own ideology, which (though "established . . . as predominant in New England" through their efforts) "contained within itself the seeds of sharp ideological conflict."[7] This was because as a system of values and feelings it simultaneously embodied both the very impulses the dominant class sought to repress and those upon which they based their authority: "both the antinomian and Arminian structures of feeling, both the longing for liberation and the requirement of discipline and control."[8] The resulting state of affairs not only strongly encouraged the class-based division between moderate hegemonists and leveling radicals that afflicted the movement but also tended to render moderate Puritanism dysfunctional as an ideology justifying dominant class power.

In other words, in its Arminian form—when it was adopted for the purpose of advancing the interests of the men who ruled Cromwell's England or

6. Gura particularly emphasizes the attempts by the Puritan establishment to co-opt the appeal of the radicals, especially by subtly altering their ecclesiology and image (215–34 and 323–28). As I will show, however, these are only two of a number of strategies adopted by the magistrates and clergy in their ongoing struggle against radical elements.

7. Stavely, *Puritan Legacies*, 106.

8. Ibid., 33. As noted in the preface, Stavely uses the terms "Arminian" and "antinomian" in his book in a paradigmatic (rather than a theologically strict) sense. Unless otherwise noted, in this introduction I follow him in doing so, solely for the sake of argumentative consistency.

Massachusetts Bay—Puritanism inevitably ran up against both the social facts of life and some of the very values it itself most reverently enshrined (such as "the tendency of all Protestantism to affirm inner experience in defiance of external and traditional authority," and its insistence "that imposed rules and regulations were not binding on regenerate Christians").[9] For it centrally affirmed the importance of freedom, autonomy, and personal empowerment yet failed to see the inherently radical ends to which these values logically tended—above all, the fact that

> in a contradictory Puritan world in which the God who had seemed to be an old priest had been slain by the aroused saints, only to be reinstated by some of those same saints as a harsh new presbyter, the progression no bishop, no king, and no civil magistrate could and did lead many of the remaining saints on—both during the English revolution and long after—to no authorities and values of any kind, save those improvised by self-aggrandizing individualism.[10]

Rather than aid the cause of the dominant class in New England, as an ideology Puritanism thus actually cooperated with the structural class oppositions and historical changes that worked against that class's interests in the first half of the century. After 1660, furthermore, matters got even worse from the elite's point of view, as all three elements combined to intensify the crisis of authority in the region.

Perhaps the most striking example of this coalescence of ideological failure, class division, and historical change is the Salem witch trials. For as John Putnam Demos has shown, specific conditions and events at the time of the trials are not enough to explain them, let alone account for the broader phenomenon of witchcraft. The old notion that witchcraft and its persecution are primarily manifestations of local social conflict and crisis neither fully matches what is known historically about the "witches" and their accusers nor accounts for the timing of the outbreaks, either at Salem or elsewhere. In Demos's view the true causes lie beyond the specific sequence of events in Salem or the facts of its social organization and collective psyche as a

---

9. Ibid., 20. These tendencies also have other aspects, of course, ones that are connected neither with the ideology of Puritanism nor with the peculiar historical circumstances of seventeenth-century Anglo-American culture. For instance, it has recently been persuasively suggested that as an ecclesiological model congregationalism is by its nature structurally prone to exactly the sorts of difficulties over authority and autonomy encountered by the moderate Puritans; see Avery Dulles, S. J., *Models of the Church* (Garden City, N.Y.: Doubleday, 1974), and *The Catholicity of the Church and the Structure of Catholicism* (Oxford: Clarendon, 1985).

10. Stavely, *Puritan Legacies*, 77.

community, in witchcraft's relation to the culture of Puritanism. For it is the conjunction of the effects of all three of the elements in New England's authority crisis (the contradictions—and hence, dysfunction—of Puritanism as an ideology, the structural class oppositions within Puritan society, and the concrete psychosocial circumstances of life in Salem at the end of the century) that supply the context out of which the trials emerged.

The events at Salem (like the century-long witchcraft craze as a whole) were, in other words, really rooted in the strife, division, and instability that permeated Puritan society from the beginning, and in the long-term (though often sublimated) sociopsychological patterns of anxiety, revolt, and repression that resulted from them. As Demos shows, the evidence supporting this explanation is overwhelming and in particular helps explain the extent and severity of the Salem trials. For by the 1690s the conflict, contradiction, and turbulence in the region were worse than ever, and the deeper conflicts and divisions within Puritan culture were clearly exacerbated by a "social climate" that in "New England as a whole was . . . unusually strained, anxious, [and] ambivalent." Simply put, "the difficulties experienced during the preceding fifteen years had added up to an almost intolerable sum: the wars" had been "more devastating, the epidemic illnesses more prevalent and 'mortal,' " and (in the aftermath of the Restoration, the Glorious Revolution, King Philip's War, the Half-Way Covenant, and the revocation of the First Charter) "the constitutional [and religious] changes more unsettling, than in any earlier period of the region's history." As a result, even for a society prone to conflict, "the early 1690's seem . . . to have been a time of extreme and pervasive anxiety,"[11] a time well suited for tensions between the demands of order and those of autonomy to combine with events and express themselves in the most virulent incident of witchcraft on record—an incident that called forth repression from a dominant class long strained by opposition and now facing new challenges to its legitimacy both at home and abroad.

"The wonders of the invisible world" and their suppression by an embattled elite are, of course, not the only late seventeenth-century example of the ways in which events harmful to communal cohesion increasingly combined with New England's socioeconomic divisions and Puritanism's ideological contradictions to undermine the power of the dominant class. Other

11. John Putnam Demos, *Entertaining Satan: Witchcraft and the Culture of Early New England* (Oxford: Oxford University Press, 1982), 381–86. See also Paul Boyer and Stephen Nissenbaum, *Salem Possessed: The Social Origins of Witchcraft* (Cambridge, Mass.: Harvard University Press, 1974).

examples can be found to prove the point, even in the history of one family. The public life of John Winthrop, for instance, was to a real degree dominated by a series of individual crises that mostly reflect this larger interplay of forces, from the Antinomian affair and the endless, class-driven disputes between the deputies and the magistrates, to more complex rivalries among various political factions and geographic interests within the Bay Colony. Yet although these attest to the difficulty the first generation of Puritan leaders had in imposing order on their fellow settlers, the political fortunes of later generations of Winthrops and Mathers provide evidence that (despite continuing high status) as time passed members of the dominant class generally found governance an even harder business than it had been for their ancestors. (Indeed, the life of Cotton Mather alone famously suggests just how far-reaching the tendencies toward erosion were.)[12]

However, for reasons that will be dealt with shortly, the example that is most relevant to the story of John Milton and Unitarian New England is that of the general fortunes over time of New England's first literary and intellectual elite, the clergy. They not only particularly well illustrate the ways in which the broader difficulties raised for the dominant class by its radical opponents and ideological contradictions were made worse by events; they do so in a manner that sets a pattern for their late eighteenth- and early nineteenth-century successors in the game of cultural politics: the Unitarian literati of the generation before Emerson.

The position of the first generations of the New England clergy was a particularly tenuous one calling for all the leadership skills at their disposal.[13]

12. For the fortunes of the Winthrop family, see Richard S. Dunn, *Puritans and Yankees: The Winthrop Dynasty of New England, 1630–1717* (Princeton, N.J.: Princeton University Press, 1962). The particular case of the Mathers as representatives of the eventual decline in elite authority (both civil and clerical) is variously treated by Robert Middlekauff, *The Mathers: Three Generations of Puritan Intellectuals, 1596–1728* (New York: Oxford University Press, 1971); David Levin, *Cotton Mather: The Young Life of the Lord's Remembrancer, 1663–1703* (Cambridge, Mass.: Harvard University Press, 1978); Kenneth Silverman, *The Life and Times of Cotton Mather* (New York: Harper and Row, 1984); and Mitchell R. Breitweiser, *Cotton Mather and Benjamin Franklin* (Cambridge, Eng.: Cambridge University Press, 1984).

13. In *Puritan Legacies* (101–8) Stavely incidentally summarizes the historiographical issues and literature concerning clerical power—and elite power generally—in seventeenth-century New England. As will be obvious, I do not accept the older view that the clergy's influence was pervasive between the Antinomian crisis and the beginning of the eighteenth century, a position that results to some degree from the privileging of texts produced by the dominant class. The classic example of this error is the still standard (and assuredly, estimable) treatment of the intellectual high culture of colonial New England and its declension, Perry Miller's two volumes on *The New England Mind: The Seventeenth Century* (New York: MacMillan, 1939) and *From*

Not only were they faced with the same religious diversity, class opposition, social change, and antinomian imperatives that bedeviled their civil counterparts; they also ran into manifestations of Puritanism's internal divisions and ideological contradictions peculiar to their profession. As a consequence, these first American intellectuals scarcely had the authority to which they pretended and throughout the seventeenth century had to resort to a variety of strategems in order to reassert their ecclesiastical, social, and political power.

Their first problem was that their understanding of their calling was itself complicated in ways that mirror the ideological contradictions of Puritanism in an almost textbook fashion. On the one hand, like ministers of other mainline Calvinist churches they claimed a divine sanction for their office, yet they were seriously committed as well to the principle of the priesthood of all believers. As a result, they found themselves caught in an uncomfortable position (midway between the sacerdotalism of Rome and the radically antihierarchical propheticism of the Anabaptists and Spiritists) that clearly reflected the more general moderate Puritan attempt to balance a felt need for order against one for freedom. Whenever they tried to exercise power they therefore laid themselves open to their own contradictory feelings about their office: feelings in which notions of godly calling and authority conflicted with the typically Protestant anticlericalism they themselves, as bitter opponents of Laud and Rome, also shared.[14]

Further, whatever effect these ideological contradictions had on their battle with the Anglicans back home, in the New World they obviously also made the moderate Puritan clergy vulnerable to attack by the more consistently leveling radicals in their midst. This was all the more true because they had for a while themselves moved in the direction of the radical camp. Indeed, in the early 1630s both the clergy and the magistrates had briefly sounded a great deal like the very people they were soon to condemn. For they had thought of Massachusetts Bay as a place where the Spirit would empower the saints, as a place where the justified would be free of the constric-

<hr>

Colony to Province (Cambridge, Mass.: Harvard University Press, 1953). See also his *Nature's Nation* (Cambridge, Mass.: Harvard University Press, 1967), esp. 14–49. (It is still possible to take this view, of course, as Harry S. Stout somewhat inconsistently does in *The New England Soul: Preaching and Religious Culture in Colonial New England* [New York: Oxford University Press, 1986], esp. 13–64, which generally defend the power and influence of the first-generation clergy.)

14. See David D. Hall, *The Faithful Shepherd: A History of the New England Ministry in the Seventeenth Century* (Chapel Hill: University of North Carolina Press, 1972), 3–47. This is the best history of the New England clergy during the first three generations of colonial settlement, and as the reader will note, this introduction is extensively indebted to it.

tions of the corrupt English church and so could live as a sanctified community awaiting the millennium. A few years later, therefore, when this millennial dream had come up against both of the other constituent elements of New England's crisis (the realities of life in the New World and the deep class divisions that beset their culture), the colonial clerical leadership was in a weakened position to deal with those for whom the original, Spiritist vision of "a city on a hill" was still alive.

As David Hall has put it, "the tribal myth of the Puritans, that sense of themselves as a holy people set apart from the world," had seemed for an instant to be an accomplished fact in the New World. Even the most staid members of the ruling circles had briefly "thought themselves pure and New England a new Israel." They soon discovered, however, that "the land meant liberty of other kinds than those [moderate] Puritanism sanctioned: the liberty that flowed from a general weakening of restraints, the liberty of local self-government, the liberty of a zeal that could turn into Antinomianism, the liberty of disorder." Moreover, faced with this excess of the very tendency toward radical freedom they themselves had momentarily harbored, they then in addition had to confront yet another shocking truth: the hard facts of life in the new colonies (which, with problems of immigration, social and religious diversity, religious indifferentism, economic hardship, and the like, proved to be no New Jerusalem). The result was that by the time of "the Antinomian crisis" of 1636–38 the overwhelming majority of the preachers (like other members of the elite) were fast abandoning their flirtation with radicalism. Increasingly worried that they might be losing control, they were fast heading toward the other pole in their culture, having been "forced . . . to reconsider what was right for New England—how much freedom, how much order," was appropriate.[15]

One particularly significant factor in the clergy's decision to move toward a paradigmatically Arminian position was their socioeconomic and political interests as professionals within the dominant class. For despite its power to create temporary millennial dreams, if coming to America did anything, it most assuredly raised the status of the clergy and reinforced their adherence to the interests and ideology of the moderate party. This was because in England they had been in a situation that inevitably "shaped" their "stance and social attitudes." Like their Anglican counterparts, Puritan clerics were, whatever their social origins, definitely men who "had to earn a living in the world," men well below "the gentry [who] as a class looked down upon

15. Ibid., 88 and 92.

them." They were men who "had to struggle for rewards in a pluralistic, competitive society," men who felt keen "frustration" at "the gap between their self-conception" as ambassadors of Christ "and the place they actually held in the English social system" (particularly as their situation within the English church made them dependent upon the favor and protection of the wealthier laity, who endowed their lectureships, presented them to benifices, paid their salaries, and defended them against the power of the king and his bishops).[16] By contrast, when they came to New England, first-generation clergy suddenly found themselves "at the top of society. The migration . . . made possible an enormous leap in social status for the ministers [because] immigration largely freed them of the class of gentry who looked down on their profession in England, while in wealth and prestige they now ranked higher than any other group save the magistrates." This "high status translated into real power in town affairs and the colony governments," and like any group within a dominant class, it soon became apparent that "if necessary they would use" this power "to protect their position in society."[17]

That they would have difficulty in doing so became clear almost immediately, as their attempt to find "some middle way between" prelatry and antinomianism, to find "a definition of the minister's authority that checked the risk of majority rule while retaining the [central congregationalist] principle of free consent," quickly ran afoul of both the religious diversity and antihierarchical instincts of their parishioners.[18] Moreover, their initial response to this opposition, the formation of an alliance with the rest of the dominant class in order to obtain "laws to ensure the security of the churches, to suppress dissent, and to guarantee sufficient maintenance" for themselves, was also a failure. And so, despite tastes of "real power"[19] as early as the mid-1640s, it was "clear that the preachers could no longer rely on the automatic support of the state" and that they were rapidly slipping back toward the frustrated position they had had in England as well. Regarded with both deference and suspicion by the common folk, and ill supported by the laity among the elite, they discovered that in bourgeois fashion "they would have to compete with other groups for the favor of the state" once more.

Nothing illustrates the clergy's lack of success better than the fact that while the resulting "competition . . . sealed their alliance with the magis-

16. Ibid., 66–68.
17. Ibid., 152.
18. Ibid., 112.
19. Ibid., 130–31.

trates, who proved more sympathetic to their social goals"[20] than the more popularly elected deputies, even this entente rapidly disintegrated in the years after the Antinomian crisis. This was mostly because the polarizing tendencies that hobbled moderate Puritanism in general were also operative among the dominant class laity. "Men of Winthrop's social class were" also walking an ideological and pragmatic tightrope between the claims of order and those of freedom, and so in their relations with the clergy they were equally the victims of the cultural contradictions of Puritanism. Thus, even though both they and the ministers were attempting to pursue their mutual self-interest in forming an alliance against their class enemies, neither the clergy nor the laity were willing to bury their typically Puritan urge toward individualism and antiauthoritarianism. Despite the fact that "the threats to order in the 1640s convinced" the clergy "that the strength of the civil magistrate was needed to sustain their position," and despite their shared desire for a "strengthening of the social order against the forces of disruption," the ministers as a result found their civil counterparts difficult allies, and over and over again their successes were canceled out by the latent antinomianism and endemic anticlericalism of the magistrates (by the fact that men like Winthrop were just "not used to giving way before the ministers, especially when their interests clashed").[21]

Moreover, the woes of the clergy only increased later in the first half of the century, since as their socioeconomic position rose over the next three decades,[22] and as the divisions within New England intensified under the pressure of events, they provoked ever more resentment from their flocks. Their dominance of the church and education, along with their influence in politics, was consequently even more at peril, and so their next attempt at solving their problems, not surprisingly, fared no better than their first. For in the absence of consistently reliable support from the laity within their own class, they tried to rest their authority upon "formalized, institutional [forms of] protection [that] replaced voluntary, loving bonds between themselves

20. Ibid., 145.
21. Ibid., 122 and 130.
22. As Hall notes elsewhere, despite the fact that many second-generation clergy faced unemployment due to an oversupply of ministers and congregations that favored English-educated preachers, "few of" those who persisted in their vocation "died poor; the average size of their estates placed the ministers within the wealthiest 15 percent of colonists." Furthermore, "marriage patterns" confirm "the high rank of the group" as well as its ties to the dominant class: "The richest men in New England, the merchants of Boston, agreed to frequent marriages between their daughters and young parsons, while often marrying themselves into ministerial families. Altogether, a Harvard education paid off in the seventeenth century" (ibid., 183).

and the people."[23] Rather than make more appeals to a resentful population or continue to depend on the magistrates to defend their interests, they tried to find institutional and intellectual ways of reconceiving the nature of "church membership, church government, and the definition of their office" so as to increase their power.[24] These ranged from the early device of founding Harvard College (which, as Harry Stout notes, was specifically meant to provide an educated ministry inimical to "civil and ecclesiastical chaos")[25] to such later gambits as the contractualization of the terms of clerical service, the formation of mutually supportive ministerial associations, and the promotion of theological and ecclesiological innovations meant to decrease lay influence and reassert the quasi-sacerdotal status of the ministry.

Like their alliance with the magistrates, however, these various institutional reassertions of authority ironically only deepened the opposition to what was fast becoming the Standing Order; and by 1679, when the last synod called by the civil authorities in Massachusetts Bay was held, it was clear that a "politics of declension" had set in. For in addition to the sheer momentum of the growing tensions within the region, the series of ecclesiastical and political changes already mentioned in connection with the Salem trials cut to the heart of continued governance by the local elite, by pushing New England toward "toleration of dissent [and] submission to the English king, and" by encouraging yet more "quarrels within the church" itself. When combined with the particularly destabilizing events of the last decades of the century and a series of well-documented changes in late seventeenth-century New England's congregational life, spirituality, and professional and generational relations, the result was that the original position of the clergy as the sole spiritual, intellectual, and cultural leaders of their communities was largely compromised—as were all such theocratic pretensions they might continue to harbor.[26]

23. Ibid., 146.
24. Ibid., 199.
25. Stout, 57–58.
26. Hall, *The Faithful Shepherd*, 228. In addition to Stavely's *Puritan Legacies* and the Hall title just cited, the three best sources of information about the gathered congregations of seventeenth-century New England (especially concerning the ways in which Puritanism's contradictory dynamics affected its spirituality and internal politics) are Patricia Caldwell, *The Puritan Conversion Narrative: The Beginnings of American Expression* (Cambridge, Eng.: Cambridge University Press, 1983); Edmund S. Morgan, *Visible Saints: The History of a Puritan Idea* (Ithaca, N.Y.: Cornell University Press, 1963); and Hall's more recent *Worlds of Wonder, Days of Judgment: Popular Religious Belief in Early New England* (New York: Knopf, 1989). For the pub-

To be sure, the clergy tried to maintain their position by many other means as the century neared its end. For instance, they deployed a number of pastoral and liturgical devices aimed at defusing tensions and incorporating the disaffected or indifferent within their congregations: including the Half-Way Covenant, Solomon Stoddard's evangelical extension of the Communion to the unregenerate, covenant-renewal ceremonies, and the first efforts at revivalism. Similarly, at times they also attempted to accommodate themselves to the political changes going on around them (the most notable example being their effort after the Restoration to adapt the original language of the Bay polity—with its emphasis on the covenanted nature and eschatological thrust of New England's errand—to their region's new status as a province of an imperial monarchy).[27]

Yet the most significant means by which the ministers (and the dominant class generally) sought to deal with their lack of authority was through the revision of the ideology by which they had justified their rule. For at century's end, faced as they were with the persistent antinomies and class cleavages of their culture and staggered by the shock of events, New England's clerical and lay leaders had also come to be impressed by the success moderate Puritanism had had in establishing its dominance in England after 1688. Inevitably, they associated this success with the new ideology that accompanied it, a refiguring of moderate Puritanism that took shape out of that series of convergent philosophical, scientific, and theological influences (Newtonianism, Lockeanism, empiricism, latitudinarianism,

---

lic and generational pressures under which the clergy operated and the means by which they sought to maintain their influence by adapting to them, see Hall, *The Faithful Shepherd*, and Emory Elliott, *Power and the Pulpit in Puritan New England* (Princeton, N.J.: Princeton University Press, 1975). The first two parts of Stout's book (13–123) are also useful, even though he takes a too sanguine view of the clergy's position.

Finally, the gradual declericalization of the lettered classes and the decline of the ministerial monopoly on higher education from the 1690s on are discussed incidentally but effectively in a number of accounts of the triumph of the bar as the career of choice among the American elite starting in the middle and late eighteenth century. The most recent and best of these is Robert A. Ferguson's *Law and Letters in American Culture* (Cambridge, Mass.: Harvard University Press, 1984); others are Charles A. Warren, *A History of the American Bar* (1911; rpt. New York: Howard Fertig, 1966); Richard Beale Davis, "The Early American Lawyer and the Profession of Letters," *Huntington Library Quarterly* 12 (1949): 191–206; Perry Miller, ed., *The Legal Mind in America from Independence to the Civil War* (Garden City, N.Y.: Doubleday, 1962); and John P. McWilliams, Jr., *Political Justice in a Republic: James Fenimore Cooper's America* (Berkeley: University of California Press, 1972).

27. Stout, 67–181, gives a good account of these strategems, although once again his belief in their efficacy betrays a faith in the dominance of the clergy that seems somewhat misplaced.

and Arminianism [in the strict sense]) that constituted "the moderate enlightenment."[28] And so, they adopted as their own the new paradigm of authority of which these ideas formed the constituent parts—an ideology they hoped might secure their interests more effectively than had been the case in the past.

Originally, of course, the New England dominant class had rested its right to govern on an ideology that reflected the reality of "social and economic conflict" in Britain at the time of its members' emigration. The result was a system of values that mirrored their position as rising townsmen and small-holders caught between the traditional dominant class in English society and the lower orders. They thus on the one hand affirmed a general belief in liberty, because it was "essential for resistance to" those who opposed their attempts to take over the established structures of society; yet driven by the fear that "too much freedom might lead men to forget theological and social orthodoxies," they on the other affirmed the importance of order as a defense against the "Antinomians, democratical spirits, and Levellers" who sought to displace them in turn.[29]

In Massachusetts Bay, however, the specific form of this intellectual defense of moderate Puritan interests was a bit different from the one in England (even though its main features first took shape in the mother country). Going further than most of their transatlantic cousins, the emigrant dominant class adopted an ideology in which all human relations (whether societal, interpersonal, or divine) were to be understood in terms of a biblically sanctioned covenant. As Perry Miller put it, in New England "political doctrine" became "part and parcel of the theological, and the cord that" bound them "all . . . together" was "the covenant." This was because of the key role of the covenant as a concept in the anthropology that underlay their understanding of human salvation. As Calvin's New England theological interpreters explained these matters,

> individuals, in a natural state, before grace has been given them, are
> at absolute liberty to do anything they can, to lie, steal, murder. . . .

28. The phrase "moderate enlightenment" is Henry F. May's, whose *The Enlightenment in America* (Oxford: Oxford University Press, 1976) is not only the best general history of the intellectual life of eighteenth-century America, but the best introduction (3–101) to this stage in its development. See also Jay Fliegelman, *Prodigals and Pilgrims: The American Revolution against Patriarchal Authority, 1750–1800* (Cambridge, Eng.: Cambridge University Press, 1982), 155–94, for another excellent account of how these ideas influenced early eighteenth-century American high culture.

29. Miller, *The New England Mind: The Seventeenth Century*, 430.

But when men become regenerate they are then at "liberty" to do only what God commands. And God commands certain things for the group as a whole as well as for each individual. Regenerate men, therefore, by the very fact of being regenerate, come together, form churches and a state upon explicit agreements, in which they all promise to live with one another according to the laws and for the purposes of God. Thus the government is brought into being by the act of the people; but the people do not create just any sort of government, but the one kind of government which God has outlined.

Miller goes on to say that in such a government, though "the governors are elected by the people," they are "elected into an office which has been established by God." As such, they partake of His authority, and so deserve a deference worthy of the same; for "when men have made a covenant with God they have thereby promised Him, in the very terms of that agreement, to compact among themselves in order to form a holy state in which His discipline will be practiced." This is why a John Winthrop "can . . . insist that though the government of" a covenanted state like "Massachusetts is bound by fundamental law, and though it takes its rise from the people, and though the people elect the officials, still the people's liberty in Massachusetts consists in a 'liberty to that only which is good, just, and honest.' "[30] For such a commonwealth was established for a divine and holy end, and this end not only sanctions the suppression by the elite of license, subversion, rebellion, and antinomianism but also empowers the ministers and magistrates (once they have been elected) to act as the final earthly arbiters of its destiny in all matters.

Of course, as Miller himself elsewhere suggests, this notion of a divinely ordained, covenanted balance between liberty and order—with a strong emphasis on the latter and its supervision by the dominant class—was in many respects just an early stage in a wider change in the ideology of power in seventeenth-century Europe that was related to the rise of capitalism. It was a part of that "universal tendency in European thought" at this time "to change social relationships from status to contract, . . . it was one expression of late Renaissance speculation, which was moving in general away from the ideas of feudalism, from the belief that society must be modeled upon an eternally fixed hierarchy to the theories of constitutional limitation and

30. Perry Miller, *Errand into the Wilderness* (Cambridge, Mass.: Harvard University Press, 1956), 148–49.

voluntary origins, to the protection of individual rights and the shattering of sumptuary economic regulations." Indeed, as Miller points out, so pervasive was this movement in Europe that the English theologians upon whose work New England's ideology and polity were based had earlier actually gone so far as to insert "the federal [i.e., covenant] idea into the very substance of divinity," changing "the relation even of God to man from necessity to contract, largely because contractualism was becoming increasingly congenial to the age and in particular to Puritans."[31]

Yet as Miller himself only partly acknowledges, this theory of society is also an almost perfect projection of the moderate Puritan party's contradictory interests, since it is really an intellectual middle way between submission to the patriarchalism of defenders of the old order, like the bishops (or, later, Sir Robert Filmer), and surrender to the radical conclusions that logically flowed from its own contractualism, voluntarism, consensualism, and popularism (the very concepts that would come to the fore in increasingly democratic, subversive ways over the next two centuries).[32]

The use of the concept of the covenant in Anglo-American reformed theology itself illustrates this, since in using this idea to set "forth the character of God with greater precision" than had hitherto been the case in English Protestantism, the authors of the federal theology (as this revision of Calvinism was known) were deeply motivated by a keen sense of their own self-interest. Thus, they began by very prominently laying "to rest [those] doubts about moral obedience and personal assurance" that were (respectively) near the core of Arminius's neo-Pelagianism and Mrs. Hutchinson's views on regeneration and sanctification—something that had the calculated effect of discrediting the theologies of both their Laudian and radical opponents (the "Arminians and Antinomians"),[33] who in religion as in much else rejected the moderate Puritan position and tended toward the opposite poles of Protestant culture. Furthermore, their doctrine of the covenant itself comprises a masterly—albeit contradictory—attempt to satisfy both the Puritan rage for order (by maintaining Calvin's hierarchical view of the "ontological relation" between God and the human race as "a connection determined by

31. Miller, *The New England Mind: The Seventeenth Century*, 399.
32. For the patriarchal tradition in seventeenth-century English political thought, see Gordon J. Schochet, *Patriarchalism in Political Thought: The Authoritarian Family and Political Speculation and Attitudes Especially in Seventeenth-Century England* (New York: Basic Books, 1975).
33. Miller, *The New England Mind: The Seventeenth Century*, 378. Here the terms "Arminian" and "antinomian" are used in their technical as well as their paradigmatic sense. (The Laudians, on the whole, were notorious followers of Arminius, and Mrs. Hutchinson, of course, was the archetypal New World antinomian.)

brute necessity and the ineluctable order of things") and the equally strong Puritan desire for freedom (by trying to limit what this patriarchal divine Monarch would actually be allowed to do). For it introduces a kind of bourgeois constitutionalism into matters of salvation. In a direct parallel to the moderates' political theory, it posits that the relationship between God and that part of humanity who comprise the Elect (itself a kind of soteriological dominant class) is almost—although technically, not *quite*—governed by a tradesman's agreement, in which the divine Master "forgoes what is His by right divine [and], preferring a spontaneous to an enforced service," in a "gesture [that] is pure graciousness . . . limits Himself to a contract." This contract is what the federal theologians termed "the Covenant of Grace," and it is this covenant that balances the Puritan need for hierarchy with that for equality, thereby providing a moderate blueprint for the ordering of a regenerate church, state, and community in the regenerate soul's relationship to God. As in the later relation of Crown and Parliament under the settlement of 1688, the Covenant of Grace is "an agreement of unequals upon just and equal terms," an arrangement that maintains divine superiority and human inferiority and yet also establishes "an equally certain but more honorable relation of assent" between God and man, " 'in which God promises true happinesse to man, and man engages himself by promise for performance of what God requires.' "[34]

As the centerpiece and pattern of a broader ideology, the problem with this middling, constitutionalist, self-interested theology was twofold. First, even at the beginning of the century the conflicting impulses it tried to mediate were too great to be successfully negotiated, and later historical developments in New England made this task only more complicated. As a result, in Miller's view, "the federal theology and the covenant theory of the state" erected alongside it quickly proved "unstable" in both theory and practice. From the start, the Puritan leadership "had to reckon . . . with the consequences of their own teaching," and later they "were hard pressed to explain why what had been sauce for Charles I should not also be sauce for" John Winthrop and his successors. Moreover, as the eighteenth century neared, yet another problem arose. For this ideology had arisen in "a transitional age," one in which the claims of reason and faith could still be easily reconciled.[35] In the increasingly rationalist intellectual atmosphere of the last decades of the century, however, this was no longer so simple, even in a peripheral but progressively less isolated colony like Massachusetts. As a

34. Ibid., 376.
35. Ibid., 422 and 430.

consequence, any ideology that rested its proponents' authority on divine will and such sanctions as were implicit in violating it was bound to become increasingly suspect. Not surprisingly, therefore, the New England dominant class soon discovered—more than a little to their discomfort—that the very centrality of religious dogma to their ideology was now itself a problem. In their "mingling of nature and religion, of civil law and divine law . . . they believed they had . . . shown the findings of reason to be one with the tenets of faith" (and so confirmed their own authority as a class empowered to rule a covenanted society), but they did "not foresee, even in 1660, how short the time would be, once men had commenced thinking in this fashion, until the findings of reason would suffice of themselves, until the compact and the deductions of logic would provide the content of political wisdom, and politicians would no longer be obliged to heed the requirements of faith."[36]

The works of John Locke, the most influential English philosopher of the age, alone illustrate the intellectual sea change confronting the province's leaders at the end of the seventeenth century, if only because by resting his view of authority (whether political or familial) upon "a descriptive and politically neutral anthropology" he "rejected far more than [the genetic] patriarchalism" of the defenders of divine right. In addition "he replaced" the biblical "premises" upon which authority in Puritan New England rested as well, discarding them as "parts of a world view or belief system that was being undermined by the growth of historical consciousness, by the rise of empirical science and philosophy, by the growth of deism, and by social and political events themselves."[37] Instead, he justified "the existence of political authority . . . by an appeal to something more functional and tangible than divine mystery or the nature of things": the self-interest and collective will of the body politic itself. The result in the *Two Treatises of Government* and elsewhere was an almost wholly secular account of the nature of civil authority, a view of the state in which "the purpose of government" is unconnected with issues of salvation; the exercise of power is limited "in general, to" the protection of "the life, liberty, and property of [its] citizens"; and even such carefully prescribed powers are themselves neither irrevocable nor absolute.[38]

Locke's notions of authority were, of course, no less bourgeois in spirit than those of his moderate Puritan predecessors, whether in England or

36. Ibid., 431. Of course, Miller was notorious for his emphasis on the rationalist element in New England Puritanism (and seventeenth-century European thought generally). Yet as a generalization, his description of the transitional nature of the federalist theologians' mixture of the religious and the secular seems true.
37. Schochet, 259 and 268–69.
38. Ibid., 260.

America. On the contrary, in fact, they were advanced in aid of the victors of 1688. His political writings in particular were a bold attempt to address the problems and contradictions still confronting moderate Puritanism as it tried to solidify its hold on English society (primarily by recasting the constituent parts of its ideology in order to press home the attack on the remnants of patriarchalism and divine right and to answer the strengthened antinomian tendencies of a secular and antihierarchical age). Moreover, their effect (when combined with that of his educational and philosophical writings) was to lay the groundwork for the new ideological structure by which the eighteenth-century Anglo-American dominant class quickly came to justify its hold on power. For it was by taking Locke as a starting point that defenders of dominant class interests sought to revise the relative claims of order and liberty in order to strike a more workable balance between the two, a balance they hoped would alleviate the social tensions and polarities in their culture by establishing a more amiable and egalitarian (but still hierarchical and classist) relationship between governors and governed.

This new ideology coalesced rapidly from a number of sources during the eighteenth century—including some (like the Scottish Common Sense School later on) quite suspicious of Locke and the potentially radical implications of his thought[39]—and seemed for a while to solve the problems confronting the dominant class, by offering a revised model for the behavior of civil rulers, ministers, husbands, and parents towards those in their charge. Known as "consensualism," it posited that governance, if it were to be successful, could no longer be effected (as in the past) through appeals to revelation and divine decree. Rather, those in authority would have to modulate more subtly between the Arminian and antinomian polarities of their secularizing, mercantile culture and (in the context of Locke's contractualism) use appeals to reason and self-interest and an emphasis on "the primacy of the social bond, [the] affections, and disinterested benevolence"[40] to establish voluntary but deferential relationships between themselves and those they ruled.

39. Despite their general admiration for him, Locke was nonetheless thought by many eighteenth-century thinkers to be too conciliatory in various respects to the antinomian tendencies of their culture. Thus, an admirer of his (markedly consensualist) educational writings, like Isaac Watts, could praise them as works "that . . . retaught a Protestant nation the greatest article of its own faith: the doctrine of rational voluntarism," while also implying that they betrayed a certain naïveté toward the fact that "the dangers of license" in child rearing were "as great as those of tyranny" (Fliegelman, 19). Similarly, one reason for the popularity of the Scottish Common Sense School later in the century was a widespread fear that Locke and his followers were too optimistic about the efficacy of the benevolent exercise of authority in resolving the conflicting impulses still threatening dominant class power.

40. Ibid., 25.

According to the consensualists, the magistrate or monarch, the preacher, the parent, or the merchant, was thus in authority, not by the grace of God or on account of mere genetic priority, but because in exercising authority he or she fulfilled a social purpose that sprang directly from the rights of those over whom he or she had power. For the most all-encompassing of human rights, they argued, was that of being educated and improved, of being aided in the process of one's maturation and the development of one's autonomy; and the way those in authority could accomplish this end (while not losing control over those they governed) was through the indirect exercise of their power using such stratagems as: education and tuition by example, didactic appeals and moral suasion, pleas for voluntary consent and plays on self-interest, displays of affection, acts of benevolence, and expressions of fellow-feeling. Having benefited from these and other constituent elements of the mentorial relationship—so the theory went—the subject or the student, the layman, the child, or the worker, would then realize the continuing advantages of respecting those in authority; and so, upon reaching full maturity, he or she would voluntarily agree to take his or her rightful (though deferential) place within the established order of family, church, state, and society (thus in effect recognizing the hold on power gradually won by the formerly Puritan, bourgeois dominant class after 1688).[41]

The many English and Scottish authors advancing broadly consensualist views were widely read on both sides of the Atlantic in the century following the Glorious Revolution and had a particularly far-reaching effect upon the New England elite (many of whom had, in any case, been moving independently toward similar conclusions about the nature of authority themselves). In the specific instance of the New England clergy this exposure to consensualism and the thought of the moderate enlightenment generally resulted in a sustained recasting of the terms of the New England Way. It was a course of action not without difficulty, given the potentially or actually heterodox aspects of Locke's philosophy and that of many of his contemporaries; indeed, much of this new, more rational and empirical worldview was diametrically opposed to the assumptions that had informed the federalist theological tradition. Yet whatever their position across the theological spectrum, the extent of the changes going on in Europe was such that the colonial clergy had little choice but to reflect at length upon them—so much so that the

41. Fliegelman provides the best treatment of the consensualist ideology, its history, and impact, with special attention to its principle literary manifestations and proponents, and to its influence in America.

religious literature of eighteenth-century congregationalism almost every-where bespeaks their effort in this regard.[42]

The very fact that the ministers were willing to go to such lengths and abandon or modify much of their intellectual heritage in order to try out con-sensualism suggests the degree of urgency they felt in finding an ideological solution to the problems facing them. As Harry Stout notes, by "the middle decades of the eighteenth century" the social divisions they and other mem-bers of the dominant class confronted were more troublesome than ever. "Never before were there so many changes, on so many fronts, in so conten-tious an atmosphere." The region, like the rest of British North America, was at a "critical 'takeoff' period in the American colonies' evolution from a 'traditional' to a 'modern' society," and the resulting "social transforma-tion," spurred by "demographic growth and economic development," exac-erbated both the earlier socioeconomic divisions and the endemic polarities they had spawned. "Traditional social categories were about to explode and splinter in many directions," with devastating effect upon "New England's decentralized and inherently unstable institutions."

As Stout further shows, in the case of the church this explosion took the form of another series of "crises of authority," largely centered around "in-creased disputes between ministers and their congregations over clerical au-thority, ministerial salaries, and theological orthodoxy." The result was still another clerical retreat, since "instead of peace and continuity"—let alone unchallenged power—the first generation of eighteenth-century ministers was rapidly "forced to create from the fragments of a once-coherent hierar-chical social ethic a more democratic configuration" than "their predeces-sors would . . . have recognized—or endorsed."[43] Later, furthermore, things got even worse, since although (according to Henry May) "the established New England clergy of the second half of the eighteenth century" were hardly "a negligible force" and could still use their traditional position and status to "exert formidable power,"[44] their "position" (like that "of the late

42. In addition to Fliegelman, see also Kenneth Silverman, *A Cultural History of the American Revolution* (New York: Crowell, 1976), and Kenneth S. Lynn, *A Divided People* (Westport, Conn.: Greenwood Press, 1977), particularly for consensualism in the latter half of the eigh-teenth century. The impact of Locke and other writers of the moderate enlightenment on Amer-ican theology and church life is the focus of much of May's discussion of this period (see esp. 3–25 and 42–115); see also Elliott, *Power and the Pulpit*, 136ff., for examples of the independent efforts of New England clerics to move in much the same direction as their English contemporaries.

43. Stout, 185–86 (with terminology from sources cited 356, n. 1).

44. May, 51.

colonial clergy" in other regions) "was unenviable. Their authority was limited, their status insecure, their duties at once all-important but ill-defined. Where they were still centrally important, they were denounced and lampooned. Far worse, where the indifference of the age had spread most widely, they were beginning to be ignored." Indeed, "their most common complaint was not either heresy or apostasy, though both were serious, but rather the growing 'neglect of the ordinances.' Too many people were staying away from church, and above all too few were making the efforts demanded as the price of church membership" (efforts that could effectually bring them within the minister's sphere of influence).[45]

Predictably, as in the previous century, the New England clergy tried out a variety of strategies during the decades leading up to the Revolution in response to this further erosion of authority. The most striking of them was their adoption of consensualism as a means of ideologically shoring up their own position and, by extension, that of the rest of the region's elite as well. This can especially be seen at the time of the Great Awakening; for even if the general place of that series of revivals in the history of the clergy's decline is still a matter of controversy,[46] the New England congregationalist preachers who figured in it were almost all at least to some degree consensualists bent upon reaffirming their profession's authority and its traditional moderate course between the polarities of their culture.

For instance, an Arminian in both the theological and paradigmatic senses like Charles Chauncy could thus be typically defensive about his calling's professional and social standing and represent "an extreme aspect of the intellectualist tradition that emphasized the 'understanding' and strict clerical control over congregations." Similarly, his chief opponent, Jonathan Edwards, could—despite protestations to the contrary—speak out of a "voluntarist, [antinomian] tradition that emphasized the 'affections' and favored more active lay involvement in church affairs."[47] But in point of fact, neither Chauncy nor Edwards was exclusively drawn toward one pole or the other in their culture; rather, both were trying to come to terms with a changing social reality, and both turned for aid to the new model of authority in the hope that it would once more allow them to

45. Ibid., 48.
46. Stout, for instance, at times gives somewhat contradictory evidence about its ultimate effects (see 185–232).
47. Ibid., 203.

occupy the middle ground—and so preserve the central standing of the preacher a while longer.[48]

Chauncy and other congregationalist Arminians tried to do this by gradually becoming wholehearted consensualists who refashioned their image of God and the ministry alike to fit the new view of how those in authority were to behave in an age of mixed government and a decent respect for the autonomy of those under it. Although they thus followed the precedent of the federalist theologians by projecting their understanding of authority in secular matters into their understanding of their relationship with God, their deity was no longer that of federalism—let alone the God of Calvin. He was instead now a divinity fit to reign under the Whig Constitution: One Who had forsworn His kingly divine right in order to rule in a limited and indirect fashion (not as a monarch, but as a loving father who sought to bring His earthly children to salvation through a consensualist program that respected their autonomy even as it pressed them toward a voluntary acceptance of His grace and ordinances). As such, He also provided a pattern for His representatives on earth (who in light of their past and present difficulties over authority in any case no longer cared to present their role in the semihieratic terms of the previous century). For Chauncy and those like him realized that if the clergy's former ideological figuration of their office had failed to help establish their authority then, it was even less likely to do so now. They believed, therefore, that they must instead refashion themselves professionally as the benevolent consensualist mentors of their communities—as men whose authority arose, in fact, not from an imitation of Calvin's patriarchal God but from an imitation of Christ, our fellow son and brother. For in the Son's example of self-sacrifice, kindness, and moral tuition, they felt that one found both the best model of ministry and the one that had the greatest chances of success (because it most effectually encouraged the affectionate

48. In addition to the sources already mentioned, other good treatments of the Great Awakening and the general situation in early eighteenth-century New England include: the introduction to Alan Heimert and Perry Miller, comps., *The Great Awakening: Documents Illustrating the Crisis and Its Consequences* (Indianapolis, Ind.: Bobbs-Merrill, 1967); Heimert's *Religion and the American Mind from the Great Awakening to the Revolution* (Cambridge, Mass.: Harvard University Press, 1966); James W. Jones, *The Shattered Synthesis: New England Puritanism before the Great Awakening* (New Haven, Conn.: Yale University Press, 1973); and J. William T. Youngs, Jr., *God's Messengers: Religious Leadership in Colonial New England, 1700–1750* (Baltimore: Johns Hopkins University Press, 1976). The theology of the Old Lights is specifically treated in Conrad Wright, *The Beginnings of Unitarianism in America* (Boston: Starr King Press, 1955), and that of Edwards (and its European connections) in Norman Fiering, *Jonathan Edwards' Moral Thought in its British Context* (Chapel Hill: University of North Carolina Press, 1981).

submission of souls to the Father by showing His equality with—and yet superiority to—us in His Son).

The Arminian clergy were thus not above using the doctrines of the hypostatic union and the Incarnation to support this attempt to solve their
problems about matters of hierarchy and equality, order and liberty. Indeed,
they felt that an incarnate god infinitely superior to and yet just like us, Who
during His earthly life exercised exalted powers with restraint, benevolence,
and a concern for human moral independence, was just what they needed as
they sought a model by which they might assert authority and yet not provoke opposition. For being moderate, fourth-generation, dominant-class Puritans, they still wanted to walk the line between the Arminian and antinomian polarities of their culture, only now with a new ideological cover; and
a consensualist Jesus provided them with sanction for this of the most com-
pelling sort.

In the case of Jonathan Edwards and the "New Lights," on the other
hand, the traditional nature of their theology (especially their patriarchal figuration of the deity and their semihieratic view of the ministry) would seem
to place them totally at odds with consensualists of Chauncy's ilk. Yet they
too had to operate within the same social circumstances and deal with the
same cultural contradictions as the Arminians; nor were they any less exposed than Chauncy either to the literature of consensualism or to its prestige
as the ideology of the English (and increasingly, the American) dominant
class. And so, whether evangelizing a restive frontier population or arguing
on behalf of New England's traditional beliefs, their thoughts and actions
were no less "politically" determined and only somewhat less influenced by
consensualism than those of their chief clerical rivals.

A case that illustrates this point is their revision of the Puritan morphology
of conversion. For though they would hedge it about or deny it in order to
preserve orthodoxy, in promoting the Awakening, Edwards and the others at
one level broke with tradition and effectively validated two dimensions of religious experience that had generally been regarded with distrust by moderate Puritan divines of the previous century: the religious affections and—admittedly, more by implication—mystical or contemplative experience. In
doing so, they clearly veered toward the antinomian pole in their culture. Yet
looked at from another (perhaps more cynical) perspective, this move was
not, in fact, a break with tradition at all. Indeed, it very much followed the
practice of the seventeenth-century clergy, since by emphasizing the pivotal
role of the affections in the process of conversion and by coming closer to
admitting the possibility of direct experience of the divine, Edwards and

the rest were, like their predecessors, trying to co-opt one of the most powerful factors in the traditional appeal of Puritan radicalism: its willingness to entertain and commend forms of conversion other than the cognitive or ethical.[49]

Faced by ever more chaos and dissent, and appalled by the lack of evangelical fervor in the church, they chose, in other words, to correct one of established New England congregationalism's long-standing weaknesses (its psychologically deficient spirituality), lest that weakness continue to undermine the influence of the established clergy and give aid to their class and sectarian enemies. What seems at first to be a benevolent and pastorally pragmatic move thus turns out to be yet another clerical attempt to co-opt antinomianism within the New England Way. One sign of this is that although by this concession Edwards and his followers allowed a wider range of religious experience to be regarded as putatively valid than had been the case in the past, and though they also thereby accorded a relatively greater degree of power and self-validating authority to individual experience than formerly, Edwards's famous exchanges with Chauncy reveal how concerned they were lest this endorsement be misinterpreted as neglect of the demands of order. In typical moderate Puritan fashion, Edwards feared the very antinomianism he was charged with fomenting and was nearly as committed to the Arminian side of the Puritan paradigm as his more technically Arminian contemporaries. As a result, in both his writings and his ministry, he went out of his way to try to preserve and extend the traditional role of the clergy as communal intellectual and spiritual leaders by stressing the control he and other like-minded clergy sought to exercise over participants in the Awakening.

The Edwardsian morphology of conversion both in theory and in practice hardly marks an abandonment of the ideological tradition of moderate Puritanism, therefore. Contemporary circumstances and the proven problems of the moderate position had merely driven Edwards, like Chauncy, toward his own revision of the old understanding of authority, a revision he hoped might enable him to deal anew with the conflictions of his culture. For though not really a consensualist, Edwards faced the same set of problems that gave rise to consensualism and responded with a less radical, but nonetheless cognate, restructuring of the ideology his generation of the dominant class had inherited. Moreover, similarly, though the chief defender of theological federalism,

49. I am here indebted to the distinctions made in Walter Conn, *Christian Conversion: A Developmental Interpretation of Autonomy and Surrender* (New York: Paulist Press, 1986). A recent historical treatment of these issues is Charles L. Cohen, *God's Caress: The Psychology of Puritan Religious Experience* (New York: Oxford University Press, 1986).

he also understood the prestige of the learning that accompanied the new consensualist ideology, and so sought to use it to make the New England Way intellectually persuasive to those educated in the wake of Locke and Newton. This is why in a work like his *Treatise on the Religious Affections* he adopted the psychology and philosophy of Locke, Hutcheson, Shaftesbury, and other consensualist writers. For it allowed him simultaneously to do three seemingly disparate things: to defend the understanding of conversion originally developed within the matrix of federalist Calvinism; to extend that understanding (for the reasons just discussed) so as to validate the affective as a variety of religious experience; and, at the same time, to make the traditional Puritan view of metanoia comprehensible to those who had utterly rejected the patriarchalism with which Calvin's God had become associated. Similarly, his rapprochement with consensualism also explains why there are surprising parallels between Edwards's systematic theology (which consistently reexplains the federalist position on divine sovereignty, total depravity, freedom of the will, and the like in the language of Locke and the rest) and the new ideology. For in a world in which the dominant class was increasingly committed to "that ultimate [bourgeois] reconciliation sought by the mid-eighteenth century—in theology as well as in politics—between a just authority and a circumscribed but real liberty, between the psychological necessities of submission and assertion," an old concept like praevenient grace had more intellectual currency if it could be understood as a Lockean "simple idea"; and Edwards's "understanding of the relation of formal to efficient cause, of man's will to God's," in *The Freedom of the Will* would be more persuasive if, in surprising ways, it resembled (as it does) the views of even so unlikely a consensualist analogue as Rousseau's *Emile*.[50]

If, in his lifelong effort "to keep the past upon her throne," the third president of Nassau Hall thus proved himself only a tactical consensualist (a denizen but not a full citizen of the eighteenth century), later "disciples of Edwards" like "Joseph Bellamy and Samuel Hopkins" show just how strong the pull of the new ideology eventually came to be. Beginning in the 1750s and 1760s they were even more ineluctably driven than their master toward consensualism, eventually being "obliged to make [even further] concessions" to the new way of thinking. Thus, for example, although in their "so-called New Divinity" they were still "unwilling to compromise the orthodox [federalist] stand on" such matters as "innate depravity and moral inability,

50. Fliegelman, 34–35.

Bellamy" and the rest soon "offered a new theory of the atonement that" had the effect of moving "New England theology in the direction of the new [consensualist] politics—away from will and toward law," by imposing "on God the same expectations the Glorious Revolution [had] imposed on the monarchy and the new [consensualist] pedagogy" had similarly imposed "on parents."[51]

As Edwards's own experience in Northampton alone attests, however, neither the New Lights' more complex, intellectually compromised reassertion of clerical authority nor their attempts to seize ground from the radicals fared any better than Chauncy's Arminianism did in dealing with the endemic—and now irritated—contradictions of Puritan culture. The Awakening and the itinerant evangelicalism that followed in its wake, in fact, if anything, made things worse, leading to an even greater disintegration of ecclesial unity and clerical prestige all around.[52]

This does not deny, of course, that the history of that disintegration during the remainder of the colonial period is complex. There is, for instance, plenty of evidence that the tides of dissent against the Standing Order ebbed and flowed in the years leading up to the American Revolution. There is also even evidence of a resurgence of clerical influence during both the Seven Years' War and the events leading up to the Eighteenth of April, 1775 (though interestingly enough, largely in connection with the persistence of a covenant rhetoric modified by consensualism). But in the end, the facts underscore the themes enunciated thus far: that the social divisions and cultural polarities of New England and late colonial America in general were exacerbated by socioeconomic change during the course of the eighteenth century, and that in the resulting atmosphere of crisis, consensualism functioned (either directly or incidentally) as the means by which the clergy and other members of the dominant class pursued their traditional policy of attempting to justify and so ensure deference to their authority. Much social and ecclesiastical history supports this view of the pattern of tensions in the region and their deleterious effects on the elite (especially the clergy). Moreover, it also explains why toward the end of the colonial regime the ministers moved once more to center stage. For at the time of the taking of Quebec or the Stamp Act, they could, for once, play out their own antinomian instincts in

51. Ibid., 167 and 169.
52. So great were the disintegrative effects of the Awakening, in fact, that Stout is hardly alone in regarding "the decade 1735–1745" as "the most critical period in colonial New England's intellectual and religious history" (208). For example, Stavely, *Puritan Legacies*, 101–97, not only corroborates this but also gives a particularly vivid example of its effects on the lives of a parson and his parishioners in one Massachusetts town.

concert with those of their lay brethren, as they now had external enemies who for a time allowed them (with renewed fervor for the region's traditional typological self-understanding) to deflect the antiauthoritarian imperatives of their culture toward those old Puritan bogies: papist France and the English monarchy.[53]

As this implies, the coming of the American Revolution did not solve the problems of the New England dominant class, nor did it change their habits in trying to turn those difficulties to advantage. For in that struggle the region's clerical and lay leaders (like those of the new nation as a whole) consciously sought to mediate between the polarities of their culture. Thus, on the one hand, they were determined to forge an ideology of resistance to imperial oppression. To do so, they drew upon a number of currents in contemporary culture (including broad patterns of eighteenth-century religious dissent, radical Whiggery, Protestant millennialism, and Yankee particularism) that tended to encourage the antinomian tendencies within their society. Yet because their class interests and practical problems as members of an elite had not disappeared with the departure of the last royal governor (even if, for a while, they fooled themselves into thinking that they had), they also continued to maintain their traditional concern with satisfying the claims of order. The result was a contradictory rhetoric of revolution that simultaneously employed both the language of consensualism and that of radical antihierarchicalism—a language so fraught with contradiction that, whatever its short-term success, in the long run it paradoxically set the stage for the final decline of their influence by century's end.

The first major feature of the American Revolution from an ideological point of view is, therefore, the degree to which the dominant class in New England and elsewhere gave in for a while to their culture's deep reservoirs of antinomian feeling. For both in hearkening back to the "Puritan revolution of the seventeenth century" as "precedent" for their own and in turning to "the Commonwealth and Radical Whig" traditions to help frame their arguments for independence, the members of this class were playing to the deeply antiauthoritarian strain in Anglo-American culture. At the same time, however, this development lay athwart their equally strong need to affirm the demands of order in consensualist terms, an expression of bourgeois self-interest manifested most notably in their many arguments for independence grounded in the writings of Locke and the Common Sense School.

---

53. For evidence, see Stout, 231–55.

The result was a contradictory cultural moment that has been called "the revolutionary enlightenment": a time when consensualist rhetoric (which turned the model of a benevolent, mentorial relationship between governors and governed against the King of Great Britain) mixed freely with more radical sentiments that were fundamentally leveling, "enthusiastic, and religious in spirit."[54] Indeed, so completely did ideas of social contract and natural rights taken from the consensualist "bestsellers of 1775"[55] get mixed up with notions of negative liberty and antihierarchicalism, that in New England in particular there was arguably at least as "much in common between [the] millennial and sectarian movements" long associated with antinomianism "and the new revolution of the late eighteenth century" as there was between the latter and the thought of "Locke or Hume or Voltaire, Rousseau and Paine."[56]

As has already been suggested, the temporary consequence of this move toward accommodating elite self-interest with the radical elements within the culture was that the dominant class (and the ministry in particular) was not only "more unified than it had been for some time" but more influential as well. In fact, in New England and elsewhere it seemed "to some of the clergy, [that] the Revolution was a heaven-sent opportunity to restore unity and arrest decline." By projecting their culture's antinomianism onto such traditional external enemies as the Crown, the Pope, and the Anglican church, "Arminians, moderate Calvinists, and ultra-Calvinists" all thought they could deflect the effects of this structure of feeling away from themselves. They hoped, in other words, that their mutual hatred of bishops, their treatment of George III as "the Great Beast himself, and America ever more clearly [as] the theater of Armageddon," and their demands for "religious as well as civil liberty" would restore their popularity with the mass of

54. May, 154–59. Fliegelman, 36–154, demonstrates just how extensively the ideology of consensualism inserted itself into political debate at the time of the Revolution. In particular, he shows how it came to inform dominant-class treatments—both literary and otherwise—of the question of independence (with elite advocates of freedom arguing for the necessity of revolt against a tyrannical father figure who had failed in his consensualist obligation to raise his colonial children to a mature state of independence, while dominant-class advocates of loyalism depicted those same colonial children as ungrateful prodigals disobeying a kindly consensualist monarch). See also Gordon S. Wood, "Rhetoric and Reality in the American Revolution," *William and Mary Quarterly*, ser. 3, 23 (1966): 3–32, and especially Bernard Bailyn, *The Ideological Origins of the American Revolution* (Cambridge, Mass.: Harvard University Press, 1967), which remains the best general account of the ideological structures justifying the Revolution, particularly the radical Whig and republican strain in eighteenth-century Anglo-American thought.

55. This phrase is from part of Fliegelman's title for chapter 2 of part 1 of his book.

56. May, 154.

New Englanders—and hence, their cohesion and authority as a profession as well.[57] Similarly, by using the same strategy, secular members of their class also sought to speak effectively to the province and the rest of British North America in "lay orations [that] were distinctly sermonic in form" and content;[58] by mixing the tones of the jeremiad and reasoned consensualist appeals with radically antiauthoritarian rhetoric about the nature of personal rights, they sought at least temporarily to move the focus of long-standing class resentment away from themselves and toward the government of Lord North (thereby marshaling it to revolutionary effect).

It was a gambit that was in a sense successful, moreover, since men of the dominant class were not only leaders in the Revolution but were also able to a surprising degree to co-opt contemporary radical feeling into what Sacvan Bercovitch has called a secular "typology of mission." The "pattern" of this typology "was well established by the last decades of the eighteenth century," and it gave men of the class that had long provided New England with ministers and magistrates a chance to act as the privileged interpreters of America's new republican covenant. In this extension of the covenant theory of the state to America as a whole,

> Washington could be enshrined as saviour, his mighty deeds ex-
> pounded, his apostles ranked, the Judas in their midst identified,
> the Declaration of Independence adequately compared to the Ser-
> mon on the Mount, the sacred places and objects (Bunker Hill, Val-
> ley Forge, the Liberty Bell) properly labeled, the Constitution duly
> ordained (in Emerson's words) as "the best book in the world" next
> to the New Testament, and the Revolution, summarily, "indissolu-
> bly linked" (as John Quincy Adams put it) with "the birthday . . .
> of the Saviour," as being the social, moral, and political correlative
> of "the Redeemer's mission on earth," and thus, "the first irrevo-
> cable pledge of the fulfillment of the prophecies, announced directly
> from Heaven."[59]

Yet as Bercovitch's description suggests, a closer look reveals that such attempts to appeal to antinomian sentiments as a means of fostering elite control could not for long escape either the legacy of Puritanism or the facts of postrevolutionary life. Despite their effectiveness before and during the war, these ideological appeals were, in fact, yet another muddled compromise be-

57. Ibid., 160–61.
58. Stout, 276.
59. Bercovitch, *American Jeremiad*, 129.

tween the demands of order and those of freedom; and as such, they were just as prone to exploitation by the enemies of the dominant class as earlier justifications of elite power had been. For instance, the very phrase by which the New England clergy's chief contribution to revolutionary political thought is known ("covenant republicanism") suggests just how earnestly they sought to adapt the covenant theory of the state (and the traditions of elite hegemony it endorsed) to the spirit of the times by putting it in the service of egalitarianism. In a reprise of their classic position, these descendants of the Puritan moderates sought to create "a new rhetoric" that affirmed liberty and yet also stressed the need for stability and hierarchy in the context of a "social order and political authority that upheld the people in their jealous defense of liberty and legitimated their resistance to unjust tyranny."[60] However, as has already been shown, whether in the seventeenth or the eighteenth centuries, such attempts to pursue a middle course between the polarities of the culture had long proven ineffective, and as an ideological construct "covenant republicanism" fared no better.

Similarly, "the same pattern of bifurcated speech" adopted by the Yankee clergy when speaking to inhabitants of their own region—as opposed to the rest of the nation—also manifested the same deep confliction. For in discourse intended for national consumption, they took an affirmative stance towards liberty:

> When justifying resistance in orations intended for print and widespread dissemination, ministers emphasized the secular vocabulary of "rights and property" that all colonists shared in common. Like lay orators, pamphlet writers, and newspaper editors, they pointed to England's betrayal of her own constitutional heritage. . . . Words like these were calculated to arouse the largest possible number of colonial patriots. At the same time, however, they provide few clues to the message New Englanders routinely heard at home. . . . In local oratory the message audiences heard most frequently was that the struggle with Parliament involved far more than questions of home rule or even, for that matter, who should rule at home; the issues involved nothing less than the preservation of *Sola Scriptura* and New England's privileged position at the center of redemptive history [doctrines intimately connected to the federalist theology and the more hierarchical view of authority it enshrined].[61]

60. Stout, 274.
61. Ibid., 284.

The result, as elsewhere, was a language of authority and freedom that in every way contradicted itself (even as to its intellectual heritage); moreover, as such, this language created still another point at which its dominant-class authors were vulnerable to the domestic reapplication of their own arguments. For once the external British threat had been disposed of, such an unstable amalgam of federalist theology, contractualism, and radical Whiggery could hardly prevent newly independent Yankees from feeling the same toward the republican successors of Thomas Hutchinson and General Gage as their ancestors had toward John Winthrop. In fact, it was actually the successful prosecution of the Revolution that brought to a head the potential for antinomian self-assertion that had been growing in the culture all along, thereby finally giving the lie to these attempts to co-opt it. As Harry Stout has put it:

> Not surprisingly, the chief source of strength within the new republic—its celebration of liberty—was also the chief source of internal strain and confrontation. The cry of "liberty or death," it soon became apparent, was lifted as easily against habits and traditions *within* American society as it was against outside threats. Like many abstract terms, "liberty" was expansive and contagious; a protean shape whose outline could never be fixed. It threatened to contain as many meanings as there were speakers trumpeting its glories and invoking its protections. Without the restraining mechanisms of monarchies, aristocracies, standing armies, mercantile controls, or state churches, there was no telling how far Americans might go in reforming and restructuring their society, or where it would all end.[62]

Thus, although Henry May is right in asserting that in the end "the Revolution" never went as far as it might ("it was more than a colonial revolution, but far less than a complete social upheaval"),[63] its results were clearly enough by the 1790s to have the New England dominant class and their counterparts elsewhere scared. For in its wake "institutions which, on the surface, had no direct bearing on the issue of independence were vulnerable to libertarian criticism and condemned; social assumptions that once commanded respect were questioned and replaced by more democratic principles. This revolution, it soon became apparent, involved . . . nothing less

62. Ibid., 312.
63. May, 179.

than a restructuring of institutions on all levels of society."[64] Furthermore, this leveling tendency was associated with a wave of disorder so great that many members of the elite came to conclude as never before that both New England and America generally were simply ungovernable—let alone open to consensualist persuasion. For although "riots, mob actions, and the raising of semi-private militias were recurrent features of American civil life before the Revolution, in the decades" thereafter "the country was threatened by civil insurrection in the doctors' riot in New York, Shay's Rebellion in western Massachusetts, and the Whiskey Rebellion in Pennsylvania. Mob violence was endemic; there were fist fights in state and federal legislatures; ordinary people took to the streets, destroying property and beating men; dueling became widespread; 'everything . . . seemed to be coming apart, and murder, suicide, and drunkenness were prevalent.' "[65]

In New England one consequence of this state of affairs was the final "loss of mastery" by the Standing Order, who "only gradually, and with great discomfort," realized that their revolutionary indulgence of the antinomian impulses in their culture "had helped create an engine for change and reformation that they ultimately could not control." This not only "laid the basis for their own demise as the single voice of authority in their local communities"[66] but also permanently compromised any future attempts at recouping their losses. Indeed, after their generally successful effort to exert influence during the Revolution, so marked was the eclipse of the ministry (as manifested in the continued growth of deism, unbelief, and indifference, increased denominational competition, the failure of traditional political alliances with the mercantile and legal classes, and yet more demands for the democratization and laicization of church polity) that by the beginning of the nineteenth century it was nearly complete, even in those parts of the area that for a while retained a quasi-establishment.[67]

64. Stout, 312–13.
65. Jane Tompkins, *Sensational Designs: The Cultural Work of American Fiction, 1790–1860* (New York: Oxford University Press, 1985), 48. Tompkins cites Gordon S. Wood's introduction to *The Rising Glory of America, 1760–1820* (New York: George Braziller, 1971), 10. See also his *The Creation of the American Republic, 1776–1787* (Chapel Hill: University of North Carolina Press, 1969).
66. Stout, 313.
67. Bernard Bailyn, ed., *Pamphlets of the American Revolution* (Cambridge, Mass.: Harvard University Press, 1965–) is the most readily available source of information on political propaganda during the Revolution; and Philip Davidson, *Propaganda and the American Revolution, 1763–1783* (Chapel Hill: University of North Carolina Press, 1941) is the standard history. In addition to Ferguson, 3–33, and Stout, 259ff., which treat the particular contribution of the New England clergy (especially the Calvinist "black regiment") to the Revolutionary cause and

The clergy's disempowerment was not the only consequence of this latest combination of events with New England's long-standing class divisions and cultural polarities, however. Elite literary authority was also compromised in the decades after the Treaty of Paris, largely because the revolutionary generation of dominant class male authors in New England (as in America generally) suffered from the same contradictions and confronted the same dilemmas as their clerical counterparts.

On the one hand, they too were deeply committed both to the maintenance of order and to consensualism as an ideological means to that end. For whatever their individual social origins, as educated men they ipso facto belonged to the dominant class and so shared both its interests and—with the exception of a few conscious radicals—its views on matters of authority as well. Moreover, consensualism had also become central to their professional self-understanding as authors. This was not only due to its general prestige in the Anglo-American world but also because by the 1770s educational leaders (from Edward Holyoke and his successors at Harvard to such diverse figures as Provost Smith of the College of Philadelphia and Edwards's eventual successor at Princeton, John Witherspoon) had made consensualist texts the mainstays of the college curriculum. Writers educated in these institutions as a result generally saw their role (whether as poets and essayists or political and philosophical authors) as being akin to that of the consensualist preacher. In a clear colonial parallel to the contemporary English co-option of letters for bourgeois ends, they had been taught that preaching and poetry are " 'like two colors' that 'melt into one another by almost imperceptible shades till the distinction is entirely lost' "[68] and that therefore they should regard themselves as having the same authority and purpose as that of the establishment minister: to act as consensualist didacts and use their pens to gain the affectionate and voluntary submission of their fellow citizens by educat-

---

their problems both during and after the war, Carl Bridenbaugh, *Mitre and Sceptre: Transatlantic Faiths, Ideas, Personalities, and Politics, 1689–1775* (New York: Oxford University Press, 1962), and Nathan O. Hatch, *The Sacred Cause of Liberty: Republican Thought and the Millennium in Revolutionary New England* (New Haven, Conn.: Yale University Press, 1977), deal with the decline of the ministry in influence and status throughout the revolutionary and postrevolutionary periods. A number of interesting individual examples of clerical attempts to influence political events at this time are also provided in Donald Weber's *Rhetoric and History in Revolutionary New England* (New York: Oxford University Press, 1988).

68. John Witherspoon, *Lectures on Moral Philosophy and Eloquence* (Philadelphia: William W. Woodward, 1810), 198 [cited in Emory Elliott, *Revolutionary Writers: Literature and Authority in the New Republic, 1725–1810* (New York: Oxford University Press, 1982), 32]. Elliott, 3–54, discusses the impact of consensualist texts upon secular intellectual life, thus supplementing Fliegelman's more extensive account.

ing them and furthering their religious, cultural, political, and moral progress to the point where they would realize the superior virtue and wisdom of their teachers.

Graduates of Harvard or students of Witherspoon, like Freneau, Brackenridge, and Madison, thus learned that in being writers they were to be participants with the clergy in the exercise of elite leadership. For by providing a didactic theory of literature and a moderate, bourgeois view of its sociocultural purpose, their teachers did more than reinforce these budding authors' professional and class interests; they also explicitly taught them to function as members of a clerisy dedicated in good consensualist fashion to ensuring their own central role in republican culture. Paradoxically, therefore, although the appeal of the ministry as a career choice was itself on the wane among young members of the dominant class in the late eighteenth century, it was at this very time that the didactic, consensualist ideals most associated with the Arminian clergy became associated with a life given over to letters—especially if, as was more and more often now the case, it were combined with the law.[69]

Unfortunately, like the preachers, almost all the writers of the revolutionary generation also bought at least partially into the antiauthoritarianism and millennial leveling then popular in the country at large. Indeed, throughout

69. Although one can still point to a number of prominent individuals during this period who (like Timothy Dwight) were quite literally preacher-poets, the law was increasingly the career of choice for those in the dominant class in need of a profession, especially if they were of a literary bent. As Ferguson and others already cited have shown (see above, n. 26), this was because of the relative decline in the prestige and influence of the clergy, the final secularization of education and urban life, the prominence of political issues from 1763 on, and the simple fact that authors needed a remunerative and yet leisured profession in a society whose lack of a court, a large publishing industry, and traditions of patronage all necessarily tended to make belles lettres a part-time endeavor. In addition, the fact that the bar had a jealously maintained reputation for learning, classical scholarship, and the neo-republican sentiments associated with the common law and the English "country party" tradition also made it a haven for those who sought to combine scholarship, letters, and politics as a means of wielding influence through belles lettres and courtroom and legislative oratory.

These issues are dealt with by a number of scholars. The fullest (and most accurate) treatment of the literary and cultural reception of the classics in eighteenth-century America is Meyer Reinhold, *Classica Americana: The Greek and Roman Heritage in the United States* (Detroit: Wayne State University Press, 1984), esp. 23–173. The ideological connections among the classics, literary neoclassicism, republicanism, and the legal profession are summarized in Ferguson, 59–84. In addition, Howard D. Weinbrot's *Augustan Caesar in "Augustan" England: the Decline of a Classical Norm* (Princeton, N.J.: Princeton University Press, 1978) is also useful in outlining the English background to this intellectual constellation, as are Bailyn, *Ideological Origins*, and Daniel Walker Howe, *The Political Culture of the American Whigs* (Chicago: University of Chicago Press, 1979), which chart the effects in America of the other cultural strands mentioned here (the common law, the English "country party" tradition of resistance, etc.).

the 1770s and 1780s their themes were "the rising glory of America" and the blessings of "liberty and independence." Later, therefore, when they ran up against the consequences of this maneuver (as antihierarchical feelings began to be refocused on them and men of their class, and as postcolonial socioeconomic and political instabilities increased) the rush of many of them toward the Arminian pole of their tradition was every bit as rapid as that of their clerical counterparts. As Emory Elliott has put it—with perhaps insufficient regard for the many New England precedents for this event—"the writers and ministers who had entered the Revolution with such optimism and high hopes for America" now "found themselves in a struggle for the survival of values and traditions which only a few years before they had assumed to be permanent."

> What soon became apparent . . . was that the revolution of mind taking place in America was conducive neither to the arts nor to religion. Even before the fighting was over, the ministers and the poets began to comprehend the emergent threat to their social status and intellectual authority. Politicians and patrons who had been so encouraging to the arts turned cool; congregations grew sullen and rebellious; literary journals failed; literary works by Americans sold poorly. For many of the clergy and for most of the men of letters who lived in America during the last decades of the eighteenth century, the American Revolution seemed to involve a betrayal. As the more perceptive writers and the ministers realized, the changes being brought about were only signs of a radical shift of attitude within the American populace that could constitute a serious threat to traditional religious and intellectual authority. Unless the men of letters could establish new grounds for asserting their intellectual leadership in the society, they would find themselves at the mercy of public favor on the one hand and the power of political and economic interests on the other.

As Elliott goes on to note, this chain of events on the whole led dominant class intellectuals to become decidedly pessimistic. "At worst they feared that the new nation would become a cultural and spiritual wasteland, a new Sodom where social anarchy and moral corruption reigned, [and] at the least they foresaw a diminishing of" their own "role . . . to . . . social insignificance." Even though in the end "religion did survive, . . . [and] literature also endured,"[70] they believed, therefore, that they were fast arriving at the very position the clergy had tried so hard to avoid for the previous century and a half.

Of course, there was obviously a degree of hysteria in these complaints (something not unknown among authors even in our own day). Yet the threats to dominant class interests were real, as was (with the exception of a few genuine Jacobins like Freneau and Barlow) the movement from the late 1780s on, at various speeds, of America's male dominant class writers away from the antinomian pole in American culture. This return to the satisfaction of the claims of order was most pronounced in Federalist New England (although it can be found at a slower pace in other areas and other circles— even Jeffersonian ones—as well),[71] and its result was the production of texts that were consciously didactic and consensualist in their emphasis on the need to guide individual and communal nurture toward social harmony (so much so that many of them are distinctly monitory in tone).

For example, although it is not by a New Englander, Charles Brockden Brown's *Wieland* was written "in 1798, the year of the Alien and Sedition Acts." Appropriately enough, therefore, it is both a meditation upon consensualist themes common throughout the second half of the eighteenth century and also "a terrifying post–French Revolutionary account of the fallibility of the human mind and, by extension, of democracy itself" (one in which two clear manifestations of the current antinomian tide, "ventriloquism and religious enthusiasm, . . . seem with a sardonic literalness to call into question all possible faith in the republican formula *vox populi, vox Dei*"). For in Brown's view and that of many members of the elite, the Terror had confirmed their worst fear: that the international upheavals of the preceding quarter century had produced a culture of political seduction, untrammeled self-interest, and the manipulation of mass feeling conducive to the likes of Robespierre and Aaron Burr. Moreover, as the novel's plot makes clear, even worse in their eyes was the "epistemological terror and moral confusion" that seemed to accompany democracy, since it appeared to them to have all but overwhelmed parental and dominant class attempts at exercising authority. And so, *Wieland*'s

70. Elliott, *Revolutionary Writers*, 35–36. For other accounts of the postrevolutionary crisis and its effect on literary authority, see Tompkins, 40–93, and May, esp. 153ff.
71. "Federalist" is used here (and generally hereafter) in its party political rather than its theological sense.

subtitle, *The Transformation,* refers not only to the transformation of [the character] Wieland but to a broad historical transformation, the shift from a world that assumed stable forms and fixed relations between appearance and reality and between man and society to a world sensitive to shifting values, deceptive appearances, mixed motives, and most significantly, the tyranny of language over things, rhetoric over logic. A secure world has been made insecure and that, Brown announces, is the price of its having become "free." [Moreover,] by placing his novel in the decade before the American Revolution, Brown suggests, by implication, that the great conflict for American independence, rather than merely being a result of that larger "transformation," decisively hastened it.

For "in this transformed world both freedom of rational inquiry and the enthusiast's belief in religious determinism lead to fatal consequences," and "the 'benevolent scheme' of nurture and cultivation, the great enterprise of the Enlightenment" (and the backbone of consensualism's defense of bourgeois authority), has become "mocked and perverted" in a stark "betrayal of the American promise of liberty."[72]

Brown's vision of the dark side of the Enlightenment's moon was by no means unique. Other writers of the dominant class, both in New England and elsewhere, saw the same signs in the upheavals of their times and tried to shore up their consensualist defenses against the antinomian flood tide surging about them. In some cases they did so positively and (as in the hagiographical literature surrounding George Washington) tried to provide the nation with more potent consensualist authority figures;[73] but more commonly they wrote negative, cautionary tales (like Trumbull's revised *M'Fingal,* Tyler's *The Contrast,* and Brackenridge's *Modern Chivalry*) that satirically extolled the authority of the educated and gentle, and attacked the farmers and frontiersmen whom they sought to control. Yet even in circumstances such as those of the 1790s, they could not rid themselves of the conflictions of their culture, divisions that expressed themselves in the "contradictions of repub-

72. Fliegelman, 237–40. Other useful discussions of the "politics" of Charles Brockden Brown's novels include Tompkins, 40–61, and Cathy N. Davidson, *Revolution and the Word: The Rise of the Novel in America* (New York: Oxford University Press, 1986), 212–53. A more general survey of the shifting literature of consensualism in the last two decades of the eighteenth century is to be found in Fliegelman, pp. 227ff.

73. Fliegelman, 197–226, gives a good brief introduction to the cultus of George Washington and its political origins. For a more lengthy account, see Gary Wills, *Cincinnatus: George Washington and the Enlightenment* (Garden City, N.Y.: Doubleday, 1984).

lican discourse."[74] This is why Washington in their writings is both archetypal rebel and surrogate king, a human like us and yet a demigod—like
Chauncy's Jesus, a typical consensualist leader whose very figural moderation between command from above and acquiescence in the popular will
left him open to attack from below. It is also why elite male poets and novelists like the Browns and Tylers and Trumbulls failed to take one side or the
other in this contest for authority decisively. For their upper-class heroes are
clearly expressions of their own fears and ideological contradictions, and so
are either ineffectual in the face of antinomian knavery or are intermittent
mouthpieces for criticism of the very upper class whose interests they defend. Similarly, their lower-class villains (like Brown's Carwin) also contradict the consensualism of their works as a whole, because they are strangely
attractive and powerful in their advocacy of radical revolution (thereby be-
speaking the personal difficulty their creators had in resisting the antinomian side of their inheritance).

   Indeed, when these contradictory impulses and their manifestation in consensualism are added to both the effects of postrevolutionary social change on
the elite and a number of specific problems peculiar to postcolonial American authors,[75] it is little wonder that a hobbled turn toward Arminianism

---

74. Cathy N. Davidson, 154; see 151–211 of her book for an interesting treatment of the picar-
esque novel as the quintessential fictional example of the contradictions of this cultural position
(which, as she demonstrates, afflicted political Federalists and Republicans alike).

75. Perhaps the most important of the afflictions hobbling postrevolutionary elite male authors as they attempted to lead their society through belles lettres were their neocolonial cultural
loyalties. For even as the nationalism of their generation impelled them to seek a distinctively
American voice in which to address the widest possible cross section of their fellow citizens, they
continued to feel deep loyalty to the European literary tradition. This loyalty was reinforced by
the neoclassical republicanism of contemporary American political culture (see above, n. 69), a
literary conservatism born of the essentially imitative procedures of their rhetorical training and
the fear that both the educated minority at home and critics abroad would treat departures from
established models "as unpolished products of the forest." Paradoxically, the resulting disjunc-
tion in their works (between an often histrionic nationalism and formal and thematic deriva-
tiveness) fulfilled their worst neocolonial fears. For their nationalistic epics in imitation of Pope
and Homer, their slightly old-fashioned New England loco-topographical poems, and their
Americanized dramas fashioned after Addison's *Cato* and the comedies of the London stage were
received for what they generally were: "weak imitations of English or classical models" incon-
gruously translated to the New World (Elliott, *Revolutionary Writers*, 45).
   Indeed, even writers painfully aware of this dilemma produced works showing how insidious
it really was. The most famous example of this is Royall Tyler's thoroughly consensualist imitation of Sheridan, *The Contrast*, which not only enacts the confliction between order and freedom at the heart of Anglo-American bourgeois culture but also illustrates the cruelest paradox of
Federalist literature: the fact that the new republic's dominant-class men of letters failed in their
quest to become the mentors of a grateful nation, precisely because they were not successful in
achieving the very independence and maturity which (as consensualists) they themselves sought

did little to improve the authority of Federalist men of letters. The last decades of the eighteenth century, in fact, comprise nothing less than a chronicle of the disillusionment and frustration of dominant-class authors with democracy and the threat it seemed to pose to their status and power. With few exceptions, whatever the conscious political loyalties of their creators, in the end the writings of these descendants of English Dissent were fraught with contradiction. This is why in affirming the blessings of order, piety, and moderate, consensualist republicanism, an orthodox Yale preacher-poet like Timothy Dwight could combine blatant pastoral nostalgia with nightmarish visions of war and anarchy in "Greenfield Hill"; and it is also why the new nation's most consistent literary Jacobin, Joel Barlow—himself a renegade from the pulpit and New England's God—could eventually abandon his revolutionary fervor for the bitter recriminations over a failed career and a betrayed cause found in "Advice to a Raven in Russia." For however quick or slow they were to realize it, they found themselves cursed by the same social realities and delusive self-divisions that had tormented the previous four generations of their ancestors.[76]

---

to inculcate. (Ferguson, 111–19, gives a convincing reading of *The Contrast*, as [incidentally] does Davidson, esp. 192–200 and 212–15. See also Albert J. von Frank, *The Sacred Game: Provincialism and Frontier Consciousness in American Literature: 1630–1860* [Cambridge, Eng.: Cambridge University Press, 1985], 29–41, and [for a more general treatment] G. Thomas Tanselle, *Royall Tyler* [Cambridge, Mass.: Harvard University Press, 1967].)

76. See Ferguson, 95–149, and Elliott, *Revolutionary Writers*, 55ff., for examples of the ways in which individual authors dealt with the frustrations and demands of their careers in this complex cultural situation.

1

THE UNITARIAN MILTON

John Milton's reception during the last two decades of the eighteenth century offers an especially good illustration of the ways in which the contradictions of Puritanism continued to affect the dominant class. The reasons for this are not hard to find. To begin with, given his place in English history and his literary reputation, Milton would likely have been among the New England elite's pantheon in any case. It is no surprise, therefore, to find that they regarded him as "a consummate artist" and "a man of titanic stature" to such a degree that "few dared speak ill of his name." Nor is it surprising that by the time of "the early Republic . . . Americans" both in New England and regions farther south had "made him a touchstone of judgment and a model for poets." For in imitating Milton, poets such as Barlow, Dwight, Trumbull, and Freneau were at one level only paying homage to a great predecessor—as were, in prose, educators like Provost Smith, philosophers like William Livingston, men of letters like John Blair Linn and James Ralph, and political thinkers from John Adams to Thomas Jefferson— all of whom drew upon Milton as a source of ideas, "praised him as one of England's illustrious sons and extolled his lofty thought and sublime style."[1]

1. George Sensabaugh provides general evidence for Milton's high standing in eighteenth-century America in his introductory chapter, from which these phrases are taken (3–33). He also gives more detailed examples in his treatment of Milton in the prerevolutionary period (34–96). Because his account is in general *descriptively* complete, I will usually refer the reader to it when citing specific examples of Milton's reception during this period. Another brief summary is that of John T. Shawcross, *John Milton and Influence: Presence in Literature, History and Culture* (Pittsburgh, Pa.: Duquesne University Press, 1991), 139–55.

Yet in holding him in such high esteem, Milton's dominant-class American students and imitators were hardly just being naïve enthusiasts.[2] There was another reason for their approbation, one grounded in their fundamental self-interest as members of an elite. For whether they were on the political right (like Adams and Timothy Dwight) or on the left (like Thomas Paine and Joel Barlow), Milton seemed to them to be uniquely amenable to self-interested manipulation, because he spoke to—and so seemed to provide answers for—the crisis of authority that continued to confront them. Thus, for instance, these eighteenth-century Americans rightly understood *Paradise Lost* to be one of the classic representations of moderate Puritanism's confliction between the claims of order and those of liberty (something Milton expressed in the sharp contrast between the hierarchical but mutual relationship of Father and Son within the Godhead, and the epic's two main antithetical actions: the confrontation between God and Satan, and the growing opposition between Adam and Eve). Faced as they were with the same deep polarities, they also quite naturally interpreted the relationship between the Father and the Son in the poem so as to support their own visions of an ideal balance between order and freedom and made the text's confrontations between deity and demon, and primordial man and woman, the locus of all their resentments, passions, and fears.

In other words, although Milton's avowed aim in *Paradise Lost* was "to justify the ways of God to man," Americans during the Age of Reason understood that his deeper purpose had been to create a mythic justification for moderate Puritanism and its hegemonic claims. Similarly, they also saw how neatly that objective fit their own situation as men simultaneously struggling in the name of middle-class authority against both divine right and leveling. This is why when they read Milton's portrayal of Satan as an antinomian hero defying hierarchical power yet then also read his Arminian negation of the more radical implications of that portrayal, they felt the poet spoke for them. As Jay Fliegelman notes, in the tumultuous years before the Revolution, Milton's assertion "that the tyrannical God against whom Satan rages is" not real but "a projection of the arch-fiend's own rebellious pride and a reflection of the limitations of his perception" seemed to give them warrant for their own contradictory attempts to apply the brake to the very egalitarian forces they themselves to a degree supported.

Thus, as Fliegelman goes on to show, the convergence of interests and ideology between Milton and the American dominant class in the late eigh-

2. As Sensabaugh's admirable but not always probing study often implies.

teenth century explains why before the Revolution a New Divinity preacher like Joseph Bellamy could read Milton's account of the revolt of Satan more or less as the poet himself consciously intended. For despite leanings in the direction of radicalism, like the earlier New Lights, Bellamy sought to co-opt rather than affirm his culture's antinomianism; and so he found Milton's moderate position on authority supportive of his own defense of the federal theology and the figuration of dominant-class rule it enshrined. Similarly, the poet's ideological usefulness also explains why, while on one level theologically Arminian "detractors of Calvin" like Charles Chauncy and Benjamin Colman viewed the war between Heaven and Hell in an antinomian way (as a refutation of their ancestors' patriarchalist belief in a "God apart from Christ, justice apart from mercy, works apart from faith, service apart from obedience"), they also read that action in ways that reflect their more paradigmatically Arminian interests as bourgeois professionals. For even though they applauded Milton's protest in the poem against arbitrariness and tyranny, and his Protestant assertion of the equality of persons, as demonstrated by Satan's "jealousy of the favor Jehovah showed Christ"—doctrines that utterly undercut divine right—they were not true radicals. Rather, like their moderate Puritan ancestors, they were actually very much interested in suppressing radicalism; and so, they were even more glad that at the end of the poem Milton had made it clear that God (and with Him, the forces of order and hierarchy) would eventually triumph. For like the poet, they did not wish to follow through on the logical consequences of their commitment to liberty and individual autonomy and accept the full ecclesiastical implications of Satan's leveling assertion "that the Only Begotten Son was, in fact, no different from others of the angelic host who were all begotten sons."

Moreover, this is certainly why Chauncy and company also emphasized those parts of *Paradise Lost* that proved Milton to be no antinomian but instead, like themselves (and most of the Anglo-American elite after 1688), a moderate rejector of genetic patriarchy—one who, though (like Satan) he "would not brook there being but one son and others who must slavishly obey," would not wish to abolish hierarchical relationships like paternity either. For the most prominent of these passages are those in which Milton forestalled the potentially radical implications of Satan's defiance by stressing that his resistance is but an imperfect foreshadowing of the Incarnation. Because "Satan's rebellious desire to be son and not servant and Christ's offer of a new dispensation of sonship (which silently acknowledged that rebellion) are ultimately related," they could therefore dissipate the archetypal tensions within the poem between governor and governed by absorbing them into the new consensualist relationship between God and humanity exemplified by the dual nature of Christ (which in its salvific combination of humanity and divinity affirms "that part of the Christian tradition that insists upon benevolence as a primary attribute of the Deity").[3]

As this suggests, in the end, the real difference between Milton's eighteenth-century American Arminian interpreters and New Lights like Bellamy is that the former read the poem in ways that were more thoroughly consensualist. Yet the two sets of theologians were equally self-interested as interpreters of *Paradise Lost*. In this they were hardly unusual. As will be seen, the large number of Miltonic imitations written by lay poets during this period alone show how widely his works were called upon by those wishing to address matters of authority in a turbulent age; and there are many examples of the use of his prose to this end as well. It is important to note first, however, that there was another reason that dominant-class writers were drawn to Milton at the end of the eighteenth century. For if one had to search for an earlier literary figure who embodied the personal cultural authority late eighteenth-century American men of letters lacked and who also mirrored their own rather complex sociocultural position, one could do no better than John Milton.

Of course, one reason for Milton's prominence at this time was that (with the exception of a few detractors like Dr. Johnson and Noah Webster) he was held in high esteem on both sides of the Atlantic. His poetry and prose were recommended by popular rhetoricians (like Robert Lowth, Hugh Blair, and James Burgh) as being among the best models for imitation, and in both Britain and America he was ranked critically as a poetic genius second—if at all—only to Shakespeare. It was only natural, therefore, that he should be a literary model for Americans concerned about achieving greatness themselves. However, in addition, much late eighteenth-century Milton biography and criticism presented the poet as a figure who evinced the very qualities America's consensualist clerisy hoped to show in their own writing. In the view of many in the Age of Reason, he was an ideal consensualist authority figure, a genius whose sublimity of vision, moral elevation, seriousness of purpose, didactic skill, and religious inspiration all made him a fitting *alter ego* for dominant class authors, as they too tried to reestablish their leading

---

3. Fliegelman, 174. Examples of Milton's use by the New Lights and the Arminians to advance their respective positions on questions of authority can be found in the writings of Bellamy, Colman, and Chauncy (see ibid., 43–52 and 120–22).

role by bringing faith, learning, and a commitment to civic education to bear on affairs of state.[4]

Unfortunately, the elite's identification with Milton as a fellow consensualist quickly ran afoul of contradictions much like those which had characterized his own political position. During the American Revolution dominant class intellectuals had in general sought to play to the antinomianism of their culture at a time when both they and most of the other colonists were moving in a strongly antiauthoritarian direction. The chief intellectual manifestation of this was the development of a body of democratic and egalitarian ideas that form (what Bernard Bailyn has called) the most "distinctive ideological strain" in the events of 1776. Significantly, although in terms of origins "its permanent form had been acquired at the turn of the seventeenth century and in the early eighteenth century, in the writings of a group of prolific opposition theorists, 'country' politicians and publicists," the "ultimate origins" of this tradition of dissent "lay in the radical social and political thought of the English Civil War and of the Commonwealth period"; and "among the . . . progenitors of this line of . . . radical writers and opposition politicians united in criticism of 'court' and ministerial power, Milton was an important figure" (not least because his writings could easily be applied to justify America's own attempt to overthrow royal tyranny). Thus, when during the Revolution they invoked his example as precedent for their own exercise of leadership, dominant-class men of letters were unwittingly invoking the Milton who had created a heroic Satan. In the short term, this did not seem to matter, since at the very time when such antinomian defiance was most appealing, the radical strain in Milton's writings naturally made him both a transatlantic and a profoundly contemporary figure—an honorary American because he loved liberty. "Milton the radical tractarian, author of *Eikonoklastes* and *The Tenure of Kings and Magistrates*," was easy grist for the patriotic propaganda mill, and his great epic frequently and effectively expressed colonial defiance of George III as well.[5] Indeed, as Fliegelman

4. Sensabaugh, 98–110, discusses Milton's prominent place in the rhetoric books and college curricula up to about 1810. See also his discussion (3–96) for examples of Milton's positive treatment in colonial American critical and biographical works. The best recent treatment of Milton's reception in eighteenth-century England, Dustin Griffin, *Regaining Paradise: Milton and the Eighteenth Century* (Cambridge, Eng.: Cambridge University Press, 1986), 1–42, summarizes his British critical reputation in ways that are suggestive for students of Milton in revolutionary America. (Griffin also places Dr. Johnson's animadversions about the poet in useful perspective).

5. Bailyn, 34. It should be noted that Bailyn is wrong in underestimating the place of Milton's verse in this tradition.

argues, proponents of "Christian evangelicalism, rational theology, and revolutionary politics—each deeply affected by . . . [the] antipatriarchal tradition—all" came to see *Paradise Lost* as being concerned, like "themselves, with redefining sonship"; and it is this act of familial refiguring through a "heretical union" of ideas (taken from the Whig and Country party traditions) that gives "the ideology of the American Revolution its distinctive character."[6]

Yet as has also been noted, most of the dominant class increasingly wanted this redefinition of authority to be a consensualist rather than a radical one, especially as the leveling implications of the Revolution became apparent. Their Milton as a consequence quickly came to be less the justifier of regicide and more the ancestor (along with Locke, Hampden, Harrington, Neville, and Sidney) of their own moderate constitutional republicanism. For by the end of the war, the pursuit of dominant-class hegemony had again become uppermost in many of their minds, and so Milton's historically conflicted position on authority aptly fit their own mood as they tried to play to Anglo-American culture's antinomian strain (under the guise of "the typology of Christian liberty" and "covenant republicanism")—but without encouraging radicalism.[7]

Among other things, this explains the nature of most of the many quotations and allusions to Milton's writings in the newspapers and magazines of the Revolution, as well as his frequent appearances in the sermons and tracts of ministers like Jonathan Mayhew, the verse of poets like Jonathan Trumbull, and the political thought of such secular Yankee leaders as John Adams. For in these and other instances, New Englanders of a dominant class and professional background usually invoked or imitated such works as *Paradise Lost*, *Areopagitica*, *The Tenure of Kings and Magistrates*, and the *Pro Populo Anglicano Defensio* in a consensualist way that served their self-interest. In the case of *Paradise Lost*, for example, writers from the elite on the one hand thus typically portrayed George III during the Revolution as a hapless parody of Milton's God, since like the common folk they viewed their monarch as a tyrant against whom they might indulge their antinomian impulses at

---

6. Fliegelman, 174.

7. The standard treatments of the "typology of Christian liberty" (both in relation to "covenant republicanism" and otherwise) are Bercovitch's *American Jeremiad* and his *Puritan Origins of the American Self* (New Haven, Conn.: Yale University Press, 1975). John P. McWilliams, Jr., *Hawthorne, Melville, and the American Character: A Looking-glass Business* (Cambridge, Eng.: Cambridge University Press, 1984), and Michael J. Colacurcio, *The Province of Piety: Moral History in Hawthorne's Early Tales* (Cambridge, Mass.: Harvard University Press, 1984), also discuss this ideological formation and its impact on some later New England authors.

will. Yet being subject to the Arminian structure of feeling as well, they typically then also tried to blunt the radical potential of this application of Milton's poem. Often they did this by balancing their portrayal of the King as a patriarchalist god with another portrait that implicitly condemned revolution except in very special circumstances. This was their caricature of the Tories as satanic conspirators against the *other* side of Milton's deity: the God Who (both in His own relationship with Christ, and in the relationship originally ordained between Adam and Eve) had limited His power so as to establish a balance between the claims of equality and those of hierarchy. King George became, thereby, a more ambiguous figure. He was still a patriarchalist father who had denied his American offspring their right to growth and autonomy; yet he was also now one against whom only a certain kind of revolt was appropriate—rebellion, not in the name of satanic egalitarianism, but in that of the sort of moderate, consensualist relationship between superiors and inferiors that Milton's epic ultimately endorses.

At such a time of widespread antinomian indulgence, however, the hegemonist aspects of these patriotic imitations of *Paradise Lost* do not initially seem to have made much difference to their reception. It was the poems' antiauthoritarian dimension that instead seems to have struck a chord with the public. Indeed, they were so immensely popular and effective that loyalists like Samuel Seabury of Connecticut and Jonathan Odell of New York had to reply in kind. Yet the Tory sermons and poems they wrote in imitation of, or alluding to, John Milton only further confirm the barely hidden Arminian agenda behind the employment of his epic by the dominant class as a whole. For out of an even more pervasively Arminian fear of democratic empowerment, these loyalists turned to the older patriarchalist ideology in order to impose two different anticonsensualist readings upon the same Miltonic passages so popular with their Whig contemporaries: one in which the King (alternatively portrayed as Jehovah, an aggrieved parent, or God's anointed angel) righteously wreaks vengeance on those in the colonies who have disobeyed him (especially the satanic conclave gathered in Philadelphia); and another in which (as in Major Richard Rogers's verse play, *Ponteach*) Milton's Satan gives frightening self-satiric voice to the radical implications of the rebellion's antinomian rhetoric.[8]

8. Sensabaugh, 122–83 and 239–81, provides many illustrations of Milton's use before, during, and after the Revolution in relation to the crisis convulsing British North America. These include such pseudo-Miltonic poetic contributions in aid of the patriot cause as Freneau's "A Voyage to Boston" and "On the Fall of General Earl Cornwallis" (also discussed by Fliegelman, 155–58); the work of many minor Whig poets like Elijah Fitch; and that most extensive Miltonic

As this suggests, dominant-class patriot and loyalist alike read Milton's *Paradise Lost* as a political allegory that implicitly cautioned against leveling. Both were at least partially motivated by class self-interest in using Milton's greatest poem for political purposes during the War of Independence, and in using the epic (and Milton's other writings), both showed an allegiance to one or the other of the ideologies (consensualism or patriarchalism) then employed by their class to affirm hierarchical control. The only difference is that Milton's Tory admirers were more extreme in their attempt to hew an antiegalitarian course. In the case of the conflict's winners, furthermore, their misunderstanding of why they were at first so successful in applying *Paradise Lost* to current events had long-term consequences. The initial reception of their revolutionary Miltonic satires later encouraged them to hope that by imitating the poet they might continue to speak with authority to the new nation about affairs of state. Yet as the examples just cited should suggest, in this they were deluded, since the underlying reason for their ephemeral success was not what they thought it to be; rather, their adaptations of Milton's prose and their satiric uses of his verse were popular precisely because they played to the same antinomian strain in Anglo-American culture that had threatened dominant-class rule all along. After independence had been won, when they found themselves once again the targets of lower-class enmity, they discovered that neither the imitation of John Milton nor any other literary ploy would suffice to induce deference in a restive population.

The wide readership of a revolutionary-era poem like the original version of Trumbull's *M'Fingal* was thus due—in Miltonic terms, at least—to the fact that *Paradise Lost* effectively focused the antiauthoritarianism so deep in New England culture onto the King's minions. Similarly, the period's more serious attempts to imitate Milton's vatic powers at first also found an audience for the same reason. For when they drew upon the prophetic passages of *Paradise Lost* in order to encourage the happy prosecution of the struggle at hand, patriotic American poets were ringing the changes on the enthusiasm,

---

imitation during the revolutionary period: the first version of Trumbull's *M'Fingal*. Sensabaugh also summarizes the work of the Tory poets, who (with little sense of contradiction) made Milton a supporter of the King's cause. In addition, Laura E. Tanner and James N. Krasner, in "Exposing the 'Sacred Juggle': Revolutionary Rhetoric in Robert Rogers' *Ponteach*," *Early American Literature* 24 (1989): 4–18, provide an interesting discussion of the literary career of the sometime captain of Rogers's Rangers (whom they see as frontally assaulting "the 'heightened language of intense liberalism and paranoiac mistrust of power,' . . . the 'fear and frenzy, the exaggerations and the enthusiasm' that, according to Gordon Wood, are characteristic of Whig revolutionary rhetoric" [4]). By contrast, the rather different political reception of Milton in contemporary England is discussed by Griffin, 11–21.

millennialism, and utopianism that figure so prominently in the radicalism of both the Great Rebellion and the Revolutionary War. Despite the Americans' lack of true Miltonic fire, this is why there is therefore a brief but believable—and, it seems, popular—tradition of Miltonic visionary verse in America, beginning with Freneau and Brackenridge's 1770 Princeton commencement ode, "The Rising Glory of America" (in which the Archangel Michael's prediction of future history is reworked into a sanguine vision of an America freed from England's yoke), and continuing on in the triumphalist moments of satires like *M'Fingal* and Freneau's "A Voyage to Boston." Paradoxically, however, this is also partly the reason why eighteenth-century New England's two most ambitious poetic efforts (Timothy Dwight's *The Conquest of Canaan* and Joel Barlow's *The Vision of Columbus*—later recast as *The Columbiad*) came to grief after the war. For even though Dwight and Barlow's histrionically nationalistic epics obviously suffer in comparison to *Paradise Lost* on literary grounds (e.g., they are both woodenly derivative of the European epic and the Bible, and uninterestingly Miltonic when they project a utopian future for the postrevolutionary New World), their failure also has to do with the fact that both poems ran afoul of the antinomian structure of feeling. In the case of the Federalist Dwight, this was because his epic was imbued with the consensualism of the postrevolutionary dominant class and so represented a position about authority increasingly out of favor even among those Americans able or willing to read heroic verse. And in that of Barlow, it was because after his conversion to radicalism, *The Columbiad* preached a distinctly Francophile brand of revolutionary millennialism at the very time when Napoleon and the Terror were making revolutionary France synonymous with the tyranny and patriarchalism from which the New World had just escaped.[9]

9. Sensabaugh, 146–83, provides many examples of Milton's pervasive influence on the development of the popular "Rising Glory" poetry of the Revolutionary and Early National periods, as well as parallel instances of a similar Miltonic presence in other genres (e.g., that of Brackenridge's *Comus*like masque praising George Washington). See also Stavely, "The World All before Them: Milton and the Rising Glory of America," in *Studies in Eighteenth-Century Culture*, ed. Leslie Ellen Brown and Patricia B. Craddock (East Lansing, Mich.: Colleagues Press, 1990) 20: 147–64, and Bercovitch, *American Jeremiad*, 93ff., and *The Puritan Origins of the American Self*, 136ff., for the process by which these and other literary works (both in verse and prose) were used to secularize earlier typological renderings of "the myth of America" (often, as Stavely suggests, thereby contradicting Milton himself).

It should be mentioned in this context that the very neocolonial imitativeness that retarded American belles lettres in general during this period (see Introduction, n. 75) finds perhaps its most excruciating manifestation in the Federalist epics. This is largely because of the formal nature of what Barlow and Dwight were trying to do. For when, on the one hand, their

By contrast, popularly successful dominant-class Miltonic verse usually occurred in the 1780s and 1790s when authors effectively harnessed one or the other of the structures of feeling in Anglo-American culture to their purposes. During the constitutional debates, for instance, before the tide had wholly turned against the elite, dominant-class writers who favored the proposed document and its antiradical features (e.g., the system of checks and balances, an indirectly elected Senate, and judges appointed for life), were for a few years in step with the majority in their desire to correct the semi-anarchic conditions that existed under the Articles of Confederation. When they turned to *Paradise Lost* to help them argue the case for law, order, and moderate governance they thus did so in circumstances that were temporarily favorable to their cause. Moreover, they were also successful because in using the poem to stress the need for greater cohesion they avoided evoking the other side of their culture's Puritan heritage. In particular, they refocused interest away from the satanic parts of the poem and onto the "Wedding Hymn" in book IV (which they made the very type of an ideal, Arminian communitarian order). The resulting portrait of an "affectional and voluntaristic marriage" under the new moderate constitution "captured [the] American imagination" at a time when the nation was tired of war and disorder.[10]

---

contemporaries imitated *Paradise Lost* for the purpose of political satire, they were writing in a different genre and—strictly speaking, in literary terms—for a different end than Milton had been. Their poems on affairs of state and party political satires were thus not perceived as being in intertextual competition with Milton's epic, because in terms of the conventions of eighteenth-century mock heroic, their application of Satan's grand villainy to the likes of General Gage and George III made for a witty and effective play on the "kinds" of literature (one which deliberately channeled the reader's sense of diminished poetic power for conscious ends). (Ian Jack, *Augustan Satire: Intention and Idiom in English Poetry, 1660–1750* [1942; corr. ed., Oxford: Oxford University Press, 1971], offers a useful historical introduction to this self-conscious use of genre in eighteenth-century satire.) However, when, on the other hand, Dwight or Barlow attempted to imitate Milton's visionary mode by writing epics of their own, none of the refracting qualities of the mock heroic obtained; and so, their poems were seen as being in direct intertextual confrontation with *Paradise Lost*—with disastrous results. For the comparison of the shaky republic to the New Jerusalem was more than just potentially risible (despite the spread from New England of the typological habit of mind); the obvious difference in poetic power between these botched, wooden poems and their original was clear; and the debt of their triumphalistically nationalist authors to the culture of the Old World was painfully evident. As a consequence, *The Conquest of Canaan* and *The Columbiad* became bywords in their own day, and now stand as epitomes of the problems afflicting elite American literature at the end of the eighteenth century.

10. Fliegelman, 127 and 129. He devotes a whole chapter in *Prodigals and Pilgrims* to this use of Milton (123–54), and Sensabaugh, 110–17 and 195–217, also discusses it at length. For a provocative (if controversial) treatment of the impact of the "affectionate union" doctrine on late

However, as the new nation's antiauthoritarian tendencies continued to grow, and as the crisis of authority intensified, Federalists, Democrats, and Jacobins all came to see that visions of wedded New World bliss were beyond America's abilities. They consequently joined the debate over authority again with renewed vigor—often, like Trumbull (who early on in 1782 expanded *M'Fingal*, making it even more explicitly Arminian), by returning to those parts of *Paradise Lost* in which Satan appears, in order to give weight to their views. As a result, the partisan satire occasioned by the Citizen Genet affair, the Alien and Sedition Acts, the alleged Jacobinism of the third president, and later the Hartford Convention has a distinctly Miltonic cast. Once again the person of Satan and the war between Heaven and Hell were invoked in order to characterize political opponents; once again the poet's archetypal tale of the conflict between authority and freedom was used in ways that bespeak the polarities within Puritan culture. Yet there is an important difference between these later satires and those of the Revolution, because the poets' jibes were now largely aimed at domestic American targets. In deploying *Paradise Lost* in aid of their leveling attacks, the few genuine radicals among the elite thus now had the conservative elements within their own class rather than the King of England in mind, and sought to appeal to their fellow citizens' antinomian instincts in order to overturn the domestic social order rather than redress injustices originating from abroad. Poetic Federalists (though they sometimes directed their fire toward revolutionary France) were now mostly concerned with using *Paradise Lost* to rein in the domestic antinomianism they had long feared but once deployed against the King; and versifiers from the party of Jefferson, caught between their genuinely democratic instincts and a gradual recognition of their need to defend class interests in a time of radical threat, slowly came to affirm one or the other of the structures of feeling.

In the end what the writers discovered was nothing less than the dangers of using *Paradise Lost* to justify their leadership claims. For the authority figures against whom the people railed were no longer George III or Thomas Hutchinson but the local clergyman or squire or gentleman of letters; and so, the leveling spirit of the times, having no foreign outlet, increasingly took Satan for its hero, and refused to brook even such consensualist ameliorations of hierarchy as could be found in Milton's Christ. The result, as one moves

---

eighteenth-century American political thought and its roots in the Scottish Common Sense philosophy, see Gary Wills, *Inventing America: Jefferson's Declaration of Independence* (Garden City, N.Y.: Doubleday, 1978).

into the early nineteenth century (in New England at least), is a tendency either to move away completely from *Paradise Lost* as a poetic model or to be more careful in its use so as to avoid engaging the subversive tendencies it had historically encouraged. Yet as the reception of the Miltonic satire of Federalists like Fisher Ames shows, the latter course was no solution either. For as Sensabaugh points out, being more clearly Arminian in the early nineteenth century only meant being less effective with a public hostile to elite authority; and so, gradually *Paradise Lost* was abandoned as a model for political verse.[11]

A parallel pattern exists in the case of the essayists, politicians, and literary lawyers who used Milton's prose to address questions of authority. At first, in the immediate wake of the Revolution, like the imitators of *Paradise Lost*, they too drew successfully upon his reputation as a friend of freedom to advance views that played to the antinomian side of Anglo-American culture. Perhaps the most famous example of this is that of Thomas Jefferson, who even before the war was over employed the *Areopagitica* and the antiprelatical tracts in his campaign for disestablishment and other mildly radical measures in Virginia. Yet in attacking the Anglican establishment of his native state, he had an unpopular, quasi-foreign, royalist institution in his sights. The obvious merits of the case and his own sincerity notwithstanding, Jefferson could, therefore, invoke the antiauthoritarian side of Milton's Puritanism with relative impunity. It was relatively safe in the 1770s for a landed gentleman to be open to the antinomian structure of feeling in the first dawn of independence and against such a foe. Later, however, during the 1780s, when John Adams used Milton's prose to argue the case for moderate constitutionalism, he did so at a time when issues of social control were again beginning to loom large for members of his class. As a result, his employment of Milton's writings was more Arminian, since his aim was to defend the mixed, implicitly consensualist basic law he had framed for Massachusetts. Moreover, even later, toward the end of the decade—though still praising the poet as a defender of liberty—Adams attacked a work like *The Ready and Easy Way to Establish a Free Commonwealth* for its advocacy of a populist concentration of authority. He did so because in his view (as in those of Fisher Ames and many other members of the New England elite), such a proposal seemed

11. For a general discussion of Milton's place in the elite's literary response to the problems of postrevolutionary America, see Sensabaugh, 122–83 and 239–81, and Fliegelman, 197–267. Ferguson, 107–11, gives a good summary of the Federalist perspective, which, when introduced into the revised *M'Fingal*, toned down its antiauthoritarian fervor; May, 307ff. (see below, n. 17), discusses the cultural shift underlying the decline in Milton's influence outside Boston after the start of the nineteenth century.

downright antinomian and dangerous in circumstances in which America and France seemed to be in danger of falling into that alternation between disorder and dictatorship which—in the consensualist view—typified both the English Commonwealth and the republics of antiquity.[12]

Similarly, late eighteenth-century examples of Milton's use as a proof text in matters of religious and familial authority show the same drift by the dominant class toward paradigmatically Arminian attitudes. For like *Paradise Lost*, the divorce tract and the antiprelatical tracts had often been cited earlier in the century by controversialists (from orthodox neo-Edwardsians to skeptics like Thomas Paine) who had manifested a variety of affiliations toward the conflicting polarities within their culture. Yet by the end of the 1780s, the dominant class's fear of anarchy and displacement (in conjugal and social relations as much as in religious and political ones) began to predominate; and so, in New England especially, Milton was increasingly either condemned (as in the case of his views on divorce) or cited selectively only when his works furthered consensualism and the moderate approach to matters of authority it endorsed.[13]

The chief later manifestation in New England of this movement by the dominant class toward the Arminian pole in their culture was the development in the first three decades of the nineteenth century of "a Unitarian-Whig orthodoxy, emanating chiefly from Boston,"[14] which dominated the local literary scene down to the Civil War. It was an ideological formation that arose primarily because the preachers, poets, lawyers, and reviewers who authored it fit the pattern of elite intellectual affiliation established in the previous century. By reason of their personal social origin and/or professional standing, members of this group generally belonged to (and therefore had the

12. Sensabaugh, 132–46, presents convincing (if somewhat exaggerated) evidence of Jefferson's debt to Milton. He also summarizes Adams's objections to Milton's proposals for the government of the English Commonwealth and attributed these animadversions to Adams's provocation by certain radicals within the French Enlightenment who had attacked his moderate Massachusetts constitution in the name of unlimited popular sovereignty.

13. Sensabaugh, 110–17 and 195–217, gives examples of the use of Milton to discuss issues of marital and familial authority; see him also, 217–38, for examples of the poet's invocation by the theological controversialists of the day. Fliegelman's whole book is concerned with these issues and the responses of Protestant and/or consensualist writers to them; but see especially 83–194 for consensualist treatments (often using Milton) of theological and familial issues during the late eighteenth century, and 197ff. for the postrevolutionary political dimensions of what (in two chapter titles) he calls the themes of "George Washington and the reconstituted family" and "The Sealing of the Garden, Or the world well lost."

14. Lawrence Buell, *New England Literary Culture: From Revolution through Renaissance* (Cambridge, Eng.: Cambridge University Press, 1986), 44.

same interests as) Boston's socially privileged class: a caste that was still as markedly urban, Anglophile, and conservative as it had been during the Federalist era.

The Unitarian frame of mind to a large degree therefore represents yet another attempt by part of the New England elite to negotiate the terms of authority they had inherited from the Puritan past. As this implies, Unitarian literature is the physical and intellectual product of an entrenched but threatened local dominant class. Physically, this is so because it consists of texts written by gentlemen of property and learning, texts that were published in journals sponsored either by upper-class literary societies or by the theologically Arminian wing of the Standing Order;[15] and intellectually, it is true because of its content. For if the Unitarians had inherited the social status and ambitions of their ancestors, they had inherited their problems as well. In typical moderate bourgeois New England fashion, they therefore saw their writing as a means of counteracting these difficulties by inculcating the consensualist ideology (and particularly, the doctrine of "self-culture") in the hopes of regaining influence.[16]

However, by 1810 the Unitarians' inherited social position and historical circumstance had joined with the ideological contradictions of New England culture to make this task extraordinarily difficult. For one thing, as they had moved toward the Arminian pole in their culture, the mass of the people had become even more antinomian in feeling. Even in their own relatively con-

15. The elitist institutional origins of Unitarian literature are illustrated by the nature and history of the three most famous publications in which it appeared: *The Monthly Anthology and Boston Review*, which was published by the conservative, upper-class Anthology Society from 1803 to 1811, and *The Christian Examiner and Theological Review* and *The North American Review*, which were later projects of the Unitarian clergy and laity.

16. Buell, *New England Literary Culture*, 23–102, is the best summary of the Unitarians' place in the complex transition from neoclassical to romantic in New England. The ideological and historical discussion of Unitarianism that follows is indebted to it and to Ann Douglas, *The Feminization of American Culture* (New York: Knopf, 1977), which treats the continued decline of ministerial authority in antebellum America; Daniel Walker Howe, *The Unitarian Conscience: Harvard Moral Philosophy, 1805–1861* (Cambridge, Mass.: Harvard University Press, 1970), which provides a thorough account of Unitarian intellectual life; Lewis P. Simpson's introduction to *The Federalist Literary Mind: Selections from the "Monthly Anthology and Boston Review," 1803–1811, Including Documents Relating to the Boston Athenaeum* (Baton Rouge: Louisiana State University Press, 1962), 3–41, and Buell's *Literary Transcendentalism: Style and Vision in the American Renaissance* (Ithaca, N.Y.: Cornell University Press, 1973), 21–74, both of which describe Unitarian Boston's literary theory, denominational and political isolation, social conservatism, etc.; and David Robinson, *Apostle of Culture: Emerson as Preacher and Lecturer* (Philadelphia: University of Pennsylvania Press, 1982), 7–29, which gives the best brief account of the doctrine of "self-culture." I am also indebted to the sources on Unitarianism cited below with regard to William Ellery Channing, Ch. 2, n. 9.

servative region the antideferential and centripetal trends of the Revolutionary and Federalist periods had grown stronger. As a result, their attempt to reestablish themselves through a revamped consensualism—itself a last, didactic gasp of the Enlightenment—was pretty well doomed from the start. Indeed, it soon became apparent even to them that regaining consistent influence was going to be well-nigh impossible, either for them as members of the dominant class or in their individual roles as privileged professionals. Furthermore, the Unitarians' odd position as theological liberals but social and political conservatives also worked against them in this regard. For on both counts the intellectuals of what would come to be called "Brahmin" Boston were severely isolated in the regionalized culture of early nineteenth-century America. In matters of religion, for instance, there had long been a split between those New Englanders who tended toward the antinomian and enthusiastic and those whose faith had a decidedly sober and Arminian cast. By the early nineteenth century, however, this fissure was even worse than before. The ethos spawned by "the Boston religion" was simply alien to average Americans (who were either unchurched or stridently evangelical), and even among the upper classes its natural supernaturalism and perceived tendency to fall uncomfortably between Christianity and Deism were increasingly uncongenial. As a consequence, the Unitarians were never numerous outside their eastern Massachusetts stronghold, and even locally among their own class they gradually lost ground to the less heterodox (though—in both the paradigmatic and theological senses—equally Arminian) Episcopalians.[17]

Similarly, the Unitarians were also hampered in their attempted reassertion of influence by their political isolation. There are two reasons for this. The first is that by the time of its demise, what Henry May has called their "ancestral Federalism" had become a disabling projection of their own deepest inner cultural divisions. For in their ideology as in their individual psyches, what amounted to a conscious Toryism competed for control with an equally strong antinomian subconscious. The former manifested itself in what May terms "their passionate love of English ways and institutions, their inveterate suspicion of France, and their strained relation to political democracy," as well as in a hankering after aristocracy. Indeed, in their most Arminian moods, many Unitarians even endorsed a kind of patriarchalism—the hope

---

17. May, 307ff., provides a particularly illuminating treatment of the Unitarians' place in what he calls "the didactic enlightenment." He describes in detail why it replaced "the radical enlightenment" among large segments of the American elite in the late eighteenth century, and why it too, by 1820, then gave way, leaving New England's Arian Congregationalists as virtually its only survivors in a sea of Evangelicals.

that "society would always be based on tradition and hierarchy, not on contract." As a result, "a surprising devotion to Burke lingered in Boston and Cambridge" throughout the first half of the nineteenth century, and "the political economy taught at Harvard qualified its adherence to laissez-faire with contempt for greed and speculation and [an] insistence on the obligation of public service." At the same time, however, (as May further notes) the Unitarians' Puritan inheritance also manifested itself in the fact that like good antinomians they "passionately believed in free speech, and [so] sought earnestly" not so much to destroy democracy as "to define the function of gentlemen in a democracy." For all their reactionary maunderings, in other words, on the whole the Unitarians were not the Tory squires they at some level wished to be. Instead, they were really the ever more divided descendants of the moderate Puritans: men whose conflicting feelings and interests led them to place their hopes in a revived consensualism, one in which, even "if aristocratic leadership in national politics was no longer possible, gentlemen could continue to lead the way through example, education, and support for rational and moderate movements of reform." Significantly, they felt that in this regard "above all, the special role of enlightened men of means was the support of a rational and uplifting literature," which would encourage "a pure and refined taste [that] could uplift democracy, and redeem it from vulgarity and greed."[18]

The results of these internal ideological conflicts were scarcely empowering, however; instead, in fact, the Unitarians' replication of the contradictory position of their ancestors tended to render them even more ineffective. For as Federalists and later Whigs, they were members of moderate conservative minority parties whose leadership was distinctly middle- and upper-class and whose policies clearly fostered dominant class interests. Rather than placate the democratic leanings of a leveling age, their political affiliations and program thus underscored the hegemonic agenda behind their high-minded consensualist professions—and so fed the resentment against them. Similarly, at a practical level, this patent self-interestedness contributed to the second cause of their political isolation: their chosen means of extending their influence. As the events leading up to the Civil War proved, the Unitarians' consensualist reliance on moral suasion and genteel literary reform, and their disdain for the rough-and-tumble of democratic politics made them seem irrelevant in a context of mounting sectional violence and constitutional crisis. Yet as everything in the prior history of their class might have

18. Ibid., 355.

predicted, with a few exceptions (like William Ellery Channing late in life), the Unitarians continued to be strongly inclined toward this indirect and nonconfrontational course of action. Even a strong individual commitment to egalitarianism and the Democratic party might not eradicate these moderate Puritan clerical instincts—as the classically conflicted views of two famous literary Unitarians, Bryant and Hawthorne, attest. For moderate, benevolent, paternalistic, but ultimately self-interested, consensualism continued to represent the historic position of Boston's religious liberals—and others who became assimilated into their subculture—throughout the antebellum period.[19]

The prominence of belles lettres in the Unitarians' plan of action suggests that in addition to their political and religious isolation, their cultural authority was affected by another circumstance as well. For they no longer had the literary monopoly their seventeenth-century clerical ancestors had enjoyed. As seen earlier, their poetry and essays had suffered by comparison with both the classics of English literature and the literature of contemporary Britain since the middle of the previous century; but now, in addition, New England's gentlemen authors had to compete with a wide range of popular domestic writers. While this competition was not always wholly hostile, its overall result was the bitter sense on their part of having lost out in the race for cultural influence—both to all sorts of popular (racy, risque, radically reformist, sentimental, evangelical, female, lower-class) American writers and to the latest generation of English competitors (Dickens, Thackeray, and the Lake poets) too.[20]

In circumstances such as these, Milton's reception was almost bound to be tinged by the same ulterior motives that had colored his treatment by the

19. Howe's *Political Culture of the American Whigs* is the best account of political and cultural conservatism in early nineteenth-century America, and his *Unitarian Conscience*, esp. 121–48, presents much evidence for its predominance in Boston. Bryant will be discussed later in this chapter and Hawthorne will be treated at length in the second volume of this study.

20. The competition between dominant-class male authors and other writers is one of the subjects of Nina Baym's *Novels, Readers, and Reviewers: Responses to Fiction in Antebellum America* (Ithaca, N.Y.: Cornell University Press, 1984). In addition, Buell, *New England Literary Culture;* Tompkins; and Michael T. Gilmore, *American Romanticism and the Marketplace* (Chicago: University of Chicago Press, 1985), also deal with the question of literary competition and the success or failure of various kinds of New England writers at it. By contrast, David S. Reynolds, *Beneath the American Renaissance: The Subversive Imagination in the Age of Emerson and Melville* (New York: Knopf, 1988), provides a more complex, less wholly competitive view of the relationship between the writers of "the American Renaissance" and their more popular contemporaries (though one which is in important ways biased in favor of the former). Weisbuch also has many useful things to say about transatlantic literary relations in the early nineteenth-century English-speaking world as well.

Federalists. For one thing, his works still remained open to readings that endorsed consensualism, and as a historical figure, he could still be seen as exemplifying the clerical model of literary authority. Furthermore, because he was part of their moderate, bourgeois tradition and because of the rediscovery in the 1820s of his treatise on Christian doctrine (which finally confirmed his Arian beliefs), Milton also seemed a plausible guide for the Unitarians as they tried to cope with their peculiar political and sectarian isolation.[21] There was, as a result, no falling off of interest in the poet in Unitarian circles after the War of 1812. Despite occasional passages criticizing *Paradise Lost* and the prose works for encouraging radicalism, he was still widely regarded by the Boston elite as a personification of the cultural authority they hoped to wield once more. Moreover, his reception by them continued to follow the generally consensualist pattern of the Federalists in the late eighteenth century. The only difference was that with the disastrous example of the Federalist epics behind them, the Unitarians and others of their class perhaps understandably did not follow Dwight and Barlow in poetically imitating *Paradise Lost*. Instead, they on the whole engaged him as a subject for critical comment only, and it is that body of criticism which proves them to be—in this as in most other things—men who instinctively deferred to tradition.[22]

At Harvard, for instance, students continued to be taught that Milton was a genius whom they might profitably emulate. Significantly, they were also taught that this imitation ought to be part of a broader pattern of consensualist self-assertion. For their teachers saw him in the same terms as the rest of the older generation of elite intellectuals: as a man whose divine inspiration, sublime virtue, intellectual breadth, and moral steadfastness

21. Phyllis Cole, "The Purity of Puritanism: Transcendentalist Readings of Milton," *Studies in Romanticism* 17 (1978): 129–48, treats Milton's influence in early nineteenth-century New England, as do a number of Ph.D. dissertations (although from an almost wholly descriptive or bibliographical point of view): Ruth W. Gregory, "American Criticism of Milton, 1800–1938," University of Wisconsin, 1938; James Thorpe, "The Decline of the Miltonic Tradition," Harvard University, 1941; John A. Weigel, "The Miltonic Tradition in the First Half of the Nineteenth Century," Western Reserve University, 1939; and Lester F. Zimmerman, "Some Aspects of Milton's American Reputation to 1900," University of Wisconsin, 1950. Of these, Weigel, 177–270, is probably the best, despite its largely British focus. In addition, two studies of Milton and individual authors exist: William M. Wynkoop, *Three Children of the Universe: Emerson's View of Shakespeare, Bacon, and Milton* (The Hague: Mouton, 1966), and Henry F. Pommer, *Milton and Melville* (Pittsburgh, Pa.: University of Pittsburgh Press, 1950).

22. By concentrating on American poetic imitations of Milton (especially in a satiric or visionary vein), Sensabaugh, 282–305, overlooks the lively critical interest in the poet and his works in eastern Massachusetts after the second war against Great Britain.

had empowered him to speak didactically from a position of spiritual, social, and intellectual superiority (thus deserving the deference of his own and later generations).

The *Lectures* of the quintessential Unitarian literary lawyer John Quincy Adams[23] are a good example of this view of the poet, since as the College's first Boylston Professor of Rhetoric he regarded his discipline as one well suited to serve the ambitions of a consensualist elite. Rhetoric was, for him, a skill that instrumentally empowered its practitioners. In the political realm this is perhaps most obvious in the tyrant and the demagogue; but according to Adams, it is even more true in the cases of the standard embodiments of consensualist literary authority: the republican preacher, poet, and gentleman lawyer or politician. This is because rhetoric is an art that fully engages all the human faculties (from reason to benevolence to the affections); and so, it is best suited to support that indirect exercise of leadership which is most appropriate alike to the career of the gentleman and to a moderate constitutional polity.

Significantly, Adams also taught that because of his ability to engage these deeper integrative forces, Milton stands virtually alone among postclassical rhetoricians (especially in his defense of liberty) as a model for students bent upon a career of public service. As he puts it at one point,

> the powers of language in all the tongues, with which we are acquainted, recognize only three degrees of comparison; a positive, a comparative, and a superlative. But climax is ever seeking for a fourth; and one of the images, in which it most indulges, is that of finding such fourth degree of comparison. Of this grandeur of imagination, which stretches beyond the bounds of ordinary possibility, the most frequent examples are to be found in the daring and sublime genius of Milton.[24]

23. Adams had, of course, early abandoned the sinking ship of Federalism over the Embargo Act and other issues, but in every other way he aptly illustrates the main literary, professional, theological, and ideological features of this subgroup within the New England dominant class.

24. John Quincy Adams, *Lectures on Rhetoric and Oratory, Delivered to the Classes of Senior and Junior Sophisters in Harvard University* (Cambridge, Mass.: Hilliard and Metcalf, 1810), II, 127. This book was a standard reference work at Harvard for several decades, and is briefly discussed in Sensabaugh, 193–95. Something of its consensualist, preprofessional tone can be seen in the *peroratio* of Adams's "Inaugural Oration" (I, 29–31). Similarly, his discussion of rhetoric's engagement of the rational, intellectual, and moral qualities of the mind also bespeaks his commitment to consensualism (I, 343–65).

This was why, in fact, the generations of Harvard men who heard or read Adams learned that Milton was "the sublimest of poets":[25] not because he was a technical virtuoso (though Adams clearly believed that to be the case too), but because he was a man of letters who had effectively guided his fellow citizens during a time of crisis. As such, Milton was, for Adams, the consensualist sage par excellence—the possessor of a persuasive authority that "sons of Harvard" might still hope to wield, as they too sought to balance the claims of order and freedom to advantage. And as this implies, it was his continued relevance to the question of authority that made the *Lectures'* consensualist view of Milton the institutional one at Unitarian Harvard long after Adams had left its chair of rhetoric. Indeed, as the comments of Edward Tyrrel Channing (the third Boylston Professor, and brother of William Ellery Channing, who from 1819 to 1851 taught Emerson, Thoreau, Lowell, Edward Everett Hale, and Charles Eliot Norton) attest, the reason that Milton continued to be regarded there as an embodiment of literary authority was because the Unitarians believed that the author (like belles lettres) ought to fulfill a strongly ideological function.[26]

Milton's treatment as a consensualist authority figure (and his writings as consensualist texts) is also evident elsewhere in early nineteenth-century New England, both among Unitarians writing outside the precincts of Harvard Yard and among non-Unitarian members of the region's dominant class as well. A good example of the latter occurs in an incidental passage written years after *The Conquest of Canaan* by Timothy Dwight, since in it, Dwight not only surreptitiously describes the poet in terms like those used at liberal Harvard but also implicitly contrasts Milton's success with his own political and literary failure (and that of men of his class):

> As genius is the power of making efforts, it is obvious that it will never be exerted, or in other words the efforts will never be made, without energy, that is, without the resolution, activity, and perseverance which are necessary to their existence. This energy can never be summoned into action, but by motives of a suitable nature and sufficient magnitude to move the mind. Nor can it act to any considerable purpose, unless attended with proper advantages. Wherever these causes do not meet, the fire will be smothered. . . . How obviously [therefore] must the real Milton have been inglorious, if he had

25. Adams, I, 409.
26. Edward T. Channing, *Lectures Read to the Seniors in Harvard College* (Boston: Ticknor and Fields, 1856), 100.

been mute; and how obviously would he have been mute, notwith-standing all his powers, if his energy had not prompted him, or if commanding motives had not summoned that energy into action.[27]

Although Milton is admittedly a peripheral presence in this passage, Dwight implicitly treats the poet just as a Unitarian like Adams would. He thus invokes the historical Milton as an illustration of those qualities which an inspired literary didact should have, saying that he was a man of genius who, prompted by "commanding motives" not his own, marshaled his en-ergies so as "to move the mind[s]" of his readers. For Dwight, Milton's di-dactic *energia* demonstrates the power of "resolution, activity, and persever-ance" in the cause of truth; and so, he stands both as an embodiment of the consensualist view of authority and as a historical counter to the disempow-erment dominant-class New England authors had experienced during the de-cades after the Revolution. The latter can be seen from the fact that Yale's most literary president only brings him up in this passage in connection with a long quotation from Gray's "Elegy Written in a Country Churchyard" (omitted from the above citation for reasons of space). As this implies, his aim in doing so is to celebrate—albeit ruefully—Milton's avoidance of his own frustration as a would-be leader. For though defeated in his own life-time, in retrospect Milton contributed mightily to the eventual triumph of his cause after 1688; and so, his example contrasts with that of Dwight and New Englanders of his type, who can currently look back on no such success (whether political or poetic). Indeed, as the Gray quotation indicates, he and men like him instead now play the role of the "village-Hampden" of the el-egy. They are would-be American Miltons unlucky in their circumstances: neocolonial figures who had, during the Revolution, "with dauntless breast / The little tyrant of" their "fields withstood," only to find themselves later politically impotent and poetically ignored. For in contrast to the author of *Paradise Lost*, Dwight and men of his stamp are now mere "mute inglorious Milton[s]," elitists who had sought "the applause of listening senates to com-mand, / The threats of pain and ruin to despise, / To scatter plenty o'er a smiling land, / And read their history in a nation's eyes"—but failed.[28]

Much of Dwight's motivation for making this self-deprecating comparison was highly personal, of course. (He had, after all, entered the lists of epic

27. Timothy Dwight, *Travels in New England and New York*, ed. Barbara M. Solomon and Patricia M. King (Cambridge, Mass.: Harvard University Press, 1969), IV, 220–21.

28. Thomas Gray, "Elegy Written in a Country Churchyard," lines 57–64 (in part), cited from *The Poems of Gray, Collins, and Goldsmith*, ed. Roger Lonsdale (London: Longmans, Green, and Co., 1969). Dwight had cited all of lines 55–65 of the poem at this point in his text.

poetry against Milton with ignominious results.) But his use of Milton as a counterexample to his own lack of cultural authority is similar to much of what one finds elsewhere in early nineteenth-century New England, particularly as one moves—in all senses—in the direction of Boston. William Cullen Bryant, for example, was both a far more successful author than Dwight and one far closer to the Unitarian subculture. Although his party loyalties were not those of most of his coreligionists and although he originally hailed from western Massachusetts, in all other respects he had adopted the run of Unitarian professional interests and intellectual commitments. His 1825 *Lectures on Poetry* provides a particularly good indication of his cultural as well as confessional allegiances, since they are typically Unitarian in their intellectual eclecticism, commitment to the aesthetics of the Scottish Common Sense School, and interest in using the philosophy of Kames and Reid to reinforce the claims of consensualism.

Thus, to take one example, although Bryant's assertion in the *Lectures* that the imagination must be subordinated to the rational will is historically an offshoot of the Scots' attempt to refute Berkeley and Hume, it also has an ideological dimension. For—Edinburgh being much like Boston—the Common Sense philosophy itself reflects the need of a bourgeois elite to negotiate the contradictions of its culture; and so, by making the imagination a creature of the rational will, the Scots (like Bryant later on) were really aiming to establish a hierarchical model of the mind by which the alleged subjectivism of their century's greatest skeptic and most philosophical bishop could be refuted. For to them such subjectivism was the most dangerous intellectual manifestation of the antiauthoritarianism of their age, a subversive philosophical position that called for a paradigmatically Arminian intellectual response on their part.[29]

29. The impact of the Scottish Common Sense School upon Bryant, along with other intellectual influences on his work, is discussed in Ferguson, 173–95.

Relatively little has been written on the history of the imagination in New England per se. However, the effect of the Scottish philosophy on American literature is the subject of Terence Martin's *The Instructed Vision: Scottish Common Sense Philosophy and the Origins of American Fiction* (Bloomington: Indiana University Press, 1961). This subject is also treated incidentally in Michael Davitt Bell, *The Development of American Romance: The Sacrifice of Relation* (Chicago: University of Chicago Press, 1980). Other discussions of early nineteenth-century American aesthetics relevant to Bryant and the Unitarians include Howe, *The Unitarian Conscience*, 174–204; the two books by Buell already cited; William Charvat, *The Origins of American Critical Thought (1810–1835)* (Philadelphia: University of Pennsylvania Press, 1936), 27–58; James Engell, *The Creative Imagination: Enlightenment to Romanticism* (Cambridge, Mass.: Harvard University Press, 1981), esp. 188–96; and Charles Fiedelson, Jr., *Symbolism and American Literature* (Chicago: University of Chicago Press, 1953).

When in the *Lectures* Bryant declares that "the imagination is the most active and the least susceptible of fatigue of all the faculties of the human mind," he is really therefore indicating his fear of its antinomian potential. For as a faculty that is "by no means passive," and as one whose "more intense exercise is tremendous, and sometimes unsettles the reason," the force with which it operates always makes it dangerous. Indeed, too much imaginative freedom can, according to Bryant, lead to enthusiasm, madness, and delusion; and so, the imagination must be controlled. The faculty that does this is the will, and Bryant believed it ought to perform a function in the mind parallel to that to which New England's consensualist writers aspired societally: it ought to establish hierarchical control over the imagination and eliminate such disordering dangers as it presents. The result of such dominance is a rightly ordered psyche: one in which the dangers of excess and enthusiasm (like those of social leveling) disappear and the imagination (deferring to the will much as the culture ought to defer to dominant-class men of letters) "pursues the path which the poet only points out, and shapes its visions from the scenes and allusions which he gives." Significantly (especially given the poem's past reception in New England), Bryant saw the "strength and cultivation" of *Paradise Lost* as the best illustration of this controlled and proper use of the imagination (particularly Milton's portraits of Satan and of Adam and Eve);[30] and so, it is really on account of their consensualist didacticism that he calls "the great epic of Milton . . . the noblest poem in our language," and "his *Paradise Regained*" an effort not "unworthy to be the last work of so great a man."[31]

As this suggests, in the *Lectures* Bryant read *Paradise Lost* very much in the manner of the eighteenth-century dominant class: both as a received text in matters of authority and as a text useful in countering antinomianism (whether psychological or political). Even in the instances elsewhere in his writings in which his use of Milton's poetry seems more sympathetic to the antinomian structure of feeling (and more congruent with his later prominence as a Democrat),[32] Bryant's Milton (like that of his predecessors) is

30. *The Prose Writings of William Cullen Bryant*, ed. Parke Godwin (New York: D. Appleton, 1884). I, 6–7.

31. Ibid., II, 363.

32. For instance, Bryant also wrote two poems in imitation of Milton's "On the Late Massacre at Piedmont," a sonnet which enjoyed an extraordinary vogue in nineteenth-century England as a model for political poems of all stripes. (See James G. Nelson, *The Sublime Puritan: Milton and the Victorians* [Madison: University of Wisconsin Press, 1963], 30–38, for examples.) Both reflect the antinomian polarity in New England culture: "The Massacre at Scio" commemorates a Turkish atrocity in the Greek War of Independence (see Jacob H. Adler, "A Milton-Bryant

shaped by the contradictory legacy of moderate Puritanism and its never-ending confliction over matters of order and liberty.

The treatment accorded the poet and his writings by commentators even more closely associated with Unitarianism's intellectual life and institutions also demonstrates the paradigmatically Arminian tone of the antebellum Milton. The following remarks by F.W.P. Greenwood in the *North American Review* are typical of what one finds in the magazines of the period:

> For ourselves, we can truly say that we never knew Milton, till we were acquainted with his prose writings. We never knew the man till then; never felt how entirely and supremely he was a poet, or, to use his own words, "a true poem; that is, a composition and pattern of the best and honorablest things." We never knew till then, what a noble, highminded being, what a contemner of littleness and baseness, what a fearless asserter of right and denouncer of wrong, how pure, how virtuous, how incorruptible, how unconquerable he was. How truly the modern poet speaks of him, when he says; "His soul was as a star, and dwelt apart." When we now compare him with his brother stars, we perceive that he has indeed his own separate heaven, where he shines alone, and [is] not to be approached. If we grant that in the single respect of genius he was second to Shakspeare, and to him alone would we grant him to be second, yet what was Shakspeare's life? . . . We think of Shakspeare's poetry, and not of Shakspeare. His name comes to us as a voice, an abstraction, a beautiful sound. But the name of Milton is inseparably united with the man himself.[33]

Greenwood's quotation here of Wordsworth's "London, 1802" should not be taken as an indication of romantic sympathies on his part. Like most dominant-class critics in early nineteenth-century America, this conservative Unitarian valued Wordsworth because he had made the same journey as he and other upper-class New Englanders had during the previous generation: from a youthful fascination with revolution to political conservatism, conven-

Parallel," *The New England Quarterly* 24 [1951]: 377–80); the other—hitherto unnoticed—his "Hymn of the Waldenses," is an 1824 composition celebrating that people's struggle for religious freedom.

33. F.W.P. Greenwood, "Milton's English Prose Works," review of *A Selection from the English Prose Works of John Milton, The North American Review* 25 (1827): 74. All attributions for authorship for this journal are from William Cushing, *Index to "The North American Review." Volumes I–CXXV. 1815–1877* (Cambridge, Mass.: John Wilson and Son, 1878).

tional morality, and a respect for traditional religious authority.[34] Moreover, as this implies, like his Wordsworth, Greenwood's Milton was also a figure cut to a paradigmatically Arminian pattern. The author of *Paradise Lost* thus here possesses all the characteristics that had recommended him to an earlier generation of would-be Yankee preacher-poets (moral elevation, nobility, devotion to virtue, and personal holiness); and yet, as in Bryant and Dwight, he is one who speaks both boldly and didactically as well. He is "a fearless asserter of right and denouncer of wrong," a leader who, like a good consensualist, guides by moral suasion and teaches by personal example, through his attachment to truth, justice, and ordered freedom. As a consequence, Greenwood's Milton clearly has authority and deserves the affection and deference of his readers. Indeed, he has an exalted rank like that of the angels because, like an ideal consensualist minister or lawyer or poet, he both practices and embodies what he preaches. This places him on a separate plane: set apart not only from other English writers like Shakespeare but also—in an implicit admission of his own failure to live at the Miltonic level—from Greenwood and his generation of New Englanders.

One of the editors of the *North American Review,* A. H. Everett, also compared Milton to Shakespeare in ways that reveal the self-interested nature of Unitarian criticism. Even more than Greenwood, however, he acknowledged the superiority of the great playwright on purely literary grounds:

> We are free to confess, that with the highest admiration for the genius and character of Milton, we do not recognise in his poetry a talent of the same order with that of Shakspeare. His touch is free and bold,— that of Shakspeare airy and elastic. The coloring of Milton is rich and true,—that of Shakspeare fresh, bright and dewy. In Milton's creations, we feel the hand of a master;—in those of Shakspeare, we forget it.[35]

34. Charvat, 73, discusses Greenwood and Wordsworth in the context of the latter's general reception in antebellum America. It is worth noting that after Greenwood succeeded Jared Sparks as editor of the *Review* he went over from the Whigs to the Democratic party. Nonetheless, as the reader will shortly see, he was no political radical, and in other ways as well was very much a typical Unitarian.

35. A. H. Everett, "Early Literature of Modern Europe," review of *Tableau Historique de la Littérature Française,* by M. J. de Chenier, and *Historia de la Literatura Española,* by F. Bouterwek, trans. J. G. de la Cortina and N. Hugalde y Mollenido, *The North American Review* 38 (1834): 174–75; for Everett's career and support of the Transcendentalists, see Charvat, 182–85.

Yet as close attention to Everett's imagery and diction reveals, his preference for Shakespeare here only thinly veils a typically Unitarian belief in Milton as an exemplar of consensualist literary authority. For though his subject does not possess "a talent of the same order with that of Shakspeare" (whose writings do not force themselves upon us, but are merely "airy and elastic," and "fresh, bright and dewy"), his Milton is a poet of absolute values (of richness and of truth). He is "a master" whose authoritative hand urges our submission, and so, implicitly, his writings only evince their antinomian qualities (of freedom and boldness) in conjunction with his intellectual dominance of his readers—a mastery effected by his employment of a rhetoric of power and hierarchy. In other words, the language Everett uses suggests that his Milton is simultaneously the bold liberator and the stern master, the creator of Satan and yet the author of the most famous literary endorsement of Calvin's God (a poet who suffers from the same cultural contradictions as Everett himself, contradictions that compelled Everett to seek him out as an Arminian literary hero).

The consistency with which Unitarians like Everett fit Milton into their ideology can also be seen if one considers their main complaint against the poet: that his characterization of Satan in *Paradise Lost* breaks the link between the imagination and morality, thereby encouraging antinomianism. Several early examples of this can be found in the *Monthly Anthology*,[36] beginning with the critic who in 1803 piously belittled Milton's Satan by arguing that his heroism is merely that of the heroes of classical antiquity. For, he asserted, there is a higher kind of heroism than the mere military prowess at which Satan or Aeneas and Achilles excel, the heroism of those true Christian champions who possess "the *moral sublime*." This "is the most essentially and universally sublime of all the species of sublimity," because it rests "on the distinctions which exist between moral good and moral evil, distinctions, as eternal, immutable and important as the Deity himself." From the perspective of that "being who can comprehend heaven and earth at a

---

36. Two other instances in which members of the Boston establishment commented negatively on Milton, accusing him of satanically encouraging Jacobinism, are Joseph Stevens Buckminster's famous 1809 Harvard Phi Beta Kappa oration, "The Dangers and Duties of Men of Letters," printed in *The Monthly Anthology and Boston Review* 7 (1809): 145–58, and J.S.J. Gardiner's "Milton's Moral and Political Conduct," in the same journal: 6 (1809): 87–88. The latter openly attacks Milton as a partisan of the mob and (even though it is by a reactionary Episcopal minister) accurately represents the response of upper-class, Unitarian Boston to Milton at its most antidemocratic, while the former, by linking Milton (and Burke) to political faction, implicitly condemns the poet as a defector from consensualism's preferred tactic of literary moral suasion. Neither piece, however, engages in the sort of aesthetic analysis of Satan in *Paradise Lost* under consideration here.

glance," the admiration aroused by a traditional epic hero like Satan "must [therefore] appear trifling and puerile"; and a poet like Milton who had made so inferior a heroism attractive must seem doubly culpable: first, because he thereby excessively encouraged the antinomian spirit of equality, autonomy, and liberty; and second, because in the process he also implicitly denied a premise central to Boston Unitarianism, that "when the might of the hero will be despised or forgotten, the goodness of the faint will find its reward in the love and esteem of the highest orders of the moral creation."[37] The Unitarians considered it essential because it was logically necessary both for their doctrines of free will and self-culture and for their consensualist view of human authority, which grounded the relationship between governors and governed analogically in the rational, predictable, and beneficient consensualism of the relations between Father and Son, and God and redeemed man in *Paradise Lost*.

The consensualist assumptions behind this complaint against Milton are even clearer in the similar criticisms made by later, more sophisticated commentators. For example, in comparing Milton to Dante in 1819 in the *North American Review*, John C. Gray had high praise for the great English Puritan. He was also honest enough about his own antinomian impulses as a New Englander to admit as well that he too was deeply moved by Milton's Satan: after all, "such is human nature that we cannot but respect the dignity with which he fills the throne even of hell, the readiness he constantly displays to be foremost to act and suffer for the advantage of his community, the lofty spirit which enables him to feel or to feign a hope in the most desperate circumstances." Yet, like his coreligionists, Gray also felt that in giving us so heroic a Satan, Milton had radically divorced the imagination from morality—and so failed in his responsibilities as a consensualist didact. This was true even when, as in the "address to the Sun" in book IV, he detected little conscious romantic satanism on Milton's part; for even there, the poet "disarms our indignation against an adversary who could acknowledge" God's perfections "so fairly." Therefore, Gray concludes, by contrast "Dante's description of the prince of hell, as well as his kingdom, short as it is, is far more appropriate than Milton's," since the Italian poet "has divested him of all that could excite even a doubtful admiration." Indeed, Dante instead

---

37. Anon., "Scraps from a Correspondent," *The Monthly Anthology and Boston Review* 1 (1803): 60. All attributions of authorship for this journal are from *The Anthology Society: Journal of the Society Which Conducts "The Monthly Anthology and Boston Review," October 3, 1805 to July 2, 1811*, edited and introduced by M. A. DeWolfe Howe (Boston: The Boston Athenaeum, 1910). (It is perhaps of some interest that the next piece in this issue of *The Monthly Anthology* is by a young William Ellery Channing—the greatest Unitarian Miltonist of them all.)

everywhere preserves hierarchical order by making it clear that it is God, and not the rebellious demon, who is to be admired. Thus, while in *The Divine Comedy* as in *Paradise Lost* Satan "preserves every where the same gloomy greatness; . . . always elicits our pity and commands our respect in the character of an 'Arch Angel ruined,' " in the *Commedia* he does so only because he was once a denizen of Heaven. Dante's Satan has no antinomian power, attraction, or light of his own, and so is less threatening than Milton's; he "may well be compared to the Sun in a partial eclipse, shedding every where around him a light faded and solemn, but by no means terrific or baleful."[38]

As this suggests, Milton's Satan still raised the prospect of Jacobinism for Unitarians like Gray well into the nineteenth century. His preference for Dante here can certainly be attributed to the fact that the Satan of *The Divine Comedy* gave readers no cause to question the divinely ordained order of things. For unlike Milton, the greatest of medieval Italian poets had lived only at the beginning of the transition from feudal to bourgeois society; and so, his Satan was not a product of the later cultural conflictions to which Milton, like New England, had been historically exposed. Furthermore, these contradictions within the region's Puritan heritage also lie behind the second reason that Milton's Satan so terrorized the critics of early nineteenth-century Boston. For in making the devil so attractive Milton did two disturbing things: first, he suggested that he personally was an unreliable consensualist role model; and second, he raised the possibility that even the most inspired preacher-poet might be seduced into abandoning the cause of order for that of leveling.

The latter was a temptation the Unitarians themselves continued to face, of course, especially as the antiauthoritarian tendencies in New England culture became more dominant. Like W. S. Shaw, they too felt the sweep of *Paradise Lost*'s subversive currents; they too were moved when, at his most self-assertive, "Milton's character of Satan exhibits wonderful powers of mind." Yet ever as loyal to their elitist tradition as to their self-interest, they just as quickly qualified such expressions of exhilaration by raising the fear that for all its attractions the poem's antinomian power is apocalyptic in nature: that its possessor—far from being a liberator—is instead "the genius of destruction" who in trying to overthrow God overthrows all order and mo-

38. John C. Gray, "Dante," review of *La Divina Commedia di Dante Alighieri*, and *The Vision, or Hell, Purgatory and Paradise of Dante Alighieri*, trans. H. F. Carey, *The North American Review* 8 (1819): 344–45. The comparison of Milton with his predecessors in the epic tradition is common during the early nineteenth century, as the examples already cited should suggest; for a discussion, see Weigel, 179–248.

rality (the one who "bears on his front the marks of thunder, does 'not repent or change, though changed in outward lustre' "). And so, when pressed, in the end Milton's Unitarian critics typically fall back on the same moralistic resolution of their contradictory impulses as Gray, asserting (lest angelic reasons not justify demonic delight) that even as he "meditates on new vengeance" the fallen angel "in the last degree of abasement and wretchedness . . . retains the memory of his ancient glory" and thus is moving only to the degree that "some trait of his celestial nature may yet be perceived in his infernal soul."[39]

The Unitarians also had to confront their cultural self-division over authority because much of the contemporary biography and criticism to which they had been exposed gave renewed emphasis to the antinomian aspects of Milton's writings. For one thing, even in the aftermath of the upheaval and revolutionary internationalism that haunt the works of the previous generation,[40] the eighteenth-century view of the poet as an ancestor in liberty's cause still had considerable currency in America. This belief was then in turn reinforced by the emergence of the so-called "Whig" school of British Milton criticism,[41] since as James Nelson has shown,

> during the early years of the nineteenth century, a pronounced reaction to the Tory biographical and critical approach to Milton occurred, signaled, in part, by Macaulay's famous essay of 1825; and by the third decade, a new and radically different approach to Milton biography was being employed by several writers sympathetic to the ideals of the dissenters, Whigs, liberals, and radicals. The new biographies written by Joseph Ivimey, William Carpenter, Cyrus Edmonds, Edwin Paxton Hood, and others were dedicated to the propagation of Milton's political and religious views and activities, and, of necessity, to the exposition of the prose rather than the poetry. This important new direction in Milton biography was accompanied by clear and concise objections to the previous biographical writings, and succinct statements as to the aims and purposes of the new.

39. W. S. Shaw, "Silva, No. 29," *The Monthly Anthology and Boston Review* 4 (1807): 370. Stanley E. Fish's argument in *Surprised by Sin: The Reader in "Paradise Lost"* (Berkeley: University of California Press, 1967), that "angelic" readings of the "demonic" elements in Milton's poem began in the seventeenth century, obviously has relevance to Shaw's response here.

40. See the discussions of Charles Brockden Brown by Tompkins, 40–93, and Fliegelman, 237–41.

41. Nelson, 74–105, and Weigel, 92–176 and 271–97, discuss the Whig tradition.

In general, the objections to Tory biography were two. First, the biographies by Dr. Johnson and his contemporaries, members of the English church and Tory party, were biased and unsympathetic to Milton, the republican and dissenter; and, in turn, this bias resulted in unbalanced and ill-proportioned biographies which overemphasized the poetry and slighted the prose. That is, the eighteenth-century biographer usually found it more congenial to talk about Milton's poetry than to discuss his prose, and Milton the poet was more appealing than Milton the man. Second, the biographies were printed in large, elaborate editions which were too expensive for the poorer classes to buy.[42]

These biographies and critical pieces circulated widely in the United States[43] and strengthened the native filiopietistic impulses that had long caused Milton to be summoned in aid of the nationalist and republican cause. They were successful with Americans in part because the British Whigs shared both the democratic values and dissenting background of their New World counterparts. They also tended, like the Americans, to link Milton's role during the English Revolution to the current fortunes of the American Republic. Macaulay (who is, as Nelson suggests, perhaps the most famous example of this 'pro-American' current in British Milton criticism) illustrates both of these points. For he praised the poet as much for his participation in events crucial to the development of Anglo-American democracy (as one who "lived at one of the most memorable eras in the history of mankind, at the very crisis of the great conflict between Oromasdes and Arimanes, liberty and despotism, reason and prejudice") as for his personal character (which was that of a figure whose "public conduct was such as was to be expected from a man of a spirit so high and of an intellect so powerful"). This was because he believed that Milton wrote at one of those rare pivotal moments in human history when "the destinies of the human race were staked on the same cast with the freedom of the English people"; and so, in a spirit as much American as English, he had "first proclaimed those mighty principles which have since worked their way into the depths of the American forests, which have roused Greece . . . have kindled an unquenchable fire in the hearts of the oppressed, and loosed the knees of the oppressors with an unwonted fear."[44]

42. Nelson, 77–78. The Whig tradition began somewhat earlier than Nelson suggests, however, with the biographies of Mortimer (1805) and Symmons (1806).
43. See Weigel, 170–76 and 295–97, for examples.
44. "Milton," The Works of Lord Macaulay (London: Longmans, Green, 1898), VII, 31.

Given this tendency to link Milton with America's own liberties, many of Macaulay's New World contemporaries not unsurprisingly agreed with his praise of the poet. The New England historian Francis Parkman, for example, went out of his way a few years later to recall the friendship and mutual admiration between Milton and Roger Williams, because (like Macaulay) he believed that the pair embodied all that was best in Anglo-American Puritanism.[45] Similarly, so un-Bostonian and un-Unitarian a figure as Rufus Wilmot Griswold justified his 1845 American edition of Milton's prose by pledging allegiance to British Whig values. Like the Whigs, he maintained that it was Milton's implacable hostility to tyranny rather than his literary skill that made him "the greatest of all human beings: the noblest and the ennobler of mankind." Moreover, he also asserted that this was the reason why the poet's prose should be of interest as much to Americans as to Englishmen: for "in the United States, where the divine right of any man to oppress his fellows is not held . . . our admiration of MILTON suffers no abatement, but rather is greater"[46] because of his defense of radical measures in the name of liberty. And so Americans, of all people, should appreciate the efforts of their English Whig cousins to justify his apologies for regicide in the face of continued Tory defamation.

Of course, in linking Milton, the "ennobler of mankind," with king killing, Griswold (a Baptist preacher turned entrepreneurial man of letters) was revealing his own indebtedness to the antinomian structure of feeling. Regicide is not only the most extreme of antipatriarchal acts but also one with which the Founding Fathers themselves had often been figuratively charged (frequently in the context of readings of *Paradise Lost*). Yet when one considers the rest of his introduction, it seems clear that Griswold did not intend to foster radicalism; rather, his comments were meant to celebrate the achievement of independence and the establishment of moderate republicanism after 1776—no more. Nowhere does he suggest that king killing or any other form of revolutionary extremism was desirable in the 1840s (the very decade in which the annexation of Texas, the Mexican War, and the growing controversy over slavery threatened to destroy that same moderate bourgeois

---

45. Francis Parkman, "Knowles's *Memoir of Roger Williams*," review of *Memoir of Roger Williams, the Founder of the State of Rhode Island*, by James D. Knowles, *The Christian Examiner and Theological Review* 16 (1834): 86. All attributions of authorship for this journal are taken from William Cushing, *Index to "The Christian Examiner." Volumes I–LXXXVII. 1824–1869* (Boston: William Cushing, 1879).

46. Rufus W. Griswold, ed., *The Prose Works of John Milton* (Philadelphia: H. Hooker, 1845), I, ix and xi. For a Southern view that closely resembles that of Griswold and the Unitarians, see the excerpts from Hugh Swinton Legaré in Edd Winfield Parks, comp., *Ante-Bellum Southern Literary Critics* (Athens: University of Georgia Press, 1962), 23–50.

order). The side of Milton that endorsed antipatriarchal radicalism is thus not really at play here, and Griswold's seeming approbation of regicide is a pose that represses the possibility of revolution in his own day.

A similar backing off from Milton's antiauthoritarianism can be seen in the comments of the Boston Unitarians. Typical is F.W.P. Greenwood, who superficially seems to be at one with the British Whigs in asserting (in his *North American Review* article) that the poet was liberty's finest literary defender, a man with a voice at once contemporary and American. This is why, he writes,

> as Americans, as lovers of freedom, improvement, and truth, we wish to see these two volumes widely circulated among our countrymen, and deeply read. They are fit manuals for a free people. They are full of those eloquent, soul stirring, holy lessons of liberty, which do something more than simply persuade and convince the mind; which give it purpose, and principle, and firm resolve; which brace up the heart, while they strengthen the understanding; which render timidity or apostacy impossible; which, at the same time that they impart the feeling of discipleship, infuse the spirit of martyrdom; because the truths which they inculcate are of such a nature, that those who receive them must contend, and if needs be, must die for them.[47]

As this passage suggests, at one level Greenwood's Milton is clearly the patriotic "honorary American" of the Revolution. His prose works "are fit manuals for a free people" and are full of "eloquent, soul stirring, holy lessons of liberty." He thus seems to play to the antinomian polarity within New England culture and to its long heritage of resistance to authority. Yet like Griswold, Greenwood, in fact, also conceives a Milton more in the moderate Puritan tradition, one who affirms the leadership claims of the class to which (by virtue of his education and profession, if nothing else) the critic himself belonged. Looked at closely, the language of this passage indicates that Griswold's Milton is less the king-killer than the preacher-poet and consensualist didact. Rather than commanding the obedience of his readers (like a patriarchalist) or preaching his own radical equality with them (like a Digger), he affirms moderate bourgeois hegemony by trying to persuade them to defer to

---

47. Greenwood, 73–74. For a discussion of the response of dominant-class authors in America to contemporary revolutionary events in Europe and what that reveals about their lack of commitment to radical change in the New World, see Larry J. Reynolds, *European Revolutions and the American Literary Renaissance* (New Haven, Conn.: Yale University Press, 1988).

his leadership. Like a good Arminian preacher, he engages in the consensualist promotion of affectionate and voluntary discipleship by teaching a political lesson from which there can be no "apostacy." He tries to convince rationally rather than make a priori claims, and to move the affections so as to make his readers loyal even unto death. Indeed, for Greenwood, Milton's prose is effective didactically precisely because it follows the sequence of tuition, controlled arousal of the affections, and deferential consent envisioned under the consensualist model (and so often attempted with such mixed results by the region's dominant-class ministers, legislators, courtroom advocates, and authors).

Greenwood's comments on Milton are, therefore, not really a call to arms, but instead a remembrance of revolutions past combined with a recommendation of his own leadership claims and those of his class. The passage just cited defines liberty in the classic consensualist way (as the freedom of each autonomous adult to choose to defer to his or her mentors and natural leaders); and as such, it both contrasts with the more leveling reception of Milton in other parts of early nineteenth-century culture (e.g., in the African-American tradition)[48] and yet parallels contemporary non-Unitarian responses within the dominant class. An example of the latter is the first book-length American biography of Milton, which was published under evangelical auspices in 1866. Its author, W. Carlos Martyn, justified this endeavor by noting that

> since, on this side of the Atlantic, the republican ideas and the ecclesiastical truths which Milton so ardently espoused and so ably expounded, have effected a fixed and lasting lodgement, and since it may, in some sense, be said that religious and political America sprang from his brain, it is somewhat singular that no American should have undertaken to present Milton's life to his fellow-countrymen, for the edification and instruction of those who stand so heavily in his debt. It certainly seems that this republic, based largely upon his ideas, and wedded enthusiastically to his religious opinions, owes John Milton at least the tribute and the grateful recognition of a biographical record.[49]

48. Carolivia Herron, "Milton and Afro-American Literature," in *Re-membering Milton: Essays on the Texts and Traditions*, ed. Mary Nyquist and Margaret W. Ferguson (London: Methuen, 1988), 278–300.

49. W. Carlos Martyn, *Life and Times of John Milton* (New York: American Tract Society, 1866), 4.

In many respects this passage too draws upon the antinomian impulse in American culture. Milton is here the poet of liberty, our ancestor in freedom's cause and ally in time of need. Moreover, Martyn bases the rest of his undistinguished book almost exclusively upon the earlier biographies of English Whig Miltonists like Charles Symmons and Joseph Ivimey. Nevertheless, the consensualist model of the didactic preacher-poet dies hard, even here. For though Martyn maintains that "the republican ideas and the ecclesiastical truths which Milton so ardently espoused and so ably expounded have effected a fixed and lasting lodgement" in America, he too tries to present these truths in an antiradical light in order to repress their subversive implications. He does this by claiming that the result of America's exposure to Milton's views on liberty ought not to be a further commitment to reform but instead (in consensualist fashion) a recognition of the need to defer to great didacts. This is true, Martyn contends, first, with regard to Milton, because in the aftermath of the Civil War his readers particularly owe this man of letters "tribute and . . . grateful recognition" for the values that had inspired them over the previous four years; and second, with regard to himself as the poet's first American biographer, since in undertaking this book he too is seeking to play the Miltonic role of mentor or didact, by writing "for the edification and instruction of those who stand so heavily in his [Milton's] debt"; and so, his subject in large measure serves as the consensualist role model for his own pursuit of an ideological agenda. Finally, from Martyn's point of view, his stance has another contemporary relevance as well, since he is writing at the end of a struggle fought (in the view of most northerners) not to abolish slavery—let alone foment radical revolution—but instead to save the Union and preserve the moderate constitutional order established by the Founding Fathers.

The Unitarians' habit of circumscribing the potentially radical implications of Milton's life and writings was also aimed at alleviating their more immediate political and sectarian isolation too. For example, a critic like Sidney Willard would ritually praise the poet for his love of freedom, declaring that it proceeded "from a great mind, a mind distinguished by independence, to a degree remarkable at the period"; yet just as typically, he would then go on to turn the poet's reputation for defending liberty to advantage by making him his ally in the struggle to maintain elite authority. Willard does this first merely because he wrote his tribute to the poet's resistance to absolutism in a review of the newly rediscovered *De Doctrina Christiana*. The publication of this book definitively proved that Milton was a Unitarian; and so, Willard's praise is not really just a paean to his subject's antinomian qualities but rather, in addition, an attempt to use the poet's prestige on behalf of his own denomination and its much-vaunted tradition of "free inquiry." For as he is quick to argue, the Miltonic spirit that defied monarchs and defended Protestant truth "at the very seat, and almost in the presence of the papal power," is best represented in his own day by Americans like himself who reject the dogmatism and mediation of the past.

Of course, as Emerson was to discover a decade later, this Unitarian spirit of tolerance was hardly intended to endorse religious radicalism. "Free inquiry" had definite limits set by the self-interest and ideology of its proponents—limits designed in the ecclesiastical sphere to help repress any tendency toward undermining ministerial authority (whether by means of "the latest form of infidelity" or evangelical enthusiasm). Furthermore, in the context of the history of denominational competition in America, Willard's tribute is scarcely disinterested in another way too. For at the time he wrote, the Episcopal church was just beginning to recover from its postrevolutionary doldrums and make inroads among Boston's largely Unitarian elite. It was, therefore, with his own denomination's flagging position in mind that Willard went on to remind his readers of the poet's attitude toward the bishops of Rome and the archbishops of Canterbury; and (in a passage whose innuendo could hardly have been missed by an audience steeped in the typology of Puritan liberty) it is for the same reason that he noted that "connected as were the affairs of church and state at that period, it was impossible that one who [like Milton] had any strong republican tendency, should bear any good will to episcopacy."[50]

A little later, Samuel Osgood (a Unitarian member of Hedge's Transcendental club)[51] was even more blunt in using Milton's libertarianism to reassert the hegemonic claims of "the Boston religion." He declared in 1854 that

50. Sidney Willard, "Milton on Christian Doctrine," review of *A Treatise on Christian Doctrine, compiled from the Holy Scriptures alone*, by John Milton, trans. Charles R. Sumner, *The North American Review* 22 (1826): 365–67.

51. Osgood's theological position was a shifting and not always clear one. He seems to have begun as a Channing Unitarian, flirted with Transcendentalism, then become a conservative Unitarian, and finally an Episcopal priest. See William R. Hutchison, *The Transcendentalist Ministers: Church Reform in the New England Renaissance* (New Haven, Conn.: Yale University Press, 1959), 39n, 116–17, and 137; and Judith Kent Green, "A Tentative Transcendentalist in the Ohio Valley: Samuel Osgood and the *Western Messenger*," in *Studies in the American Renaissance: 1984*, ed. Joel A. Myerson (Charlottesville: University Press of Virginia, 1984), 79–92.

while every age ought to remember the poet's example and so "inflame its zeal by fire from the old altars of freedom and faith," above all his generation had need of doing so.

> In our day, England has had cause to learn many a lesson at the tombs of her great champions of liberty. In new forms the priestcraft and kingcraft of the Stuarts have risen up to conspire against civil and religious freedom; and in new forms the shades of the stout Independents, with Cromwell and Milton at their head, have gone out to do battle against them. Our own country, although called pre-eminently the land of liberty, has seen something of the same conflict and needs something of the same defence. Some of our Congressional champions of absolutism might be confounded at once by the most familiar truisms of those sages of the old English Commonwealth, from whom our fathers learned their ideas of constitutional rights; and not a few of our clergy who are making Oxford or Rome the throne of their faith might with great profit diversify their liturgical studies by the careful perusal of the old champions of religious liberty.[52]

Osgood casts Milton here as a defender of liberty who engages the antinomian structure of feeling in New England culture. In an age in which "in new forms the priestcraft and kingcraft of the Stuarts have risen up to conspire against civil and religious freedom," the poet reappears alongside the shade of Cromwell to inspire Americans "to do battle against" patriarchalism once more. Yet like Hawthorne's similar invocation of "the Angel of Hadley" myth in "The Grey Champion," there is more here than meets the eye. For Milton is no Digger or Leveler or Quaker in this passage; rather, like the Lord Protector himself, he is a distinctly Arminian figure, a priest and prophet who stands before the altar of God beckoning Americans to imitate him and follow his teachings—at once "the defender of republican liberty and order against every foe."[53]

As this suggests, Osgood in this passage accurately expresses the middling position of his subject's party during the seventeenth century (its conflicted

---

52. Samuel Osgood, "Milton in Our Day," review of *The Poetical Works of John Milton*, ed. C. D. Cleveland, and *The Prose Works of John Milton*, *The Christian Examiner and Religious Miscellany* 57 (1854): 323–24. Osgood's sectarian diatribe here is all the more ironic in light of his own eventual adherence to Anglicanism.

53. Ibid., 329.

commitments both to civil freedom and political stability, and to the priest-hood of all believers and the divine authority of the clergy). Osgood and the rest of his class had inherited this position and these interests, and that is why his Milton here is a consensualist man of letters, one who instructs the people of his age from a position of superiority by means of moral suasion and personal example, thereby creating cultural authority for himself. Like his coreligionists, Osgood's aim was to rob Milton's resistance to tyranny of its potentially radical implications and ally him to the cause of elite domi-nance, and so here he created a Milton who could serve as a hero for New England's clerisy. In particular, he did this by arguing that Milton's revolu-tionary prose and political activity had historically resulted in the American Constitution. As the didact "from whom our fathers learned their ideas of constitutional rights," the poet was therefore the ultimate progenitor of a re-ceived text that had forever settled the conflict between the demands of lib-erty and those of order in a moderate fashion (thereby definitively precluding either a return to patriarchalism or the need for further revolutions). Simi-larly, as the author of *Paradise Lost*, Osgood's Milton was "among the great Christian teachers," despite whatever unfortunate (and potentially antino-mian) interest his "demonology, the mere framework of his poem," may have aroused. For his epic essentially "teaches the great contrast between rebel-lion and obedience," and resolves the issue of authority in consensualist fash-ion in favor of the latter, through its depiction of "the final deliverance of our race from sin and woe" by Christ. Indeed, this is precisely why in Osgood's Arminian view

> we need to bring forth the name of Milton now. We need him in the conflicts through which society is now passing; we need the influence of the champion of liberty without licentiousness and of religion with-out priestcraft. We need him in the struggle now going on between all true souls and the two great divisions of worldlings who are trying to stay every worthy influence, and, instead of hearing the voice, "Come up hither," are crying, "Come down to us." The idol of our time is Mammon, and his worshippers are of two classes;—in the first place, those who have all his stores, and who would put on all men the brib-ery of servitude; [and] in the second place, those who have them not, and who band together and gnash their teeth at those who have them. Milton never bowed the knee to the Mammon of his age, although asked by a king to do so. He was neither the minion of the gilded noble nor the flatterer of the restless mob. In government and religion

> he was a man who loved liberty, because he loved order, and who
> never despaired of their being one day combined.[54]

The self-interestedness of this passage speaks for itself. It is a classic, and
even brazen, statement of bourgeois fears and desires, and clearly enunciates
the ideological position by which the New England dominant class sought to
establish and preserve its hegemony for over 250 years. Osgood's Milton is
here, perhaps more than anywhere else in the contemporary critical literature, received as a consensualist authority, one whose greatness is (in the
widest sense) largely "political." Yet it is also worth noting that in the passage first cited from his essay, he makes Milton speak as well to some of
the specific political and religious anxieties then vexing Unitarian New England. For by 1854 the Boston elite had been much provoked by the Fugitive
Slave Act and other challenges to their region's political autonomy; and so,
Osgood there lumps together the traditional patriarchal enemies of American
liberty (England's monarchs and the Tory defenders of divine right) with
"our Congressional champions of absolutism" (those who, like Calhoun,
would make the Constitution into a document justifying arbitrary rule and
the dominance of one section by another). Similarly, because he was writing
in a semiofficial publication of a sect whose influence was in decline, Osgood
also equated these congressional absolutists with two other groups who
threatened Unitarian hegemony: the Tractarians (who increasingly lured
members of the upper classes away to ritualism) and the Catholics (who in the
wake of Irish immigration were beginning to swamp native Yankees numer-
ically as well).

Of course, if Osgood's essay is the plainest statement of the hegemonist
aims behind the Unitarian Milton, its nasty and bigoted tone suggests that it
represents something of a nadir in Milton's Unitarian reception as well. In
particular, the first of the two long excerpts quoted here demonstrates how
the admittedly partisan side of the poet's late eighteenth-century American
reception could darken into a bitter defensiveness in the face of the elite's
growing eclipse. For as they became more and more overwhelmed by their
disempowerment, many mid-century Unitarian Miltonists also became more
venomous when they used the poet and his writings to help reassert their
fast-disappearing hegemony. Their Milton as a consequence sometimes
ceased being a positive role model at all and instead became a kind of tribal

54. Ibid., 336 and 338.

totem to be invoked in casting spells against alien powers. Yet for all its typicality, it would be unfair to leave the story of the Unitarian Milton with the likes of Osgood at his worst, since there is still one other member of that clan of gentlemen critics who should be considered, a literary preacher whose Milton (in Osgood's words) wore "a vesture of light." This is William Ellery Channing; and it is to him and to the poet whom he called "that sainted spirit" that attention therefore must now be turned.

2

THAT SAINTED SPIRIT

The rediscovery and translation of Milton's *De Doctrina Christiana* by Charles R. Sumner in 1826[1] had a profound impact upon Unitarian Boston. Almost as soon as Sumner's edition reached New England, the denomination's chief periodicals took notice of it and rushed suitable excerpts into print;[2] thereafter they commissioned a number of reviews in order to underscore its importance. Their reason for doing so is not hard to see, since its contents suggested that Milton was a proponent of "free inquiry" and progressive theology like themselves, and so the editors of *The Christian Examiner* and *The North American Review* could use his reputation to "answer the ominous cries of the opposers of Unitarians and of some irresolutes among themselves, who, as they see one after another of what we deem the theological errors of the day attempted to be removed, are continually exclaiming—'do not go too far!'—'where will you stop!' as if in the work of reformation we *could* go too far, or as if we ought to stop *at all*, till every strong delusion, every mere device of the human understanding, or of the human passions, is utterly destroyed, and truth and goodness are all in all!"[3] As this suggests, the Unitarian elite received the *De Doctrina Christiana* in a self-consciously ideological manner and used it to address the problem of authority still confronting them. Perhaps the most interesting—but complex—example of this

1. The rediscovery, publication, and British reception of *De Doctrina Christiana* are described in the introduction to *Two Books of Investigations into Christian Doctrine Drawn from the Sacred Scriptures Alone*, ed. Maurice Kelley and trans. John Carey, *Complete Prose Works of John Milton* (New Haven, Conn.: Yale University Press, 1973), VI, 3–40.
2. Sectarian uses and/or reprints of *De Doctrina* in *The Christian Examiner* alone, for instance, include passages at 2 (1825), 423–29; 3 (1826), 186–87; and 4 (1827), 196.
3. Ibid., 3 (1826), 121.

dominant-class appropriation is that of William Ellery Channing. His 1826 *Christian Examiner* review[4] of the *De Doctrina* both epitomizes the Unitarian "economy of evaluation"[5] and yet departs from it in ways that reveal the Boston religion's ideological contradictions and tensions. As such, it is the most important treatment of Milton by any Unitarian.

Channing's conformity to, and yet dissent from, the New England Milton tradition is evident from the very start of the review. For instance, on the one hand, his treatment of the poet is less self-interested than that of his colleagues elsewhere. This is why at the outset he declares that Milton's treatise "derives its chief interest from its author" rather than from its theology. For he was much less interested in scoring sectarian points than his coreligionists were; and so, despite the poet's historical commitment to moderate Puritanism, he portrayed him not as the author of an important text in the history of liberal religion but as an irenic figure: one who "had that universality which marks the highest order of intellect" to such a degree that "poetry was as a universal presence" in his life, and "great minds were everywhere his kindred" (4–5). Similarly (again in sharp contrast to Osgood and most other Unitarians), Channing acclaimed Milton at the beginning of the essay not because he was heterodox but because he was an instance of the powers of the mind at their farthest extension—an illustration of the proto-Emersonian contention that

> mind is in its own nature diffusive. Its object is the universe, which is strictly one, or bound together by infinite connexions and correspondences; and accordingly its natural progress is from one to another field of thought; and wherever original power, creative genius exists, the mind, far from being distracted or oppressed by the variety of its acquisitions, will see more and more common bearings and hidden and beautiful analogies in all the objects of knowledge. (6)

Despite this, however, Channing's general theme in these opening pages is still the traditional one in Unitarian Milton criticism: of how the poet's "ge-

---

4. William Ellery Channing, "Milton," review of *A Treatise on Christian Doctrine, compiled from the Holy Scriptures alone*, by John Milton, trans. Charles R. Summer, *The Christian Examiner and Theological Review* 3 (1826): 29–77. Citations are from *The Works of William E. Channing, D.D.* (Boston: James Monroe, 1848), I, 3–68, with page numbers in parentheses as indicated.

5. Barbara Herrnstein Smith, "Contingencies of Value," in *Canons*, ed. Robert von Hallberg (Chicago: University of Chicago Press, 1984), 5–39.

nius and greatness of soul" exemplify literary authority and confirm the New England dominant class's historic leadership claims (28). His initial attempt to distance himself from the less attractive features of the Unitarian Milton here does not, therefore, mean that he was any less Unitarian in his overall response to the author of the *De Doctrina*. Indeed, a passage like the one just cited is itself a product of Unitarianism's philosophical, theological, and aesthetic assumptions (especially since its description of Milton's literary authority reflects the denomination's intellectual compromise with eighteenth-century empiricism). Thus, in common with other contemporary dominant-class thinkers, Channing attributed the poet's "original power" or "creative genius" neither to a divine source (like the nightly visitations of the Heavenly Muse in *Paradise Lost*) nor to the self-generated insights of the imagination (as Emerson would later do), but instead to the fact that Milton's "great and far-looking mind, which grasps at once vast fields of thought" (22), was merely an extraordinary case of the human mind's ordinary power (as described by the Scots) to synthesize by association—and so to discover and connect the analogies embedded in sense experience. As such, Channing's understanding of Milton's authority as a man of letters was implicitly consensualist. For he believed that Milton's authority ultimately arose from his possession of a power found in all human minds, a truth which made the poet different only in degree, not in kind, from the rest of humanity. Like Christ in eighteenth-century consensualist readings of *Paradise Lost*, Channing's Milton is therefore superior to the masses, yet also equal to them: a semi-divine being, yet a gifted brother as well.

As these antinomies suggest, however, even here at his most typically Unitarian, Channing reveals the real locus of his dissent from his fellow Bostonians, which went beyond a mere distaste for denominational rivalry. For his description of Milton's literary authority demonstrates how very much more paradigmatically polarized he was than any of his colleagues. This is particularly evident with regard to his views on the nature of Milton's inspiration, which are alternatively both more in keeping with the patriarchalism his ancestors had resisted and with the antinomianism they had sought to repress. Thus, on the one hand, despite his earlier statement that Milton's genius merely marked an expansion of the ordinary powers of the human mind, Channing also asserted that his subject had a *charism* that was divine in origin and a social role that was "prophetic" rather than tutorial in nature. Significantly, moreover, he did this immediately after his description of Milton as a type of the mind's analytic and associative powers by resorting to the language of hieratic patriarchalism in order to illustrate the nature of his subject's "holy calling." For he held there that poetic genius is "the most transcendent" of God's gifts (a boon from above like a free act of grace rather than a mere human mental exercise); and so, in contradiction to his earlier statement, Channing's Milton is actually far above the rest of us in the scale of being because (in an ironic twist on the clerical model of the literary calling) he was specially commissioned to convert his readers: divinely called to be their prophet rather than their Arminian pastor. His "creative energies, [and] power of original and ever growing thought" took shape in "those sacred recesses of the soul, where poetry is born and nourished, and inhales immortal vigor, and wings herself for her heavenward flight," because given what he was meant to do, he had to possess an authority that was metaphysical rather than psychological in origin. For "it is the glorious prerogative of this art, that it 'makes all things new' for the gratification of a divine instinct"; and so its creator had to have "the conscious dignity of a prophet" rather than the genteel benignity of a Brahmin man of letters, had to possess the healing power of priestly absolution rather than the hortatory influence of the lecture hall (7–8).

Of course, one could argue that this lurch toward a kind of poetic divine right is just an exaggeration of tendencies found elsewhere in Unitarianism. The circumstances of the dominant class in antebellum New England drove many of its members toward a sympathy for hierarchicalism. Moreover, Channing's coreligionists found the Scottish philosophy attractive as a bulwark against both skepticism and dogmatism precisely because it mediated the claims of reason and faith (with the result that these adherants of natural supernaturalism had little difficulty in making a concept like "the rational imagination" consonant with both their empiricism and their vague belief in the spiritual nature of inspiration). Certainly as theologians the Unitarians were much in the habit of doing something else that Channing does here, which is to retain the vocabulary of Christian orthodoxy while subverting its substance. Nonetheless, his hyper-Arminianism here as well as later in the review does go beyond the norms of Brahmin thought, particularly because the seriousness and consistency with which he employed sacerdotal language to characterize Milton's authority sets the *De Doctrina* review (along with his companion essays on Fénelon and Napoleon) apart from the didactic rationalism of most Unitarian literary criticism.[6]

At the same time, however, these opening pages also indicate that Channing was the most open of the Unitarians to the subversive, antinomian side

---

6. The Napoleon review is found in William Ellery Channing, *Works*, I, 69–166, and the Fénelon review at I, 167–215; hereafter both are cited with page numbers as indicated parenthetically.

of Milton's thought. Paradoxically, this was because by resorting to older, more hierarchical, arbitrary, and authoritarian language to describe the sources of poetic genius, he did more than just exaggerate the Arminian polarity in his culture or criticize his coreligionists for reducing inspiration to associationist psychology and common didacticism.[7] Rather, the patriarchal moments of his meditation upon Milton ironically also involved his entertainment of some radically self-empowering notions of poetic authority. And so, Channing also proved himself in this review to be the precursor of the Emerson of "The Poet" and *The Divinity School Address,* and the author of (what is arguably) the first transcendental biography.[8] For though he there extended "the analogy between art and religion to the farthest limits Unitarianism could bear, by taking seriously, so to speak, the idea of poetic inspiration, with which his colleagues only flirted,"[9] he did so as much in the direction of New England's antinomian heritage as in that of its ideological opposite.

The first third of the *De Doctrina* review (3–20), which concentrates on Milton the poet, illustrates this ideological polarization particularly well. Channing's theme in this section is that in his literary activities Milton embodied two of the three main types of genius. The first is "*moral* greatness, or magnanimity" (118), which he exemplified because "his moral character was as strongly marked as his intellectual, and it may be expressed in one word, *magnanimity.* It was in harmony with his poetry. He had a passionate love of the higher, more commanding, and majestic virtues" (31). Significantly, however, while this moral greatness pervaded his whole life and work, Channing believed that "we see Milton's magnanimity" not so much in his

---

7. Charvat, 7–26, provides many examples (both Unitarian and non-Unitarian) of this reduction of inspiration to psychology and didacticism in early nineteenth-century America.

8. Buell, *Literary Transcendentalism,* 263ff., discusses the Transcendental biography (and autobiography) as genres.

9. Ibid., 36. Buell, 23–54, is the best summary of Channing's relationship to the Transcendentalists; for another view, which portrays Channing as a crypto-idealist, see David P. Edgell, *William Ellery Channing: An Intellectual Portrait* (Boston: Beacon, 1955), esp. 113–49. Other, more standard treatments of Channing's place in the intellectual history of Unitarianism and Transcendentalism include Howe, *The Unitarian Conscience,* and Hutchison (both passim); Conrad Wright, "The Rediscovery of Channing," in *The Liberal Christians: Essays on American Unitarian History* (Boston: Beacon, 1970), 22–40; and Andrew Delbanco, *William Ellery Channing: An Essay on the Liberal Spirit in America* (Cambridge, Mass.: Harvard University Press, 1981). Little is known about Channing's early reading in Milton and Milton criticism. However, for evidence of his exposure at Harvard to the standard rhetorical texts that discussed the poet, see Arthur W. Brown, *Always Young for Liberty: A Biography of William Ellery Channing* (Syracuse, N.Y.: Syracuse University Press, 1956), 14–33 and 192.

moments of high office as "in the circumstances under which 'Paradise Lost' was written. It was not in prosperity, in honor, and amidst triumphs, but in disappointment, desertion, and in what the world calls disgrace, that he composed that work"; it was when the poet was most disempowered (when he was most like what Channing and his class felt they were becoming) that his moral greatness most shone forth (thus proving that "it is the prerogative of true greatness to glorify itself in adversity, and to meditate and execute vast enterprises in defeat" [36]).

As this cultural siting of Milton's magnanimity suggests, Channing in many ways treated Milton in this first section much as any Unitarian would. Thus, for instance, he held that in writing verse the author of *Paradise Lost* had the high moral purpose the denomination's critics recommended: that earnestness which (as Channing puts it in the Napoleon review) comes of "that sublime energy, by which the soul, smitten with the love of virtue, binds itself indissolubly, for life and for death, to truth and duty" (118). Moreover, more generally, Channing's Milton is a consensualist didact engaged upon his tutorial responsibilities toward his readers, one who illustrates the Unitarian ideal of a poet's interaction with his audience in associationist terms:

> The great and decisive test of genius is, that it calls forth *power* in the souls of others. It not merely gives knowledge, but breathes energy. There are authors, and among these Milton holds the highest rank, in approaching whom we are conscious of an access of intellectual strength. A "virtue goes out" from them. . . . The works which we should chiefly study, are not those which contain the greatest fund of knowledge, but which raise us into sympathy with the intellectual energy of the author, and through which a great mind multiplies itself, as it were, in the reader. (30–31)

In the manner of the Scots, Milton here impresses himself and his ideas upon his readers through the creation of "sympathy" or affection between them. Yet significantly, Channing's ideological move away from consensualist centrism is evident here too. For in contradiction to his consensualism and associationism, the two biblical passages to which he alludes imply that Milton possessed a moral authority utterly unconnected with these eighteenth-century formations. They suggest instead that he wrote with the patriarchal authority of one graced with a divine *charism* (with the authority of one who exercises a gift greater than the ordinary powers of the human mind, of one who relies on more than example, tuition, and moral suasion). For he wrote as one who *inspires* or breathes his spirit into others (like the Father in the Garden at the creation of Adam), thereby healing a morally sick humanity just as Christ (the One from Whom "a 'virtue goes out' " in the New Testament) did when miraculously curing the sick.[10]

Milton's moral authority as a poet thus here partakes of the divine creative power of the Father and the Son at their most hierarchical. For in Channing's two biblical allusions at this point, divine spiritual power works its will upon a passive humanity, who submissively benefit from these patriarchal actions without any of the conscious assent, active learning, or autonomous moral choice advocated by the consensualists. Channing's Milton here is, consequently, part consensualist didact and part divine miracle worker, part exploiter of common human psychological powers and part mantic bard: a figure who reflects the tendency in their disempowerment of some of New England's dominant class to hanker inconsistently after the very sacerdotalism their moderate Puritan ancestors had resisted. At the same time, however, the passage just cited moves in the opposite direction too; for its ambiguous language also potentially relocates the source of the poet's power within the self. This is because the "great mind" that here "multiplies itself . . . in the reader" could grammatically just as easily be the poet's own as that of the Deity; and so it is arguably Milton's *energia* or *virtù* (his personal presence in all his writings) that here works miracles and impresses itself upon the reader. Read in another way, in other words, Channing's characterization of Milton as the magnanimous poet is in fact, therefore, not an endorsement of patriarchalism but an anticipation of the moments of *daemonic* inspiration in Emerson. The piety of his biblical allusions as such crumples before a more satanic set of sentiments (the desire to create as God created and to cure the spiritually lame as Christ did—but not in His name); and his radical Puritan heritage as a member of the Yankee elite is laid bare in a moment of access to the tradition that would later lead Emerson to assert that Milton's true magnanimity lay in his creation of the Archfiend and in his multiplication of his *own* mind in those of his readers.

In treating his subject's moral genius, Channing in a sense gives us a Milton whose literary authority apes that of the two main adversaries in *Paradise*

---

10. Channing's first biblical reference is to Genesis 2:7 on the creation of Adam. In addition, there are three passages in the New Testament from which he may have taken the phrase "a virtue goes out of him." One contrasts the healing power of Christ to the dead formalism of the Pharisees (Luke 6:19), and the other two tell the story of Christ's encounter with a woman afflicted with an issue of blood, who touches the hem of His garment, and so is made whole (Mark 5:30 and Luke 8:46).

Lost. He is both patriarchal God and rebellious demon: a divinely commissioned poet yet one whose autonomy of soul overthrows all order. With the former Milton, Channing reminds us that he was himself really neither a crypto-Transcendentalist nor what Andrews Norton might have called an antinomian. The writings of Kames, Stewart, and Burke were formative in shaping his intellectual presuppositions, and later influences (such as the Lake poets, the Cambridge Platonists, and the Schlegels) only induced him—like Hazlitt in England—to revise the older philosophy. His critical and philosophical position "constitutes only a groundwork, not an actual beginning of the transcendental poetic." (Indeed, as the above discussion shows, in many ways he was an Arminian bent upon being a patriarchalist.) Yet in giving us the second, subversive Milton as well, Channing so manifested his need to restore some sort of spiritual meaning to the concept of inspiration (to suggest that it was more than the mere exercise of psychological association in a mentorial cause) that he also showed how hard he tried to "reach the [Emersonian] heights he celebrates" here.[11]

This tendency to exaggerate the contradictory demands that gnawed away at the moderate ideological tradition in New England can also be seen in Channing's account of the second kind of genius manifested by Milton the poet. In the Napoleon essay he defines it as

> *intellectual* greatness, or genius in the highest sense of that word; and by this we mean that sublime capacity of thought, through which the soul, smitten with the love of the true and the beautiful, essays to comprehend the universe, soars into the heavens, penetrates the earth, penetrates itself, questions the past, anticipates the future, traces out the general and all-comprehending laws of nature, binds together by innumerable affinities and relations all the objects of its knowledge, rises from the finite and transient to the infinite and the everlasting, frames to itself from its own fulness lovelier and sublimer forms than it beholds, discerns the harmonies between the world within and the world without us, and finds in every region of the universe types and interpreters of its own deep mysteries and glorious inspirations. This is the greatness which belongs to philosophers, and to the master spirits in poetry and the fine arts. (119–20)

At the most obvious level, this quotation merely reflects the transitionalism of Channing's thought: on the one hand, it manifests the heterogeneous

11. Delbanco, 110.

philosophical influences upon the Unitarian mind (e.g., the Scottish philosophy's "rational intuitionism," the "moral sentiment" views of Hutcheson and Shaftesbury, and Burke's writings on the sublime);[12] yet on the other, his exposure as well to English romanticism (since the phrase "master spirits" is from one of Wordsworth's Milton sonnets, "Great Men Have Been Among Us").[13] In addition, however, the passage demonstrates Channing's tendency to break with Unitarianism and explore the conflicting forces within consensualism as well. This becomes particularly clear when one remembers that Wordsworth was as much a product of Anglo-American culture's bourgeois contradictions as Channing; and so, however brief, his sonnet's textual presence here opens up both the Napoleon and *De Doctrina* reviews for ideological inspection.

The similarities between Wordsworth and Channing begin with the fact that the former ascribed Milton's genius to the same magnanimity, intellectual prowess, and active virtue as the latter. Significantly, Wordsworth did so for the same classist reasons as his younger New England contemporary. Consequently, Wordsworth's Milton (like that of the Unitarians) is a conflicted, consensualist figure. He is a Milton who speaks for liberty (thereby satisfying the recessive antinomianism of middle-class gentlemen on both sides of the Atlantic), yet one who also affirms the demands of order, community, and hierarchy. Not surprisingly, therefore, in the sonnet from which Channing took the phrase "master spirits," Wordsworth celebrates not radical revolution but the bourgeois Whig constitution of 1688 (the "single volume" or "code" on account of which England had avoided the anarchy of revolutionary France):

> Great men have been among us; hands that penned
> And tongues that uttered wisdom—better none:
> The later Sidney, Marvel, Harrington,

12. See Howe, *The Unitarian Conscience*, 27–68 and 174–204, for the various intellectual currents behind this passage.

13. As with many aspects of his intellectual life, the exact shape and extent of Channing's familiarity with English romanticism is unknown. For instance, as Cole notes (129–34), he corresponded and had personal contact with both Wordsworth and Coleridge; but the evidence for this comes largely from the writings of his nephew and namesake, who in this as in much else sought to make the elder Channing over into a Transcendentalist. In the absence of a journal or records of his reading habits, his own writings consequently themselves become the main evidence of his interest in the Lake poets and other romantic writers; in general, therefore, the *De Doctrina* review should be compared with the material anthologized in J. A. Wittreich, Jr., ed., *The Romantics on Milton: Formal Essays and Critical Asides* (Cleveland, Ohio: Case Western Reserve University Press, 1970).

Young Vane, and others who called Milton friend.
These moralists could act and comprehend:
They knew how genuine glory was put on;
Taught us how rightfully a nation shone
In splendour: what strength was, that would not bend
But in magnanimous meekness. France, 'tis strange,
Hath brought forth no such souls as we had then.
Perpetual emptiness! unceasing change!
No single volume paramount, no code,
No master spirit, no determined road;
But equally a want of books and men!

Similarly, class interest also explains Wordsworth's treatment of Milton in the other sonnets in this group (especially in "London, 1802" and "It Is Not to Be Thought of That the Flood"); for though in them he once more praises the poet as a defender of freedom, he does so by evoking England's aristocratic history and asserting the poet's superior personal position (thus again affirming the equal need for authority and social hierarchy).[14]

Yet Wordsworth's Milton here is also significantly different from Channing's because he is merely conflicted and lacks the hyperpolarized quality seen thus far. Nowhere in these sonnets is the Englishman quite as patriarchal either as he later in life became or as Channing is in the Napoleon and *De Doctrina* reviews; and nowhere—as he had in his youth—did he tilt in an antinomian direction to the degree Channing at times does here. The latter fact is especially evident both in the passage just cited from *Napoleon* and in those parts of the *De Doctrina* review in which Channing betrays his deep yearning to affirm the demands of liberty and equality. For example, when in the above portion of the Napoleon review he incorporates a phrase from the Milton piece (the contention that "never was there a more unconfined mind" than his [6]) and, in doing so, inflates the mind's analogy-finding power to the point where it comes close to being a generative, esemplastic faculty, he actually relocates the source of poetic authority away from Nature and Nature's God to the soul's "own deep mysteries and glorious inspirations." The result is a moment of self-assertion akin to that of Satan in building Pandemonium, when "from its own fulness" Milton's imagination creates "lovelier and sublimer forms than it beholds" (thus annihilating objective reality in

14. The Milton sonnets are cited here from William Wordsworth, *Poetical Works*, ed. Thomas Hutchinson, rev. Ernest de Selincourt (Oxford: Oxford University Press, 1936), 244.

the standard romantic way).[15] Similarly, in his discussion of the poet's intellectual genius in the *De Doctrina* review, many of the examples he uses follow
up on this satanic moment and radicalize the common Unitarian belief that
poetry "in its legitimate and highest efforts . . . has the same tendency and
aim with Christianity; that is, to spiritualize our nature" (9). For by exploring just what such a spiritualization might entail, Channing consistently
commits the same "sin" as Milton had in creating Satan in *Paradise Lost*. He
breaks the link between poetic authority and morality, thereby suggesting
that like his subject, he too at times can forget his role as a teacher and reg-
ister his approval of amoral beauty.

The most striking example of antinomianism in his discussion of Milton's
intellectual genius, however, is where Channing likens the poet's "attribute
of power" ("his sublimity [which] is in every man's mouth") to the satanic
desire to be *as* God. He begins innocently enough, with a compliment worthy
of Adams's Boyleston *Lectures*, declaring that John Milton's "name is almost
identified with sublimity. He is in truth the sublimest of men. He rises, not
by effort or discipline, but by a native tendency and a godlike instinct, to the
contemplation of objects of grandeur and awfulness. He always moves with a
conscious energy" (12). Yet it quickly becomes apparent that for Channing
the poet shared these qualities with his most controversial creation:

15. Mention of the esemplastic power raises the issue of Channing's familiarity with Samuel
Taylor Coleridge. Although he was obviously more than slightly acquainted with Coleridge's
thought, the precise extent of his reading is again unknown. However, in addition to the major
poems, he almost surely knew the *Biographia Literaria*, which also uses Milton to speak to contemporary philosophical issues. Of particular interest is the fact that Coleridge cites the poet's
writings to support his brand of idealism at a number of significant points in the book. The
famous chapter XIII ("On the imagination, or esemplastic power") thus opens with an epigraph
from *Paradise Lost* on the organic unity of creation under the Divine Reason; and in chapter X,
Coleridge uses another passage from Milton to support his central distinction between the Reason and the Understanding—asserting that because of Milton's prestige, this distinction "was
[thus] *confirmed* by [an] authority so venerable" as to be irrefutable. Similarly, in Coleridge's
eyes, Milton's very existence also proved the truth of this distinction. For it was self-evident to
him that as "Milton had a highly *imaginative*, Cowley [had] a very *fanciful* mind. If therefore I
should succeed in establishing the actual existences of two faculties generally different, the no-
menclature would at once be determined. To the faculty by which I had characterized Milton
[Reason], we should confine the term *imagination;* while the other [Understanding] would be
contra-distinguished as *fancy.*" (*Biographia Literaria or Biographical Sketches of My Literary
Life and Opinions*, ed. James Engell and W. Jackson Bate, vol. VII of *The Collected Works of
Samuel Taylor Coleridge* [Princeton, N.J.: Princeton University Press, 1983], part I, 295, 173–75,
and 84 respectively.)
There are, in addition, other, nonphilosophical parallels between Channing and Coleridge on
Milton. The most important touch upon two aspects of the *De Doctrina* review discussed here:
their mutual admiration for his love of liberty (for Coleridge's comments, see Wittreich, 279)
and their distinction between Shakespeare's impersonality and Milton's organic presence in his
writings (see Coleridge, *Biographia*, part II, 27–28).

Hell and hell's king have a terrible harmony, and dilate into new grandeur and awfulness, the longer we contemplate them. From one element, "solid and liquid fire," the poet has framed a world of horror and suffering, such as imagination had never traversed. But fiercer flames than those which encompass Satan, burn in his own soul. Revenge, exasperated pride, consuming wrath, ambition, though fallen, yet unconquered by the thunders of the Omnipotent, and grasping still at the empire of the universe,—these form a picture more sublime and terrible than hell. Hell yields to the spirit which it imprisons. The intensity of its fires reveals the intenser passions and more vehement will of Satan; and the ruined archangel gathers into himself the sublimity of the scene which surrounds him. This forms the tremendous interest of these wonderful books. We see mind triumphant over the most terrible powers of nature. We see unutterable agony subdued by energy of soul. (15)

Channing contends here that in Satan Milton imagined a wholly evil character who was nevertheless a fellow creator with imaginative powers like his own. For like the sublime author of *Paradise Lost*, the Evil One triumphantly embodies the power of the creative imagination to overcome the limitations imposed by sense experience. His agony generates a horror beyond that of the phenomenal fires about him, and he creates a Miltonic "darkness visible" out of himself that overpowers the natural sublime of Hell (which "yields to the spirit which it imprisons"). "The mind" of the demonic creator is "triumphant over the most terrible powers of nature. We see unutterable agony subdued by energy of soul." Like Milton or any other poet of authority, Satan is a master spirit whose "energy of soul" reaches out, comprehending and giving higher form to the realm of experience. Indeed, the fallen archangel almost overgoes his poetic creator in this regard, since he "is a creation requiring in its author *almost* the spiritual energy with which he invests the fallen seraph" (16) [italics added].

By his approval of this aspect of the epic, Channing engages the subversive structure of feeling with a delight one finds nowhere else in Unitarian criticism. For a moment at least, he revels in Satan's antinomian power to overthrow order and in the creative freedom from didactic responsibility which that power implies. Yet paradoxically, there is also an equally exaggerated Arminianism here, as Milton's fallen angel is traditionally patriarchal in his triumphant imaginative activity, which is utterly disconnected from such voluntaristic consensualist formations as mentorship or self-culture. Indeed, in a devastating inversion of Channing's earlier description of Milton's moral genius, he replicates his mind in those of his readers merely for the egotistical pleasure of doing so; and in impressing himself upon others (like the Father with His commandments in the Garden), exercises authority merely for its own sake. For as Channing sees it, the reader of *Paradise Lost* has little choice as to whether he or she will voluntarily submit to the Fiend's agony of soul, and there is no didactic purpose to Milton's presentation of that torment in any case. Instead (with Channing's full approval), the archetypal preacher-poet here abandons his consensualist responsibilities and gives his readers a vision of naked power and evil incarnate that overwhelms rather than persuades (thereby creating not autonomous moral reflection but the *frisson* of awe under duress).

This breakdown of consensualism into its constituent polarities can be seen a little later too, even though the critic sounds more typically Unitarian in his insistence on the link between morals and letters:

Some have doubted whether the moral effect of such delineations of the storms and terrible workings of the soul is good; whether the interest felt in a spirit so transcendently evil as Satan, favors our sympathies with virtue. But our interest fastens, in this and like cases, on what is not evil. We gaze on Satan with an awe not unmixed with mysterious pleasure, as on a miraculous manifestation of the *power of mind*. What chains us, as with a resistless spell, in such a character, is spiritual might made visible by the racking pains which it overpowers. There is something kindling and ennobling in the consciousness, however awakened, of the energy which resides in mind; and many a virtuous man has borrowed new strength from the force, constancy, and dauntless courage of evil agents. (16)

The ideological tensions in this passage are expressed in the divergence between Channing's theme and his imagery. On the one hand, his conscious purpose is to link Milton's authority as a writer to religious and moral orthodoxy. This is why he refutes complaints about Satan's attractiveness by declaring that "our interest fastens, in this and like cases, on what is not evil" in his character. For if "the energy which resides in [the] mind" of the Fiend can be interpreted as giving readers "new strength" (on account of the moral lessons they can learn from his "force, constancy, and dauntless courage"), then Milton's reputation as a didact may be upheld. Yet the passage's imagery tells a different story, since it makes it clear how tempted Channing was to take another view of "the all-enduring, all-defying pride of Satan, assuming so majestically Hell's burning throne, and coveting the diadem, which scorches his thunder-blasted brow" (15–16). For at some level he really did believe that in this instance Milton's authority was divorced from conventional morality and faith; and so, he knew his argument was false here even as he made it.

As this suggests, however much Channing believed Satan to be "a miraculous manifestation of the *power of mind*," in the end, the demon was for him a necromancer who created a "mysterious pleasure" that "chains us" and puts us under "a resistless spell." Indeed, so bewitched and drawn into forbidden waters was he by this projection of Anglo-American culture's antinomian propensities, that he here only escaped from his "awe" at such self-validating, self-generated, amoral, imaginative authority by means of a sophistical argument (which bravely attempts to restore the Unitarian link between poetic genius and didacticism).[16] Put simply, he had been tempted beyond his measure by Milton's Satan to believe in the annihilating power of the imagination with regard to experience; tempted to separate morality and art; and tempted to believe in the divinity of the poet as well as his inspiration from within. And so, it is no surprise that a little later he figuratively ran away in desperation from his own (and Milton's) satanism, declaring that now "from hell we flee to Paradise, a region as lovely as hell is terrible, and which, to those who do not know the universality of true genius, will appear doubly wonderful, when considered as the creation of the same mind, which had painted the infernal world" (18). In doing so, he was turning with relief to the prelapsarian bliss of Adam and Eve, to the heavenly rewards of a life lived according to the precepts of his own Christian faith: to a "higher happiness" than that of our first parents, "a happiness won through struggle with inward and outward foes, the happiness of power and moral victory, the happiness of disinterested sacrifices and wide-spread love, the happiness of boundless hope, and of 'thoughts which wander through eternity' " (18). He was turning, in other words, to a moment in *Paradise Lost* that in the history of Milton's American reception had had strong consensualist associations: to Adam and Eve's original relation of loving but hierarchical mutuality, which had long mythically enabled upper-class New Englanders to reaffirm their allegiance to the Anglo-American bourgeois tradition.

Moreover, this nostalgic look back towards Eden is a reassertion of Channing's consensualist loyalties in another way as well, because it is probably

16. See Cole, 134–35.

also a deliberate revision of the *locus classicus* of "romantic satanism": the third of Hazlitt's 1818 *Lectures on the English Poets*. This lecture ("On Shakspeare and Milton") resembles the *De Doctrina* review in a number of ways. Perhaps unexpectedly, some of these are paradigmatically Arminian (for despite their *very* different politics, the English radical had necessarily been exposed to that structure of feeling in Anglo-American culture too).[17] Yet more significantly, Hazlitt's portrait of Milton's Satan also resembles Channing's in its appeal to their common antinomian heritage. Indeed, in this regard the similarities between their descriptions are many and striking: for both, Satan had a presence of soul that overwent the torments of Hell; for both, that power proceeded out of the amoral depths of the demon's imagination; and for both, this unfettered, creative power was an expression of the subversive side of Milton's own genius. The crucial difference is that Channing flees from the very antinomian possibilities in which Hazlitt (who asserted that Satan's defiance is "the most heroic subject that ever was chosen for a poem") positively reveled.[18] For the New Englander could not long rest easy

17. Hazlitt's exposure to the Arminian structure of feeling is evident in a number of places in the Shakespeare and Milton lecture. For example, like Channing, he was interested in exploring Milton's status as a man of genius. He too saw that authority as being exercised in the literary, political, and religious realms, and he too believed that Milton had a spiritual elevation which set him apart from his contemporaries. Consequently, he believed that "the spirit of the poet, the patriot, and the prophet, vied with each other in his breast," and that in each area of endeavor this spirit gave him a patriarchal authority Hazlitt could not help but admire: for "he had his thoughts constantly fixed on the contemplation of the Hebrew theocracy, and of a perfect commonwealth; and he seized the pen with a hand just warm from the touch of the ark of faith. His religious zeal infused its character into his imagination; so that he devotes himself with the same sense of duty to the cultivation of his genius, as he did to the exercise of virtue, or the good of his country. . . . He thought of nobler forms and nobler things than those he found about him. He lived apart, in the solitude of his own thoughts, carefully excluding from his mind whatever might distract its purposes or alloy its purity, or damp its zeal. 'With darkness and with dangers compassed round,' he had the mighty models of antiquity always present to his thoughts, and determined to raise a monument of equal height and glory . . ." (*The Complete Works of William Hazlitt*, ed. P. P. Howe, after A. R. Waller and Arnold Glover [London: J. M. Dent, 1930–34], v, 56–57).

18. A good example of the way in which Channing at times mirrored Hazlitt's romantic satanism is the following passage, in which the latter proclaimed that though Satan be "an outcast from Heaven, Hell trembles beneath his feet, Sin and Death are at his heels, and mankind are his easy prey." As in parts of the *De Doctrina* review, it was the Fiend's very exuberence in overthrowing all rule and order that for Hazlitt made a virtue of his archetypally antinomian vice:

> The sense of his punishment seems lost in the magnitude of it; the fierceness of tormenting flames is qualified and made innoxious by the greater fierceness of his pride; the loss of infinite happiness to himself is compensated in thought, by the power of inflicting infinite misery on others. . . . His thoughts burn like a hell within him; but the power of thought holds dominion in his mind over every other consideration. The

with the severing of the link between art and morality (or more broadly, the loss of the comfortable consensualist framework within which contemporary doctrines of literary didacticism tended to occur). So, in the end he minutely but strategically revised the British writer's lecture: by taking the (slightly misquoted) line from Belial's speech in book II of *Paradise Lost*, which Hazlitt had used to characterize Satan triumphant amidst the fires of Hell (" 'that intellectual being, those thoughts that wander through eternity' "), and applying it instead to the joys of Adam and Eve in Paradise. It is a small change, yet one that makes all the difference, because it sums up Channing's need to hold on to the Milton of his predecessors and coreligionists, to tie his own "intellectual being" to a Milton who balanced the claims of the patriarchal Father against those of his antinomian archrival, lest the world be turned upside down once more.

This polarization can also be seen in the second third of the review (20–40), in which Channing discusses Milton's political writings. He claims there that his subject's achievements as a champion of freedom were due not only to his magnanimity and intellect but also to a third kind of genius: that for action. In proving this, however, Channing shows that he shared Unitarian Boston's diffidence about the use of force and its preference for moral suasion and "self-culture" as the means of individual and corporate reform. Not surprisingly, therefore, when he came to define active genius in the Napoleon essay he revealed that he believed this type to be inferior to moral and intellectual genius. In fact, he thought it to be almost a near occasion of sin; for like other Unitarian clerics, he felt that this kind (which he says is the basis for the authority of politicians and soldiers) was like democratic politics: it was fundamentally not disinterested enough. Indeed, it normally arose alongside a Napoleonic hubris that corrupted the spirit of its possessors by seducing them into settling for mere mastery of worldly affairs (120–22).

---

consciousness of a determined purpose, of "that intellectual being, those thoughts that wander through eternity," though accompanied with endless pain, he prefers to nonentity, to "being swallowed up and lost in the wide womb of uncreated night."

Yet this same passage also goes on to illustrate the difference between the two critics. For while they both agree that Milton's portrait of Satan's labors at the beginning of *Paradise Lost* represents a victory for the creative imagination over experience, unlike Channing, Hazlitt never backs off from his assertion that the aesthetic power of this description of the demon as "gigantic, irregular, portentous, uneasy, and disturbed—but dazzling in its faded splendour, the clouded ruins of a god" absolves the poet from all blame in so violating the didactic imperatives of neoclassical art (Ibid., v, 63–65).

In Channing's eyes, Milton was a singular exception to this pattern of moral contamination, however, because he combined genius for action with the other two types. As a result, his political activities and writings have an authority that partakes of the spirit rather than the flesh, an authority that makes him the model for the intellectual engaged in public affairs. For he loved liberty as an idea rather than as a means of redressing grievances or gaining power, and so translated the politics of his day to a higher level. As Channing put it in the *De Doctrina* review, Milton's "greatness of mind" manifested itself "in his fervent and constant attachment to liberty"; but though "freedom, in all its forms and branches, was dear to him," it was "especially freedom of thought and speech, of conscience and worship, freedom to seek, profess, and propagate truth," that he served. This was very different from "the liberty of ordinary politicians," who concern themselves with "outward rights" and transient issues. "The tyranny which he hated most was that, which broke the intellectual and moral power of the community"; and so, he accomplished the chief end for which Unitarians still entered public life in the early nineteenth century: he "threw a hue of poetry over politics, and gave a sublime reference to his service of the commonwealth" (34).

As this shows, Channing interpreted Milton's role as a political writer and activist in the terms most congenial to his audience. He presented the poet as the successful embodiment of the clerical model of the literary career, one who preached ideal liberty to a divided nation. For unlike Cromwell, his Milton was never self-serving and never lost sight of the principles of freedom on account of exigency. Instead, he was just what Unitarian Boston's clergy and poets themselves wanted to be: a high-minded defender of dominant-class authority who sought to preserve bourgeois interests by idealizing them. A good example of this, according to Channing, is the poet's well-known polemical excesses; for as he explains in a masterful argument *ex concessis* (23–28), even the poet's scurrility was the product of "a great and far-looking mind" (22) enraptured by freedom and faced with perilous times. As such, his sharp-tongued denunciations of Salmasius and the bishops were really not the occasional political propaganda they seem but the sublime overflow of a great soul as it faced Stuart tyranny—an access of power that confirms rather than undermines his claims to be the ideal preacher, poet, and legislator:

> Liberty in both worlds has encountered opposition, over which she
> has triumphed only through her own immortal energies. At such

periods, men, gifted with great power of thought and loftiness of sentiment, are especially summoned to the conflict with evil. They hear, as it were, in their own magnanimity and generous aspirations, the voice of a divinity; and thus commissioned, and burning with a passionate devotion to truth and freedom, they must and will speak with an indignant energy, and they ought not to be measured by the standard of ordinary minds in ordinary times. Men of natural softness and timidity, of a sincere but effeminate virtue, will be apt to look on these bolder, hardier spirits, as violent, perturbed, and uncharitable; and the charge will not be wholly groundless. But that deep feeling of evils, which is necessary to effectual conflict with them, and which marks God's most powerful messengers to mankind, cannot breathe itself in soft and tender accents. The deeply moved soul will speak strongly, and ought to speak so as to move and shake nations. (24–25)

Milton's greatness of action in this passage complements rather than works against his magnanimity and intellectual genius (here called "great power of thought and loftiness of sentiment"). He acts, not out of a lust for power and worldly gain, but because he bears a divine commission to judge, to prophesy, and to educate. Thus, it is his fulfillment of the clerical model of the writer's social role (rooted in consensualism) that justifies his slanders and insults. For as freedom's "most devoted and eloquent literary champion" he knew that "liberty was in peril. Great evils were struggling for perpetuity, and could only be broken down by great power. Milton felt that interests of infinite moment were at stake; and who will blame him for binding himself to them with the whole energy of his great mind, and for defending them with fervor and vehemence?" (24). In addition, however, Channing's defense of his subject here reflects something else. This was his own personal disdain for controversy—a feeling in which he seems to have gone somewhat beyond what his class demanded. In comparison with his coreligionists, he was clearly not about the business of writing a political or sectarian tract for the times. Thus, there is no direct use of Milton either here or elsewhere in the *De Doctrina* review to attack party enemies (in the manner of much late eighteenth- and early nineteenth-century Anglo-American Milton criticism). Similarly, Channing largely eschews the nationalistic associations of the American Milton tradition as well. Indeed, more than any other Unitarian Miltonist, in this part of the review he made the poet a defender of liberty for its own sake and stressed not his subject's party loyalty but his utter devotion to principle and his willingness to risk blindness and death in its defense.[19]

Yet Channing's complicity here in the elite's traditional hegemonic reception of John Milton belies the same tension-filled polarization that elsewhere marks his account of the poet's genius. For though his Milton be an idealist "bearing the voice of a divinity" and a man "commissioned" by a higher power to lead from a position of spiritual superiority, his moderate, consensualist authority as a teacher or mentor promoting self-culture merely overlays deeper, largely unconscious fissures of thought and feeling. One can see this in Channing's description of the poet's active genius, which, like his earlier treatments of Milton's moral and intellectual prowess, ascribes it to two paradigmatically opposite sources. The first is patriarchal: the preacher-poet's divine inspiration as one of "God's most powerful messengers to mankind." It was this a priori commission as a medium for the voice of the Divinity that allowed Milton "to speak so as to move and shake nations" (thus ironically justifying his sometimes polemical tone on the same basis as the divine right of kings or the spiritual authority of bishops). The other source (which reflects the continuing antinomian element in New England culture) is his personal spiritual energy and *virtù*, "the voice of a divinity" speaking from within, not *the* Divinity from on high. This source (which resonates behind the vagueness of Channing's wording) undercuts the hierarchical claims implicit in the first and also severs the connection between active genius and conventional morality that the latter affirms. For notwithstanding his status as a divine messenger, it is Milton's sheer energy as a poet and as a man that here explicitly justifies his actions, even when they violate Western culture's most cherished beliefs and ethical standards. The bitter foe of Salmasius thus "ought not to be measured by the standard of ordinary minds in ordinary times," not just because his excesses were done in the name of freedom, but because he was a "deeply moved soul." Indeed, his depth of

19. Indeed, on this score early British reviewers of the *De Doctrina* review could not have been more wrong when they asserted that it was merely a transatlantic version of the politically partisan Milton criticism of Symmons and Macaulay (see Robert E. Spiller, "A Case for W. E. Channing," *The New England Quarterly* 3 [1930]: 55–81). For not only was Channing personally unsympathetic to such polemical writings; he well knew that confrontationalism and satiric embroilment were considered beneath the dignity of the Unitarian clergy (especially in light of their commitment to consensualism). Moreover, there were few cases in America of the kind of Tory criticism that goaded the British Whigs into action—exceptions being the anonymous "Thoughts on Milton," *United States Literary Gazette* 4 (1826): 278–90, and the two instances cited in Chapter 1, n. 36. It was only later, as the controversy over abolition heated up, that Milton once again became a polemical political resource for the New England elite (e.g., for Channing [see next note] and for others like Whittier [see Zimmerman, 247–80]).

soul excuses a list of aberrations that would have seemed signs of the veriest antinomianism to John Winthrop: for that self-generated authority allows him to be "violent"; to seem "perturbed"; and even—in moments of "uncharitable" inspiration—to dispense with the most abiding of the three theological virtues. Only the phrase that the charges against him are "not . . . wholly groundless" indicates Channing's unwillingness to abandon the connection between morality and art entirely.

These antinomian currents in Channing's thought become even clearer in the gloss he provides to the above passage:

> We have offered these remarks as strongly applicable to Milton. He reverenced and loved human nature, and attached himself to its great interests with a fervor of which only such a mind was capable. He lived in one of those solemn periods which determine the character of ages to come. His spirit was stirred to its very centre by the presence of danger. He lived in the midst of the battle. That the ardor of his spirit sometimes passed the bounds of wisdom and charity, and poured forth unwarrantable invective, we see and lament. But the purity and loftiness of his mind break forth amidst his bitterest invectives. We see a noble nature still. We see, that no feigned love of truth and freedom was a covering for selfishness and malignity. He did indeed love and adore uncorrupted religion, and intellectual liberty, and let his name be enrolled among their truest champions. (25)

Channing's purpose here was to condemn Milton's moral lapses while defending their overall political effect. His subversive sympathies come through, however, because his language is remarkably similar to that which he had used a few pages earlier in describing that other master of political rhetoric: Satan in *Paradise Lost*. Thus, Milton the polemicist is here, even at his worst, merely (like Satan) a fallen archangel, a god in ruins. In his bitterest remarks upon Salmasius "we see a noble nature still" and can still sense the "ardor of his spirit," his unfettered energy of soul. Despite his lapses into asperity, like the demon upon the fiery lake, he yet bears traces of his former glory. Moreover, just as this same fallen glory had almost enthralled Channing once before, so the critic only barely escapes here too. At the end of the passage he just manages to slip away from the seductive grasp of the poet's rhetorical antinomianism (with its appeal that the reader disregard the claims of order and propriety) and, as before, retreats from the radical implications of his own critical language. He instead reconnects Milton's literary power to more orthodox sources (his selfless love of "truth and freedom," and adoration of "uncorrupted religion, and intellectual liberty") and so, in typical New England dominant-class fashion, undercuts the very radical conclusions toward which his own feelings tended (by maintaining that the Milton of the Civil War and the Commonwealth had erred and fallen into bitter invective not because of his own self-divinizing fullness, but because— by too ardently translating the issues and personalities of his day into the language of ideal liberty—his genius for action had too fully fulfilled the consensualist commission of the preacher-poet).

On a number of occasions later in his life (most notably when he abandoned moral suasion as a tool in the abolitionist struggle),[20] Channing also had to justify the use of force or forceful language in defiance of his personal inclinations and Unitarian custom. He had to defend his sense that such immoderate, unclerical behavior was correct, even if it smacked of the very radicalism that had long threatened his own kind. Just as he did in this second section of the *De Doctrina* review, he took pains in each instance to mask his approval of force and forceful language by invoking the external, divine sanction implied by the doctrine of Christian liberty. For he consciously sought (as here) to justify force while suppressing any sympathy for the antinomian structure of feeling that was itself the source of his desire for reform. It is a suppression that is apparent in other parts of the *De Doctrina* review as well, his remarks on Johnson's *Life of Milton* being a case in point. Like most Unitarians, he could not attack Johnson with the relish of a Macaulay. The former's literary prestige in New England was still too high for that.[21] But in distinguishing between Johnson and Milton as two different kinds of genius, Channing not only disparaged the former's patriarchal Anglicanism and Toryism (38) but also unwittingly again revealed his own ideologically moderate cultural contradictions:

> We doubt whether two other minds, having so little in common as those of which we are now speaking, can be found in the higher walks of literature. Johnson was great in his own sphere, but that sphere was

20. Delbanco, 116–53, demonstrates that the roots of Channing's gradual conversion to abolitionism lie in the sort of approbation for sublime moral action expressed here. Furthermore, Howe, *The Unitarian Conscience*, 236–305, suggests that Channing's eventual change of heart on slavery was due to his departure from the common Unitarian understanding of moral leadership as implying an opposition to engagement in everyday politics.

21. Boston's conservative literary regard for Johnson is illustrated by the selections from *The Monthly Anthology* in Simpson's *The Federalist Literary Mind*. For the general political and social conservatism of Unitarian Boston, see Howe, *The Unitarian Conscience*, 121–48.

comparatively "of the earth," whilst Milton's was only inferior to that
of angels. It was customary, in the day of Johnson's glory, to call him
a giant, to class him with a mighty, but still an earth-born race. Milton we should rank among seraphs. Johnson's mind acted chiefly on
man's actual condition, on the realities of life, on the springs of human action, on the passions which now agitate society, and he seems
hardly to have dreamed of a higher state of the human mind, than was
then exhibited. Milton, on the other hand, burned with a deep, yet
calm love of moral grandeur and celestial purity. He thought, not so
much of what man is, as of what he might become. His own mind was
a revelation to him of a higher condition of humanity, and to promote
this he thirsted and toiled for freedom, as the element for the growth
and improvement of his nature. (37–38)

On the one hand, Channing objects to Johnson here because he represents
a form of literary authority that operates entirely with reference to "human
action" and "man's actual condition." As such, he is merely a quotidian genius who failed to fulfill the didact's responsibility to lead his readers to
higher virtue. Milton, by contrast, is ever bent upon promoting self-culture,
and so emblematically affirms both the clerical model of the literary career
and its consensualist assumptions. He "burned with a deep, yet calm love of
moral grandeur and celestial purity. He thought, not so much of what man is,
as of what he might become . . . and to promote this he thirsted and toiled
for freedom, as the element for the growth and improvement of his nature."
He is, in short, a worthy model for all of Channing's gentlemanly readers, as
they too sought to create works that idealized their own authority. Yet as
some of the language in this passage should indicate, there is another, more
satanic element at work here too. For the "revelation of a higher condition of
humanity" toward which Milton strove and encouraged others was explicitly
self-generated. "His own mind was a revelation to him," a revelation linked
neither to Holy Writ nor to such rationally verifiable proofs as the Common
Sense could provide. While seemingly orthodox in its origin and effects (in
its moral grandeur and celestial purity), in other words, Milton's authority
actually has a heterodox, antinomian source here as well; and so, Channing
contradicts himself, in effect saying that Johnson's relative inferiority epitomizes the more general inferiority of writers who follow the consensualist,
Unitarian line and take their imaginative authority from a source outside the
self. Indeed, when this passage is read in the light of its subversive element,
the author of the *Life of Milton* clearly seems to have failed to comprehend his

"king-killing" subject's genius, because he could not do what Channing incompletely does here: which is (like Emerson in *The Divinity School Address*) to translate the language of Unitarian self-culture into that of self-revelation.

The same breakdown of consensualism into the antinomies it attempted to reconcile can also be seen in the last part of the review (40–68), in which Channing turns to Milton's religious writings. He is once more torn between an antinomian desire to valorize the spiritual experience of the poet and an Arminian need to place some limits on the empowerment that experience generates. He thus begins by criticizing Milton's theology (including that of the *De Doctrina Christiana*) because it lacks the personal imprint—the energy of soul—found in his verse and political prose. In this field, Milton is too unoriginal, too much in thrall to the language and thought of tradition, for Channing. This is largely because

> Milton aims to give us the doctrines of revelation in its own words. We have them in a phraseology long familiar to us, and we are disappointed; for we expected to see them, not in the language of the Bible, but as existing in the mind of Milton, modified by his peculiar intellect and sensibility, combined and embodied with his various knowledge, illustrated by the analogies, brightened by the new lights, and clothed with the associations, with which they were surrounded by this gifted man. We hoped to see these doctrines as they were viewed by Milton in his moments of solemn feeling and deep contemplation, when they pervaded and moved his whole soul. (40)

Channing's phraseology here is classically antinomian in the way it both presages Emerson in *The Divinity School Address* and echoes the Spiritist tradition within radical Puritanism: for like the former, he complains that John Milton failed to speak religious truth as it existed "in the mind of Milton"; and like the latter, he contends that he settled instead for the collective historical experience of the Church (Tradition) and "the language of the Bible" (Revelation) as his guides. And so, while this passage indeed stands as an early New England example of the "romantic-expressivist principle of organic form,"[22] it is also an instance of a much older and more pervasive set of ideas and feelings in the region's culture. Yet as the remainder of the third part of the review shows, Channing was too timid to follow up the chief

22. Buell, *Literary Transcendentalism*, 147.

inference of his antinomianism in this passage: that a poet's religious vision might actually become disconnected from Christianity altogether (thereby in its self-generated and self-validating contemplations actually becoming what Andrews Norton would call "the latest form of infidelity"). Just as he did earlier with Satan in *Paradise Lost*, Channing therefore fled the subversive consequences of his antiauthoritarian feelings and, instead, went on to give his readers a Milton more amenable to the theologians of Unitarian Boston: one who rephrases and modifies the doctrines of traditional Christianity, but never challenges the priority of the Christian revelation itself. This is why Channing concludes the passage just cited by finding that despite the poet's traditionalism of thought and language, "still there are passages" in the *De Doctrina* "in which Milton's mind is laid open to us." For he consistently interprets these moments as providing precedent not for enthusiasm or religious radicalism but for the neo-rationalism, theological Arminianism, and tentative biblical criticism of early nineteenth-century Harvard (55–56).

Indeed, in general, Channing's treatment of Milton is more typically Unitarian in the last third of the review, since he mostly uses his subject to bolster his denomination's position. For instance, in a rare show of partisanship, he writes that the newly rediscovered tract under his review is important because it enables Unitarians to "take Milton, Locke, and Newton, and place them in our front, and want no others to oppose to the whole array of great names on the opposite side. Before these intellectual suns, the stars of self-named Orthodoxy 'hide their diminished heads' " (46). This is why, as an early exponent of "free inquiry" and "liberal religion," the poet should be listened to by early nineteenth-century Americans confused by competing denominational claims;[23] for

> he would probably stand first among that class of Christians, more numerous than is supposed, and, we hope, increasing, who are too jealous of the rights of the mind, and too dissatisfied with the clashing systems of the age, to attach themselves closely to any party; . . . who contend earnestly for free inquiry, not because all who inquire will think as they do, but because some at least may be expected

23. Ibid., 23–54, discusses the Unitarians' competition with those of other faiths, including their presentation of themselves as a liberal, nondenominational denomination above the sectarian fray. See also Hutchison, 1–21, and Elizabeth R. McKinsey, *The Western Experiment: New England Transcendentalists in the Ohio Valley* (Cambridge, Mass.: Harvard University Press, 1973), for accounts of Unitarianism's attempts to increase its influence and break out of its Boston enclave.

to outstrip them, and to be guides to higher truth. With this name-
less and spreading class we have strong sympathies. We want new
light, and care not whence it comes; we want reformers worthy of the
name; and we should rejoice in such a manifestation of Christianity, as
would throw all present systems into obscurity. (48)

However, even here, at its most conventional, the *De Doctrina* review once
more shows how ideologically polarized and unstable Channing's critical
stance was. For although in the above quotation he invokes Milton's Arian-
ism as precedent for his own (theologically and paradigmatically) Arminian
position, his language ("We want new light, and care not whence it comes;
we want reformers worthy of the name; and we should rejoice in such a manifestation of Christianity, as would throw all present systems into obscurity")
is radically antinomian. Only the qualification that such reform must be
Christian shows that in a muddled way he sought to resolve his ideological
self-confliction in favor of the Arminian structure of feeling.

Yet even in this Channing fails; for although with this qualification the
passage just cited seems to add to the chorus of self-congratulatory Unitarian
praise for the *De Doctrina Christiana,* Channing is here neither as robustly
nor as narrowly sectarian as he might have been. Indeed, while he was obviously glad that the *De Doctrina* proved Milton to be his theological predecessor, in general he did not stoop (in the review or elsewhere) to the snide
remarks about Anglicanism and Roman Catholicism one finds in Osgood.
Moreover, ironically, his restraint on this point contrasts sharply with both
the Unitarians and their Trinitarian competitors, who alike used his *De Doctrina* review for sectarian ends. For during his own lifetime, Channing was
attacked over the Milton essay from the Trinitarian side by the Reverend
Frederick Beasley of New Jersey in a pamphlet that denied the theological
import of the *De Doctrina* and made much of those passages in *Paradise Lost*
bearing an anti-Unitarian cast.[24] And after his death, the American Unitarian Association issued a truncated, propagandistic version of the essay as part
of a disreputable (and slightly paranoid) campaign against both Trinitarians
like Beasley and what they saw as the twin evils of "Puseyism and Popery."[25]

24. Rev. Frederick Beasley, *A Vindication of the Fundamental Principles of Truth and Order, in
the Church of Christ, From the Allegations of the Rev. William E. Channing, D.D.* (Trenton, N.J.:
Justice, 1830).
25. In addition to Osgood and the other examples cited in Chapter 1, another instance of this
sectarian use of Milton can be found in a note to an article by G. E. Ellis on this subject in *The
Christian Examiner* 35 (1844): 301.

(The latter differs in a number of telling ways from the original *Christian Examiner* version:[26] for instance, the Association abridged Channing's comments on the *De Doctrina* itself so as to increase emphasis on the poet's proto-Unitarianism; they downplayed his comments on the poet's more orthodox opinions; and above all, they excised the first two-thirds of the review, with the result that the more ambiguous currents in Channing's thought are missing—especially his sympathy for the antinomian structure of feeling.)

Despite Channing's willingness at times to characterize Milton the theologian as a Poet in the Emersonian sense (a self-inspired visionary bearing his own gospel),[27] and despite his unwillingness to use that same Milton in aid of sectarian extremism, however, he ultimately denied neither the necessity of churches nor of sects. The final pages of the review show, in fact, that he was to the end still an Arminian committed to consensualism and the clerical model of the writer's role. Thus, when he complained there that Milton sometimes "did not draw more from the deep and full fountains of his own soul" (67), this never led him to acknowledge the logical (antinomian) conclusions of such a remark; and when he asserted that Milton's theological writings "taught and exemplified that spirit of intellectual freedom, through which all the great conquests of truth are to be achieved, and by which the human mind is to attain to a new consciousness of its sublime faculties, and to invigorate and expand itself for ever" (68), he deliberately placed limits on that expansion. Indeed, in his conclusion Channing characteristically praised the *De Doctrina Christiana* as "a testimony to Milton's profound reverence for the Christian religion, and an assertion of the freedom and rights of the mind" (64)—a sentence whose parallel structure demonstrates his bourgeois faith in the possibility of reconciling the contradictory claims of order and liberty, his belief that "reverence for the Christian religion" and the "assertion of the freedom and rights of the mind" are necessarily one and the same.

The third section of the *De Doctrina* review, in short, essentially enacts a foreclosure of possibilities. For by his attempt to impose a conventional res-

26. William Ellery Channing, *The Character and Writings of John Milton, Memorable Sermons*, No. 17 (Boston: American Unitarian Association, n.d.).

27. In this last part of the review Channing's polarized position can also be seen in his response to those of Milton's theological opinions which by Unitarian standards were socially subversive. For instance, he was, on the one hand, sympathetic (48–51) toward Milton's speculations about creation *ex nihilo* (something that seems to bespeak his own antinomian flirtation with imaginative self-generation [see Delbanco, 33–54, and Howe, *The Unitarian Conscience*, 27–68 and 174–204]). Yet by contrast, he was generally also highly critical of Milton's radical challenges to conventional dominant-class New England views on morality (e.g., concerning divorce and polygamy [see 51–55]) and Protestant church order.

olution upon the polarities of feeling he himself had earlier revealed, Channing indicated that his allegiance was finally to the Unitarian economy of evaluation as it arose out of the sociocultural situation and ideology of his class. Appropriately enough, therefore, the final passage of the *De Doctrina* review is an act of repression, a moment when Channing denied his desire to give in to the antinomian side of his culture and declared his loyalty to the values of upper-class Boston:

> In offering this tribute, we have aimed at something higher than to express and gratify our admiration of an eminent man. We believe, that an enlightened and exalted mind is a brighter manifestation of God than the outward universe; and we have set forth, as we have been able, the praises of an illustrious servant of the Most High, that, through him, glory may redound to the Father of all spirits, the Fountain of all wisdom and magnanimous virtue. And still more; we believe that the sublime intelligence of Milton was imparted, not for his own sake only, but to awaken kindred virtue and greatness in other souls. Far from regarding him as standing alone and unapproachable, we believe that he is an illustration of what all, who are true to their nature, will become in the progress of their being; and we have held him forth, not to excite an ineffectual admiration, but to stir up our own and others' breasts to an exhilarating pursuit of high and ever-growing attainments in intellect and virtue. (68)

The Milton of this final passage is the ultimate preacher-poet, the embodiment of the American clerisy's didactic aspirations, a "servant of the Most High" sent to minister to his readers. Good consensualist that he is, through his poetry and prose, and by his example, he teaches others to love God and virtue, a process of tuition that will culminate in ever more maturity and self-cultivation, as his readers progress through life. He thus effaces whatever patriarchal or antinomian elements may have emerged during the course of the review, and reassures Channing's original Unitarian readers of the essential rightness of their own leadership claims and of the hegemony those claims promised to restore.

However, this final portrait should not retroactively invalidate the other versions of John Milton sketched in by Channing in the review: the poet who could be almost satanic in his willingness to overthrow the past and assert his own truth, yet (paradoxically) be almost like Calvin's God in his patriarchal use of power. Indeed, precisely because of these other, more polarized elements in Channing's Milton, it should be no surprise to learn that later, as Ralph Waldo Emerson outgrew the evaluative economy of Unitarianism, he turned to the *De Doctrina* review to help him clarify his own thoughts on the nature of authority. For despite youthful poverty, by virtue of his own and his father's profession, and his education, he too was a clerical member of the New England dominant class; and so, not surprisingly, he began where his mentor had left off.

3

EMERSON AND MILTON

Ralph Waldo Emerson was introduced to John Milton and the scholarship that had grown up about him at a young age. As early as 1815, he wrote to his brother to say that he had started Johnson's *Life of Milton*;[1] and in the next few years references to other Milton critics and biographers abound (especially those of the British "Whig" school). His list of "Books Read" from 1819 to 1824, for instance, notes that as an undergraduate he had looked at Charles Symmons's biography of the poet (the text that had set off the Whig reevaluation at the start of the century); and that he had also borrowed an unnamed edition of Milton's prose.[2] Seven years later he turned to Symmons once again, when he took a copy of that critic's biography and edition of the poet's prose out of the Harvard Divinity School Library;[3] and about the same time he also borrowed Henry John Todd's six-volume collected edition of Milton from the Boston Athenaeum—perhaps because he wanted to read

1. *The Letters of Ralph Waldo Emerson*, ed. Ralph L. Rusk (New York: Columbia University Press, 1939), I, 10; hereafter cited by page and volume number parenthetically in text as *Letters*.
2. This edition of Milton's prose may very well have been that of Charles Symmons as well. For the two citations, see *The Journals and Miscellaneous Notebooks of Ralph Waldo Emerson*, ed. William Gilman, et al. (Cambridge, Mass: Harvard University Press, 1960), I, 397 and 399; hereafter cited by page and volume number parenthetically in text as *JMN*. (Passages from *JMN* are quoted here in the final version written by Emerson as indicated by the editorial markings and apparatus of the Harvard edition. Bracketed items and other changes not in *JMN* are my own and are introduced for the sake of clarity.)
3. Charles Symmons, ed., *The Prose Works of John Milton, with a Life of the Author* (London: T. Binsley for J. Johnson, [etc.], 1806). See Weigel, 86 and 172–73, on the importance of this edition. Emerson's later borrowing of it from the Harvard Divinity Library is noted by Kenneth W. Cameron, comp., *Ralph Waldo Emerson's Reading* (Hartford, Conn.: Transcendental Books, 1962), 50.

an account from a different political perspective.[4] Finally, during the 1830s he twice cited Francis Jenks's patriotic 1826 American edition of the prose (*JMN*, IV, 375, and VI, 385), a work whose introduction repeats many of the Whiggish sentiments found in another book Emerson also used at this time, Joseph Ivimey's staunchly dissenting British biography.[5]

Moreover, Emerson's earliest comments on the poet bespeak his adherence both to the ideological assumptions and formations of Unitarian Boston and to its tradition of using Milton in support of them. For example, during the early 1820s his philosophy of mind was much like that of his Harvard mentors. He too ascribed great analytic and synthetic powers to the imagination, but fearful of that faculty's potentially unsettling effects, like Bryant, gave it no generative role and limited its operations to the association of sense experience.[6] The same fear of psychic antinomianism also led him to espouse the typically Unitarian position that the writer should always aim to confirm communal values and experience rather than express individual imaginative insights. For as he notes in an 1824 *Journal* passage, it is only by eschewing self-expression and affirming the rational order of the phenomenal world that the poet can arrive "at general laws, [and] the connexion of associated principles," thereby through the "enlargement of meaning in words which [this] permits" fulfilling his didactic role in society (by reaffirming the public nature of knowledge: the fact that it is the result of "the grand discovery that hundreds of laborious minds promoted").

As this suggests, the Unitarian view of the mind led Emerson to a similarly Unitarian view of the rights and duties of the man of letters. For him (as for

4. Henry John Todd, ed., *The Poetical Works of John Milton*, 6 vols. (London: Bye and Low for J. Johnson, [etc.], 1801); discussed by Weigel, 18–19 et passim. Todd's biography is the most scholarly and least partisan of the older Tory treatments; moreover, along with the edition to which it was attached, it was the one against which all other early nineteenth-century editors, critics, and biographers measured themselves. Emerson's use of it is recorded in Kenneth W. Cameron, comp., *Emerson the Essayist* (Raleigh, N.C.: The Thistle Press, 1945), II, 154 and 180.

5. Emerson's later purchase of Francis Jenks, ed., *A Selection from the English Prose Works of John Milton* (Boston: Bowles and Dearborn, 1826), is recorded in Walter Harding, comp., *Emerson's Library* (Charlottesville: University Press of Virginia, 1967), 191. The American reprint of Joseph Ivimey, *John Milton: His Life and Times, Religious and Political Opinions: with an appendix, containing animadversions upon Dr. Johnson's Life of Milton, etc., etc.* (New York: D. Appleton, 1833), is very much in the Whig tradition. Ivimey's preface alone, for instance, illustrates the two major features that Nelson says typify this school (see above, pages 69–70): first, it opens with a characteristically partisan declaration that "the former biographers of MILTON have exhibited him principally in his character as a *poet*, but have obscured his features as a *patriot*, a *protestant*, and a *non-conformist*" (iii); and second, it complains "that the LIVES OF MILTON have usually been so large and expensive, that they have been placed out of the reach of the generality of readers" (iv).

6. Emerson's early philosophical development is discussed by Robinson, *Apostle of Culture*, esp. 72–94.

Channing or Bryant) the imagination ought to aid in the fulfillment of the Horatian dictum that art should be both *dulce et utile*. As he put it in the same *Journal* passage, "in a bare epithet," poems should not only present "a picture to astonish & delight," but "also instruct by suggesting the method of using time to most advantage in accumulating wisdom." Not surprisingly, therefore, just as it was for other Unitarians, the prime example for him of such a didactic soul at white heat was the author of *Paradise Lost* (which is why he illustrates the just-cited *Journal* allusion to the *Ars Poetica* by invoking some of the most famous lines in Milton's epic: " 'To be no more; sad cure; for who would lose / Tho' full of pain this intellectual being / Those tho'ts that wander thro' eternity?' " [*JMN*, ii, 303]).

Of course, as we have seen with Channing, given their original Miltonic context, these lines from book ii of Milton's poem also potentially ally the imagination to the antinomian creativity of Pandemonium. Yet the young Emerson here seems to have been unaware of this, and likely intended this invocation of the poet as a pious affirmation of his own adherence to the Unitarian view of art. For like the critics of *The North American Review* and *The Christian Examiner,* he had been taught to believe that the author of belles lettres had a role akin to that of the Arminian preacher, and that Milton was the greatest example of this ideal in literature. Similarly, his allegiance to the clerical model of the writer's career explains why in 1823 he called the author of *Paradise Lost* one of "that glorious company of martyrs who" in wielding the pen "took up the cross of virtuous denial." For he wished to assert that Milton was one of those of whom it might be said that "God, in the watches of the starry night, fed their imaginations with secret influences of divinity, and swelled their conceptions with showers of healing water from the fountain of paradise"; and so,

they have left inscribed in their writings frequent & bold appeals to the grandeur of the spirit which lodged in their breasts, confident that what was writ would justify the truth of their claims. The sublimest bard of all—he who sung "Man's disobedience & the fruit of that forbidden tree which brought death into the world & all our woe" [in particular] felt himself continually summoned & inspired by a Spirit within him, and which afterward he says grew daily upon me—to do God's work in the world by sending forth strains which "aftertimes would not willingly let die. Not a work to be finished in the heat of youth or the vapours of wine; nor yet by invocation of Dame Memory & her siren daughters, but by devout prayer to that Eternal Spirit who giveth knowledge," hereby he hoped to release in

some great measure the hearts of posterity from that harlotry of vo-
luptuousness, whereinto he perceived with grief his own age had
fallen. (*JMN*, II, 106–7)

Emerson's Milton here is a familiarly Unitarian one. He is an inspired didact who gently but authoritatively led his age through a body of verse that
aimed at moral reformation. Similar views can be found elsewhere at this
stage of Emerson's life. For example, in the following definition written in
1821, he begins by dividing beauty—for the Unitarians, the chief aesthetic
effect of genius—into the same three categories Wordsworth and Channing
use in writing about genius itself: "Material beauty perishes or palls. Intellectual beauty limits admiration to seasons & ages; hath its ebbs & flows of
delight. . . . But moral beauty is lovely, imperishable, perfect. It is dear to
the child & the patriarch to Heaven, Angel, Man. Intelligent being can contract no habit so vile, can pervert his feelings to no such dire depravity that
moral excellence should ever lose its charm." Emerson then illustrates the
primacy of such moral beauty (or genius) over its intellectual and active
counterparts by offering the purity and zeal of Milton's writings as examples.
Yet this invocation in addition reveals both his own youthful belief as a critic
in the consensualist ideology and his desire to exercise the authority which
that ideology promised to its literary and clerical adherants:

> And none that can understand Milton's Comus can read it without
> warming to the holy emotions it panegyrizes. I would freely give all I
> ever hoped to be, even when my airblown hopes were brilliant & glo-
> rious . . . to bewitch young hearts by eloquent verses to the love of
> goodness, to bias manhood & edify gray hairs. Would not a man die
> to do such an office to mankind? The service that such books as this
> & the "Prelaty" & Bunyan &c render, is not appreciable but is im-
> mense. These books go up & down the world on the errand of charity
> & where sin and sorrow have been[,] where malignity festers & igno-
> rance thickens, pour their balm of Gilead, & cleanse the foul humours
> & purify the channels of life. (*JMN*, II, 220–21)

The author of *Comus* here has power, influence, and a central role in his
society because he brilliantly fulfills the duties prescribed for poets under
the consensualist-inspired clerical model. Despite patriarchalist undertones
suggested by Emerson's use of such notions as prophecy and grace, Milton
basically succeeds in the tutorial business of edifying gray hairs and biasing

manhood (the errand of self-culture) by dint of his powers of persuasion. Moreover, such inspiration as he does receive from above is from a Spirit Whose workings mirror the rationalist ethics and subdued "holy emotions" of Unitarian Boston. For under that Spirit's influence, he inculcates not traditional dogmatic faith—let alone the engagement of the religious affections or mysticism—but the Arminian desiderata of charity, virtue, and enlightenment. As such, Emerson's Milton is a pillar of rational religion, unenthusiastic piety, and social conformity: a Boston saint who inspires men to adhere to public values conducive of consensus and order (one who leads his fellows out upon a course of moral self-reflection even more strictly anti-antinomian than that later set forth in the *De Doctrina* review).[7]

Emerson's passionate praise for the author of *Comus* here also identifies his own yearning for an authoritative cultural role with that of Milton at a similar point in life. He "would freely give all [he] ever hoped to be" in order to be such a didact as Milton was: "to bewitch young hearts by eloquent verses to the love of goodness" and play the literary preacher to his times. It is a sentiment one finds frequently in Emerson's private writings during the 1820s. On a number of occasions even before his graduation from Harvard, for example, he compared his own difficulties in choosing a vocation with those of his predecessor on the eve of the English Civil War.[8] In 1820, for instance, he cited "a sentence from the author of Paradise Lost—& such a sentence!" on episcopal corruption, and then recorded his own ambitions in phrases that openly echo Milton's letter to Charles Diodati:

> I wish I might be so witched with study, so enamoured of glory for a little time, that it were possible to forget self & professions & tasks & the dismal crowd of ordinary circumstances in a still & rapid & comprehensive course of improvement. How immensely would a

7. For evidence of Emerson's initial conservatism vis-à-vis Channing's more polarized views (as well as for proof of the liberating personal and intellectual influences of the older critic upon him), see ibid., 11–29, 37–40, 53–57, and 74–77. The general impact of Unitarianism upon the intellectual development of Transcendentalism has long been a topic of scholarly discussion. Buell's *Literary Transcendentalism*, esp. 21–74, and Hutchison, esp. 1–97, are good summaries.

8. Useful descriptions of Emerson's early spiritual and vocational difficulties include Robinson, *Apostle of Culture*, 30–47; Gay Wilson Allen, *Waldo Emerson: A Biography* (New York: Viking, 1981), 1–110; Ralph L. Rusk, *The Life of Ralph Waldo Emerson* (New York: Scribner's, 1949), 89–130; and Stephen E. Whicher, *Freedom and Fate: An Inner Life of Ralph Waldo Emerson* (Philadelphia: University of Pennsylvania Press, 1953), 3–15. A more recent, psychobiographical treatment of his early life is Evelyn Barish, *Emerson: The Roots of Prophecy* (Princeton, N.J.: Princeton University Press, 1989).

scholar enlarge his power could he abstract himself wholly, body &
mind from the dinning throng of casual recollections that summon
him away. . . . Perhaps this ugly disorder is peculiar to myself & I
must envy that man's uninterrupted progress, who is not obliged by
his oath to nature to answer this idle call. If this is to continue it will
weaken the grasp with which I would cling,—with which every young
man would cling, to "visions of glory." . . . if I would excel & out-
shine the circle of my peers those talents must be put to the utmost
stretch of exertion, must be taught the confidence of their own power.
(*JMN*, I, 40–41)

Moreover, the following night he returned to this theme, making the parallel
between his own vaunting hopes and those of Milton explicit by citing two
passages from the poet's writings that express his desire to defend the Church
and do great things even " 'while green years are upon my head.' " Emerson
then exclaims: "What a grand man was Milton! so marked by nature for the
great Epic Poet that was to bear up the name of these latter times. In 'Reason
of church government urged against Prelaty' written while young his
[stretched [?]] spirit is already communing with itself & stretching out into
its colossal proportions & yearning for the destiny he was appointed to fulfil"
(*JMN*, I, 41–42).

   As these entries suggest, much as he wished to forget "self & professions
& tasks," during the 1820s Emerson's personal " 'visions of glory' " were
very much centered on the interconnected problems of literary authority and
career choice. The unoriginality of his answers to these questions can be seen
both in the *Journal* passages just cited (where he equated the writing of epic
poetry with the defense of religious liberty, and the office and authority of
the poet with that of the minister), and in later entries. For instance, in 1824
he rejected medicine and the law as possible professions, confiding that despite a hereditary "formality of manner & speech," it was "in Divinity" that
he hoped "to thrive." His definition of "Divinity" at this point was a very
Unitarian one, however, one in which credal orthodoxy, piety, zeal, or even
the state of his soul mattered less as qualifications than the attainment of pulpit eloquence and the pastoral ability to move others to virtue. These were
the characteristics considered most essential for the ministry by Emerson's
Unitarian teachers, who insisted upon them because of their consensualist
understanding of dominant-class professional authority and their remembrance of the New England elite's even older hegemonic insistence upon an

educated and literary clergy.[9] Moreover, also in typically Unitarian fashion, the young Emerson's understanding of his religious vocation merged naturally with his sense of the poetic calling; and so, he went on to end this second entry by taking Milton as his poetic hero as well:

> I would learn to love Virtue for her own sake, I would have my pen so guided as was Milton's when a deep & enthusiastic love of goodness & of God dictated the Comus to the bard, or that prose rhapsody in the 3rd book of Prelaty. I would sacrifice inclination to the interest of mind & soul. I would remember [that in "Lycidas" Milton wrote] that "Spare Fast oft with Gods doth diet," . . . [and so] I will remember to curtail my dinner & supper sensibly & rise from table each day with an appetite; & so see if it be fact that I can understand more clearly. (*JMN*, II, 239–40)

There are many other examples of Emerson's identification with Milton during the 1820s and early 1830s, some of which speak quite hauntingly to his professional hopes and fears.[10] However, after about 1832 his view of the poet began to develop gradually in ways that reflect a change in his attitudes about literary authority. For like William Ellery Channing in the *De Doctrina* review, he had become increasingly polarized between the conflicting structures of feeling in his culture; yet unlike Channing his reception of John Milton shows that he tried to resolve this conflict in ways that mark him as the more astute and powerful reviser of the ideology of the New England dominant class.

One of the earliest, but most poignant, examples of how Milton helped focus Emerson's growing dissatisfaction with consensualism and the solution it provided for the bourgeois dilemma occurs at a moment when the precariousness of being middle class came home to him in significant fashion. This was when he resigned from the pulpit of the Second Church and began the transition from being a minister with literary pretensions to becoming a professional man of letters. For he recorded the vote of his congregation against

9. Robinson, *Apostle of Culture*, 7–47, gives the best account of the Unitarian clergy's professional self-understanding and its impact on Emerson's thought in the first decade after his graduation from college.

10. One of the most revealing of these is his famous recollection of "Lycidas" during his first stormy passage to Europe (*JMN*, IV, 103 and 240). Perhaps related to this is his identification of the poet's sublime character with the spirits of his two dead brothers (*JMN*, V, 453).

him then in terms that openly proclaim the author of the *Areopagitica* and the *Apology for Smectymnuus* to be his predecessor in suffering for righteousness' sake:

> *"He who would write heroic poems should make his whole life a heroic poem."*   Milton

We want lives. We want characters of worthy men[,] not their books nor their relics. As the cultivation of an individual advances he thinks less of condition[,] less of offices & property & more keenly hunts for characters. Was it Henry who loved *a man*? So do men who would not have admitted him to their presence but for charity. There are very few finished men in the history of the world. To be sure the very expression is a solecism against faith. But there are none finished as far as they go—[.] (*JMN*, IV, 54)

This meditation on the nature of the heroic life does two things. First, it marks Emerson's tendency to exaggerate one or the other of the paradigmatic impulses to which he was subject. For by associating his own role as a nineteenth-century dissenter with the poet's seventeenth-century defense of freedom, he revealed his alignment at times with the antinomian heritage of his region. In refusing to administer the Lord's Supper, he implied that (like Milton) he too was an enemy of ritualism and a partisan against a religion of forms; and in suffering for that faith, he implied here that it is him (and not his Unitarian parishioners) who really stood in the Miltonic tradition of resistance to authoritarianism. Indeed, in his eyes, by imposing even so mild a discipline upon him, his congregation had given the lie to its supposed belief in "liberal religion" and "freedom of inquiry" (concepts the Unitarians associated with Milton); instead, they had taken up the cause of sacramentalism (thereby standing in relation to their minister much as Laud had stood in relation to the Puritans of old).

Secondly and more broadly, however, this entry also marks Emerson's growing rejection of consensualism itself. For in giving in fully to the antinomian structure of feeling, he here set aside the comfortable paraphernalia of the bourgeois clergyman ("books," "relics," "offices & property") and sought a life like Milton's: a life lived as "a heroic poem." In other words, Emerson by this rejected not only the ritual authority of his church but the consensualist relationship of solicitation and tuition between minister and congregation that Unitarianism also enjoined. Instead, he declared that he would now be a *man:* an autonomous, self-reliant soul who (like the anti-prelatical Milton or Milton's Satan) is unbeholden to anyone—even to an audience. As he put it a week later in a passage that shows how much he had come to reject his former role as didact, "if the soul globe itself up into a perfect integrity—have the absolute command of its desires—it is less dependent on other men, & less solicitous concerning what they do, albeit with no loss of philanthropy" (an idea suggested to him—not accidentally—by "reading Milton's beautiful vindication of himself from the charge of incontinence & intemperance" [*JMN*, IV, 57]).[11]

There are a number of other examples during this period of Emerson's personal identification with Milton's resistance to prelate and presbyter alike, examples that also bespeak his growing openness to the antinomian structure of feeling. In 1835, for instance, he once more expressed his abhorrence of formal prayer and the sacraments—the core of his disagreement with his former congregation—by advancing the precedent of the poet's similar objections to Laudianism (*JMN*, IV, 350). A few weeks earlier, he had cited "The Doctrine and Discipline of Divorce" on the same subject, with a comment worthy of any seventeenth-century radical: "A religion of forms is not for me. I honor the Methodists who find like St. John all Christianity in one word, Love. To the parishes in my neighbourhood Milton would seem a free thinker when he says, 'they (the Jews) thought it too much license to follow the charming pipe of him who sounded & proclaimed liberty & relief to all distresses' " (*JMN*, IV, 282).

However, the most extensive example during the years leading up to *The Divinity School Address* of Emerson's use of Milton to express his polarization (especially in an antinomian direction) also reveals that his ultimate goal was to create a new figuration by which dominant-class authority might be reexplained. This is an 1835 lecture he revised three years later for the *North American Review*, with the title "John Milton."[12] In that piece he deliberately confronted his ideological heritage as a sometime Unitarian cleric and

11. This *JMN* entry is accompanied by a specific reference to Jenks's edition—"(See Vol. I, p. 239, &c.)"—a fact that suggests he was reading Milton's prose for consolation and strength during the resignation crisis.
12. "John Milton" is cited from *The Early Lectures of Ralph Waldo Emerson*, ed. Stephen E. Whicher, et al. (Cambridge, Mass.: Harvard University Press, 1959), I, 144–63. For the circumstances of this essay's original presentation as a lecture and its subsequent revision, see xiii–xxvii, 93–96, and 144–45 of that volume. This and other lectures published in this edition are hereafter cited as *Early Lectures* under their individual title, with a parenthetical page and volume reference.

Harvard-educated man of letters, recasting the view of authority found in William Ellery Channing's review of the *De Doctrina Christiana* until it more adequately modulated between the demands of order and those of freedom. The text and manuscript remains of "John Milton" might not at first suggest anything so innovative, however. To begin with, like many other Unitarian Miltonists, Emerson was much indebted to British Whig sources, both for his biographical data and for his critical opinions about matters such as the worth of Milton's prose and his love of liberty.[13] His lecture also superficially seems to endorse the portrait of the poet found in Channing's piece (which Emerson later ranked—along with the Napoleon essay—as being among "the first specimens in this country of that large criticism which in England had given power and fame to the Edinburgh Review),"[14] and he certainly used the *De Doctrina* review's middle and last sections (in which his mentor had treated Milton's political and religious writings [Channing, 20ff.]) as his structural model. The two critics' specific observations about their subject often agree as well, and Emerson's overarching goal is (in a sense) the same as that of his predecessor: to present Milton as a representative man and type of the powers of the inspired soul.[15]

13. The authorial copy of the text of the lecture version of "John Milton" (MH bMs. Am 1704.10[196]) is marked up with Emerson's changes for the later magazine revision. It is now in the John Gorham Palfrey Papers at the Houghton Library, Harvard University. The Palfrey collection also includes the working documents for the whole 1834–35 lecture series in which "John Milton" was first presented. Among these manuscripts is a sheaf of notes and draft passages for the Milton lecture (MH bMs. Am 1280.194[7]) that shows Emerson used at least two of the main Whig sources. (The importance of these notes and drafts in the textual history of "John Milton" is discussed in *Early Lectures*, I, 442–43.) The first source is Charles Symmons's biography and edition, which provided Emerson with all of the Miltonic prose quotations in the piece's manuscript and printed versions and most of the biographical information included there as well; the second is the New York edition of Ivimey's biography, from which Emerson excerpted four biographical references. (About a third of the Milton citations are specifically identified by volume and page number as having come from Symmons. These are to be found on the following leaves: one each on 21v, 22r, 23v, and 26v; and three on 23r. The four biographical references taken from Ivimey are on the following leaves of the manuscript: one each on 22r and 23v, and two on 25v.) In addition, in the notes and drafts for the lecture (as opposed to the lecture manuscript just described), Emerson also cited autobiographical passages from Milton's prose, biographical facts about him, and the opinions of earlier biographers—all as reprinted by Symmons and Ivimey. He also possibly referred there at one point to a passage from Coleridge's Milton criticism (see Wynkoop, 149–51).

14. "Life and Letters in New England," *The Complete Works of Ralph Waldo Emerson*, ed. Edward Waldo Emerson (Boston: Houghton Mifflin, 1903–4), x, 339. Later references to works cited from this edition are by individual work title as *RWE*, with parenthetical volume and page numbers as indicated.

15. Although "John Milton" is hardly a pale imitation of the *De Doctrina* review, nonetheless it is a work written both in imitation of and as an implicit rejoinder to it. Previous discussions of Emerson as a Miltonist (with the partial exception of Cole, 136–40) have largely ignored this

Yet for all these similarities, by 1835 Emerson's views on genius and literary authority had begun to diverge radically from Channing's (though along lines the latter had tentatively explored). For he was even more conflicted than Channing over the insistent claims of the two structures of feeling in his culture, and he was determined—in a way Channing was not—to find a way of solving the ideological contradictions that resulted from them. In "John Milton" he began to speak to both of these agenda by trying out a language of authority that simultaneously affirmed the autonomy and freedom of the self and yet fused that concession to antinomian claims with a more imperious and patriarchal conception of the writer's role than that ever envisaged by the critics of Unitarian Boston.

The revised version of dominant-class ideology Emerson struggled to create out of this dialogue with Channing over Milton can be seen from the start of his *North American Review* piece. Like Channing in the *De Doctrina* review (see Channing, 4–5), Emerson began by distancing himself from the sectarian interest Milton's rediscovered opus had aroused among the Unitarians:

> The discovery of the lost work of Milton, the treatise "Of the Christian Doctrine," in 1823, drew a sudden attention to his name. For a short time the literary journals were filled with disquisitions on his genius; new editions of his works, and new compilations of his life, were published. But the new-found book having, in itself, less attraction than any other work of Milton, the curiosity of the public as quickly subsided, and left the poet to the enjoyment of his permanent fame, or to such increase or abatement of it only, as is incidental to a sublime genius, quite independent of the momentary challenge of universal attention to his claims. (*Early Lectures*, I, 145)

Yet despite the ephemeral nature of the *De Doctrina Christiana*'s resulting "new and temporary renown," as he goes on to say, one must admit that by this controversy Milton "has gained, in this age, some increase of permanent praise." Indeed, "it was very easy to remark an altered tone in the criticism when Milton re-appeared as an author, fifteen years ago, from any that had been bestowed on the same subject before. It implied merit indisputable and

---

fact. These include Chester E. Jorgenson, "Emerson's Paradise under the Shadow of Swords," *Philological Quarterly* 11 (1932): 274–92; Richard Campbell Pettigrew, "Emerson and Milton," *American Literature* 3 (1931): 45–59; J. Russell Roberts, "Emerson's Debt to the Seventeenth Century," *American Literature* 21 (1949): 298–310; and Zimmerman, 186–246. Of particular interest are Wynkoop's discussion of Emerson's reading during these years (137–41) and his account of the lecture itself (161–70)—although neither suggests his debt to Channing.

illustrious; yet so near to the modern mind as to be still alive and life-giving. The aspect of Milton, to this generation, will be part of the history of the nineteenth century. There is no name in literature between his age and ours, that rises into any approach to his own" (Early Lectures, I, 145).

Though sentiments like these might seem to imply Emerson's approval of the sectarian uses to which the De Doctrina Christiana had been put during the previous decade, this is not really so. For one thing, the passage just quoted is itself modeled upon the beginning of part two of the De Doctrina review, where Channing had also commented on Milton's place in nineteenth-century culture in the aftermath of Sumner's discovery (writing that "from Milton's poetry, we turn to his prose. We rejoice that the dust is beginning to be wiped from his prose writings, and that the public are now learning, what the initiated have long known, that these contain passages hardly inferior to his best poetry, and that they are throughout marked with the same vigorous mind which gave us 'Paradise Lost' " [Channing, 20–21]). Implicitly, therefore, Emerson believed that the major example of this "altered tone" in contemporary Milton criticism was Channing's review itself—the one Unitarian response to that tract which had largely eschewed such ecclesiastical party spirit. Moreover, Emerson also distanced himself even from Channing here in ways that further underscore his distaste for this side of the Unitarian Milton. For example, whereas in the passage just quoted Channing had only indirectly condemned his coreligionists' crowing over the De Doctrina (by rejoicing in the general revival of interest in Milton's prose the tract had caused), Emerson in his opening remarks much more forthrightly expressed his disagreement with their sectarianism. Significantly, he also gave free rein to those conflicting antinomian and Arminian feelings which only more gradually and tentatively emerge in Channing (exaggerating the latter in a patriarchal direction). The result is that even on its first page Emerson's lecture tends to undermine the consensualism upon which Channing had ultimately had to fall back. From the beginning, Emerson's Milton is no didact and cultivates no relationship of voluntary tutorial submission. Rather, on the one hand, like Calvin's God, he is a powerful eminence, "a sublime genius" on the ideal and eternal level, whose hierarchy-affirming presence in the modern world is alive and so gives life; yet like Milton's Satan, he is at the same time also an autonomous self whose power is "quite independent of the momentary challenge of universal attention to his claims," a genius who asserts his will without let, hindrance, or obligation.

This initial convergence and contrast establishes the relational pattern between the two pieces, moreover, since in "John Milton" Emerson typically followed Channing's formal and structural lead, only to revise him substantively at every turn on ideological grounds. For instance, as has been shown, in the *De Doctrina* review Channing had moved from the remarks just quoted to a discussion of the twin charges traditionally made against Milton's controversial writings. One of these was that the poet's polemical tone was immoral and unchristian, a complaint Channing had refuted by declaring his subject to be a divinely inspired "master spirit" whose excesses pale in comparison with the tyranny he faced. (For in circumstances such as those of seventeenth-century England, Channing believed it only natural that a "deeply moved soul will speak strongly, and ought to speak so as to move and shake nations," whatever the normal considerations of civility and charity.)[16] Similarly, the poet's status as a "master spirit" also absolved him of the second charge: that his prose was stylistically convoluted and latinate. For in Channing's view, such a style merely reflected the poet's unusual degree of inspiration:

> A great mind cannot, without injurious constraint, shrink itself to the grasp of common passive readers. Its natural movement is free, bold, and majestic, and it ought not to be required to part with these attributes, that the multitude may keep pace with it. A full mind will naturally overflow in long sentences, and, in the moment of inspiration, when the thick-coming thoughts and images crowd upon it, will often pour them forth in a splendid confusion, dazzling to common readers, but kindling to congenial spirits. . . . Such sentences are worthy and noble manifestations of a great and far-looking mind, which grasps at once vast fields of thought, just as the natural eye takes in at a moment wide prospects of grandeur and beauty. (Channing, 21–22)

In this passage, Channing exhibits all the characteristics that made him unique among Unitarian Miltonists. Just as he did in the case of Milton's polemicism (where he had held that the poet's magnanimity placed him almost outside conventional moral constraint), he once more virtually abandons the link between didacticism and authorship in order to argue that Milton's inspiration makes him an exception to those standards of "simplicity and perspicuity" which bind ordinary writers. Milton's prose does not for him have a conventional tutorial purpose or effect: there is little ministerial

---

16. Cited and discussed in full above, pages 97–99.

care in his peremptory genius, little regard for the self-culture of his readers. Instead, as elsewhere in the review, Channing's Milton is here largely a means by which Channing may relieve the contradictions of his class's unstable ideology by abandoning consensualism and projecting his own polarization between the Arminian need for hierarchy and order (the desire to affirm the self-expression of "a great mind" higher than that of "common passive readers") and the antinomian desire for an imagination independent of convention and outside authority. The result is a view of Milton's prose that combines the divinizing and satanizing qualities (majesty, elevation, isolation, freedom, and apocalyptic energy) that characterize that most conflicted of bourgeois romantic aesthetic formations: the "terrible sublime."[17] Only the elitist concession that there may be a few "congenial spirits" who may stylistically benefit from Milton's tuition indicates that here too (as more obviously elsewhere) Channing's instinct is to tiptoe back from the vision he entertains—in this case, to the didacticism of Unitarian aesthetics.

The continuity and yet the difference with Emerson at this point is readily apparent. For the younger critic also moved from his opening remarks to a discussion of these two charges, reversing the order in which they had been treated by his predecessor. Like Channing, Emerson also admitted that one can legitimately find fault with Milton's prose style:

> Their rhetorical excellence must also suffer some deduction. They have no perfectness. These writings are wonderful for the truth, the learning, the subtilty and pomp of the language; but the whole is sacrificed to the particular. Eager to do fit justice to each thought, he does not subordinate it so as to project the main argument. He writes whilst he is heated; the piece shows all the rambles and resources of

17. For treatments of this and other formations of the sublime, and their meaning in the context of American culture, see Elizabeth R. McKinsey, *Niagara Falls: Icon of the American Sublime* (New York: Cambridge University Press, 1985); Perry Miller, *The Life of the Mind in America: From the Revolution to the Civil War* (New York: Harcourt, Brace, and World, 1965); Barbara Novak, *Nature and Culture: American Landscape and Painting, 1825–1875* (New York: Oxford University Press, 1980); Earl A. Powell, "Luminism and the American Sublime," in *American Light: The Luminist Movement, 1850–1875*, ed. John Wilmerding (Washington, D.C.: National Gallery of Art, 1980), 69–94; and especially Bryan Jay Wolf, *Romantic Re-Vision: Culture and Consciousness in Nineteenth-Century American Painting and Literature* (Chicago: University of Chicago Press, 1982). More general treatments of the sublime as a concept include Samuel Monk, *The Sublime: A Study of Critical Theories in Eighteenth Century England* (1935; rpt. Ann Arbor: University of Michigan Press, 1960); and Thomas Weiskel, *The Romantic Sublime: Studies in the Structure and Psychology of Transcendence* (Baltimore: Johns Hopkins University Press, 1976).

indignation; but he has never *integrated* the parts of the argument in his mind. The reader is fatigued with admiration, but is not yet master of the subject.

Moreover, again like Channing, Emerson went on to forgive Milton, arguing that despite its shortcomings, the peculiarities of his style are an authentic expression of great genius. "His prose writings . . . are," in fact, "remarkable compositions. They are earnest, spiritual, rich with allusion, sparkling with innumerable ornaments." This is true even though "as writings designed to gain a practical point, they fail"; for in Emerson's view, the author of *Areopagitica* and the antiprelatical tracts was not out to play the consensualist game. It therefore does not matter that Milton's prose works "are not effective, like similar productions of Swift and Burke; or . . . several masterly speeches in the history of the American Congress," because they were never meant to be attempts at political persuasion in the first place. "There is no attempt to conciliate,—no mediate, no preparatory course suggested,— but, peremptory and impassioned," like God just after the Fall, or Satan in defiance, "he demands, on the instant, an ideal justice" (*Early Lectures*, I, 146).

As this suggests, Emerson was as keenly aware of the polarities in his culture as Channing, and—even more than he—was willing to feel them in their most exaggerated form. He was also more willing to experiment with the traditionally moderate ideological position of his class and profession. This is why he goes beyond his mentor here (without even the small half-step back toward dominant-class orthodoxy one finds in the *De Doctrina* review) to uncouple his defense of Milton's style from the didactic aesthetics and consensualist assumptions of the previous generation, by using language that suggests Milton's prose has an authority that is at once paradigmatically patriarchal and paradigmatically antinomian, because it both evokes and yet reconciles individualism and dominance, and freedom and absolutism.

This reconciliation of antinomies is even more obvious in Emerson's defense of the poet against the second charge made against him: that of polemical excess. Once again, he follows the outline of Channing's argument, first condemning Milton's more extreme tactics as a controversialist. "The lover of his genius will always regret" Milton's treatment of Salmasius, he tells us, because he did not take "counsel of his own lofty heart at this, as at other times, and" write "from the deep convictions of love and right, which are the foundations of civil liberty. There is little poetry, or prophecy, in this mean and ribald scolding." Also like Channing, Emerson then justifies these moral lapses much as he did the poet's syntax, on the grounds that they are apt expressions of his imaginative power. He maintains that even at Milton's worst, in "the 'Defence of the People of England,' . . . when he comes to speak of the reason of the thing, then he always recovers himself. The voice of the mob is silent, and Milton speaks." Significantly, however, this does not happen (and the poet redeems himself from his own asperity) when he is behaving like an antinomian (one of "the mob" or "the redoubted disputant of a sect"), or when he is behaving like a consensualist moral tutor. Rather, it is when he simultaneously assuages both the structures of feeling in his culture. For in a work like the *Areopagitica* Emerson thought that Milton had managed to be a self-inspired, visionary defender of individual autonomy yet still speak with the authority of a prophet to whom truth had been revealed from above; and it was this Janus-faced quality that for him laid the basis for Milton's claims upon his readers (*Early Lectures*, I, 146–48).

Emerson's desire to get beyond the self-confliction of his predecessor and his class also explains a passage like the following one, which combines language affirming order with language affirming freedom so as to create a carefully modulated statement about literary authority:

> It would be great injustice to Milton to consider him as enjoying merely a critical reputation. [For] it is the prerogative of this great man to stand at this hour foremost of all men in literary history, and so (shall we not say?) of all men, in the power *to inspire*. Virtue goes out from him into others. Leaving out of view the pretentions of our contemporaries (always an incalculable influence), we think no man can be named, whose mind still acts on the cultivated intellect of England and America with an energy comparable to that of Milton. As a poet, Shakspeare undoubtedly transcends, and far surpasses him in his popularity with foreign nations; but Shakspeare is a voice merely; who and what he was that sang, that sings, we know not. Milton stands erect, commanding, still visible as a man among men, and reads the laws of the moral sentiment to the newborn race. (*Early Lectures*, I, 148–49)

In many respects, this passage once more merely illustrates the derivative side of the relationship between "John Milton" and the *De Doctrina* review. Emerson essentially conflates a quotation from early in Channing's essay (the one in which he too had held that "a virtue goes out" from Milton to inspire others)[18] with a paraphrased version of Channing's just-cited defense of the

18. The passage in Channing is cited above, page 86.

poet's asperity. Emerson does so, moreover, in order to make the same two points as Channing: first, that the prerogatives of the great soul absolve Milton for his verbal foul play; and second—with reference to a passage in Channing not cited above—that his subject's organic presence in all his writings contrasts with the impersonality of Shakespeare. The latter then has a corollary that provides another parallel between the two pieces: for while Emerson believed Shakespeare the better poet, like Channing he also held that Milton's personal presence gave him the greater authority as a revealer of truth.

The difference between "John Milton" and the *De Doctrina* review at this juncture is that unlike Channing, Emerson does not rush to justify Milton's scurrility—and so restore the link between morality and art—by characterizing him as one of "God's most powerful messengers to mankind." Instead, typically, he first expresses both the antinomian and Arminian sentiments stirred up by Milton's example, and then tries to combine them into a new figuration justifying dominant-class hegemony. This is why he so unreservedly takes up the blasphemous implications of the biblical references his predecessor adduced at this point. For he wanted to make it clear (as he put it a little later in this passage) that though Milton may have been a prophet (and so, a representative of an ancient, patriarchal understanding of authority), he was also a rebel because he read "the laws of the moral sentiment to the newborn race" rather than the Commandments of Moses or the Beatitudes of Jesus. Similarly, although Milton is "identified in the mind with all select and holy images," the virtue that goes out from him is not inspired by the Judeo-Christian God. Rather, this poet's *charism* as a healer is the result of an inner light untainted by intercourse with the Holy Ghost; and so, even when he most seems to play the patriarchal role of poet-priest, Emerson's Milton equally affirms the antinomianism from which Channing ultimately fled. He is holy (and therefore superior to most men), but no imitator of Christ; and his writings have the binding authority of scripture, without giving the Christian revelation priority. Indeed, this is why "better than any other he has discharged the office of every great man." For his great talent was (for Emerson) to be like Emerson: to be one who could find new things to idealize, even as he undercut all previous idealizations; to be one able "to raise the idea," not now of God but "of Man in the minds of his contemporaries and of posterity,—to draw after nature a life of man, exhibiting such a composition of grace, of strength, and of virtue, as poet had not described nor hero lived. Human nature in these ages is indebted to him for its best portrait" (*Early Lectures,* I, 149).

The same strategy can be seen elsewhere in the opening section of "John Milton," as throughout it Emerson sought to satisfy the conflicting demands made upon him by his sociocultural situation (principally, by writing as if the a priori hierarchical authority claimed by the Stuarts and their bishops had been given to Milton, the poet who in real life had most sternly opposed them). This is why his "Milton stands erect" and is "commanding" when he "reads the laws of the moral sentiment to the newborn race"; for it is when he most displaces the Ten Commandments and the Beatitudes and preaches a gospel of his own devising that he becomes the truest prophet—albeit of a god that is within as well as above. Indeed, it is in these opening pages that Emerson for the first time in his career used Milton to bridge the contradictions inherent in the ideological position of his class and profession, in a passage that presages others to come:

> But the idea of a purer existence than any he saw around him, to be realized in the life and conversation of men, inspired every act and every writing of John Milton. He defined the object of education to be, "to fit a man to perform justly, skilfully, and magnanimously all the offices, both private and public, of peace and war." He declared, that "he who would aspire to write well hereafter in laudable things, ought himself to be a true poem; that is, a composition and pattern of the best and honorablest things, not presuming to sing high praises of heroic men or famous cities, unless he have in himself the experience and the practice of all that which is praiseworthy." (*Early Lectures*, I, 150)

As this suggests, Emerson obviously no longer felt that his predecessor's consensualist solution to the problem of authority worked. He therefore here rejected that formation's root proposition (that education ought to be a gradual process of enlightened reflection and self-culture under the aegis of a clerical and intellectual elite)[19] and instead implied that Milton was his role model precisely because he had no such mediating moral tutors. As he put it, the poet's "every act and every writing" sprang in direct fashion out of his own definition of what a true poet and "a true poem" ought to be. Yet this was a definition that even as it affirmed personal autonomy reached for that " 'pattern of the best and honorablest things' " which comes from an author-

19. This is not to deny the truth of David Robinson's contention (*Apostle of Culture*, 95–111) that Emerson at this time was deeply indebted both to the Unitarian ethos in general and to the doctrine of self-culture in particular. It is merely to argue that "John Milton" is an example of the degree to which he had begun to change his views on self-culture by the mid-1830s.

ity greater than the poet's own. And so, for Emerson, Milton was again no pure antinomian, but a type of his own emerging reformulation of the ideology of the New England dominant class and the view of literary authority that went with it. He was one who tried to live according to "the idea of a purer existence than any he saw around him" (an ideal and universal standard), yet do so in a way that drew upon a truth lodged in his own soul. Deferring and yet self-asserting, he therefore had at once the authority of both the rebel and the anointed monarch; for his very self-reliance reveals that (like a pope or king) he was different in kind from ordinary men. This is why "he is rightly dear to mankind, because in him,—among so many perverse and partial men of genius,—in him humanity rights itself; the old eternal goodness finds a home in his breast, and for once shows itself beautiful. His gifts are subordinated to his moral sentiments. And his virtues are so graceful, that they seem rather talents than labors" (*Early Lectures*, I, 154).

The next part of "John Milton" describes just how the future author of *Paradise Lost* came " 'himself to be a true poem.' " Once more Emerson takes his lead from Channing, since at the parallel point in the *De Doctrina* review the latter had cited several famous autobiographical passages from Milton's prose (as well as the example of *Comus*) to prove that Milton's literary and spiritual ambitions were connected from the start. These include a quotation from the letter to Diodati referring to the fable of Ceres and Proserpine (which Channing had used along with Milton's masque to prove "how the whole spirit of poetry had descended on" the poet "at that early age" and "how his whole youthful soul was penetrated, awed, and lifted up by the austere charms, 'the radiant light,' the invincible power, the celestial peace of saintly virtue"), and a slightly different version of the dictum from "An Apology of Smectymnuus" that Emerson quotes in the excerpt from "John Milton" just discussed (that " 'he who would not be frustrate of his hope to write well hereafter in laudable things, ought himself to be a true poem; . . . a composition and pattern of the best and honorablest things' "). Channing then treats these early declarations as prefigurings of his subject's later striving toward the same ideal of perfection. He argues that one can see this, for instance, in the poet's "multifarious reading," which like the rest of his intellectual life built "up within himself" a singular "reverence for virtue." Milton's youthful studies in Plato and chivalric lore in particular not only taught him " 'what a noble virtue chastity sure must be' " but also (in combination with the regimen described in his famous account of his " 'morning haunts' ") helped him develop habits of real sanctity. And it is this habit of holiness that in the end most truly refutes the charges—especially of polemical excess—laid against him (Channing, 31–33).

As some of his language should suggest, Channing's real purpose in including these citations was not just to praise Milton; rather, he sought to use him to reinforce the consensualist view of authority as well. Similarly, the poet's intellectual earnestness, piety, virtue, and respect for convention tended in his mind to reinforce the old Unitarian link between morality and art (especially as he portrayed the poet here as someone who submitted to the authority of others—Christ, Plato, the chivalric authors—in order that he might achieve a "likeness to God" through self-culture). Emerson certainly realized that this was what Channing was doing, since in rearranging the order of these quotations from Milton and adding biographical material not included by his predecessor (*Early Lectures*, I, 150–54), he did so in ways that clearly confront Channing's whole economy of evaluation.

For instance, Emerson prefaced his recycling of Channing's citations from Milton with an attack on the major intellectual influences behind Unitarianism, who in contrast to the poet were unfit by their very philosophy "to raise the idea of Man in the minds of" their "contemporaries and of posterity." The founder of English empiricism, "Lord Bacon[,] . . . shrinks and falters before the absolute and uncourtly Puritan, . . . [his] Essays are the portrait of an ambitious and profound calculator,—a great man of the vulgar sort. Of the upper world of man's being they speak few and faint words." Similarly, the vision of human nature provided by the rest of Boston's eighteenth-century pantheon suffers from the same deficiency: "The man of Locke is virtuous without enthusiasm, and intelligent without poetry, Addison, Pope, Hume, and Johnson . . . cannot, taken together, make any pretension to the amount, or the quality, of Milton's inspirations. The man of Lord Chesterfield is unworthy to touch his garment's hem. Franklin's man," though by comparison "a frugal, inoffensive, thrifty citizen, . . . savours of nothing heroic." Even France and Germany have more recently produced nothing like him—especially not the Germany of Goethe, who fell into the temptation "to say, that art and not life seems to be the end of" all human "effort" (*Early Lectures*, I, 149–50).

Significantly, Emerson contrasted Milton so strongly with these paragons of rationalist ethics, consensualism, and calculating art because in comparison he believed his subject to be both more his own man and more a writer beholden to a higher authority. His Milton is, in other words, no mere conformist or "thrifty citizen," but a heroic enthusiast and breaker of convention; and these antinomian qualities (in Emerson's refiguring of the rhetoric of bourgeois power) without paradox give him the a priori authority of a divinely inspired bard—of one who is superior to most men in his deference to the Spirit. This is why reading the *Areopagitica* is a different experience than perusing Chesterfield's cynical letters. For in his resistance to authority Milton affirmed an ideal order (of virtue as of reality); and so, to read him is to reexperience both a moment of individual self-assertion and a moment when that individual power reveals the authority of something higher. It is a moment when (like Christ healing the halt and the lame or the British sovereign 'touching for King's Evil') the true poet knows that "in himself . . . virtue had gone out of him" (a moment when he heals both in his own name and in that of God, a point when he has the authority of divine right as well as that of Satan).

Emerson then reorders and revises Channing's account of the Milton quotations, which appear at this point in both pieces, in ways that undermine his predecessor's confused and tentative resolution of the tensions within their culture. He too brings up the fable of Ceres and Proserpine to which Milton had referred in the letter to Diodati; but instead of using it to argue for the poet's piety and dependence upon divine inspiration, Emerson uses the story to epitomize Milton as one who pursued the " 'perfect model of the beautiful in all forms and appearances of things' " (as a man "enamoured, if ever any was, of moral perfection"). For in keeping with his general aim of bridging the paradigmatic divide in New England culture so that he might accrue authority, these goals affirm a vague sense of cosmic hierarchy and order, yet do not detract from Milton's autonomy by making him seem to defer to orthodox Christianity (with its notion that poetic inspiration originates in religious assent). Similarly, Emerson also follows Channing here in believing that "mastery of language" and rhetorical skill bespeak a mere "secondary power" in comparison to that provided by true spiritual inspiration. But his notions of where such visitations come from are purposely vague, as his aim is to blur the competing claims of autonomy and hierarchy, by asserting both that the great soul's inspiration comes from *within* and that it does so only because it bears an original relation to the Truth of God (*Early Lectures*, I, 153–54).

Moreover, although Emerson, like Channing, next invokes the poet's " 'morning haunts' " and "the spirit of 'Comus,' " his aim is to deny the conventionally moralistic tone of this part of the *De Doctrina* review. To be sure, he too believed that Milton's early spiritual discipline illustrated his deliberate cultivation of virtue and love of chastity. *Comus* is for him, as for the great Unitarian, "the loftiest song in the praise of chastity, that is in any language. It always sparkles in his [Milton's] eyes. It breathed itself over his decent form. It refined his amusements. . . . It engaged his interest in chivalry, in courtesy, in whatsoever savoured of generosity and nobleness. This magnanimity shines in all his life" (*Early Lectures,* i, 155). Yet the poet's love of chastity and pursuit of virtue do more in "John Milton" than establish him as a paragon of sexual morality; and his penchant for chivalry and engagement with Plato are hardly in Emerson—as in Channing—a nostalgic hearkening after the idealized authority of an age long dead. Instead, Milton's purity and morality, like his courtliness, provide Emerson with yet another means by which he may assuage the opposing sets of demands imposed upon him. The young poet's character thus affirms the absolute, God-given, patriarchal authority of those who (like Milton) are pure and moral, while also suggesting that such traits stem from a source unbeholden to society's mores and revealed texts: the natural empowerment of the great soul. Indeed, as Emerson goes on to note with regard to a passage from the same part of "An Apology for Smectymnuus" used by Channing, Milton himself said that it was " 'his mind,' " rather than any authority on chivalry, which " 'gave him' " the leveling belief that no king is needed to make a man a gentle knight and true; and it was his mind too (rather than an old book like Plato or the New Testament), which gave him the anticlerical faith that no oath or ceremony can make a man virtuous. Milton believed instead that the source of true gentility, like that of true inspiration or true chastity, is internal and natural—and, in being so, is Heaven-sent; this is why he declared " 'that every free and gentle spirit, without that oath of chastity, ought to be born a knight; nor needed to expect the gilt spur, or the laying of a sword upon his shoulder, to stir him up, by his counsel and his arm, to secure and protect' attempted innocence" (*Early Lectures,* i, 155).

The rest of Emerson's lecture revises the later two-thirds of the *De Doctrina* review, where Channing discussed the poet's defense of liberty. The latter had presented Milton's love of religious freedom as an instance of his commitment to the doctrine of "Christian Liberty, under which head may be included the discipline of the church, the power of ministers, and the rights of the people" (Channing, 57). Both the language of Anglo-American Protestantism and of this sentence suggest, however, that Channing's assumptions here are those of a bourgeois parson. For the concept of "Christian Liberty" he uses had historically served middle-class clerical interest. When he writes that "in Milton's views of the church and the ministry, we have other proofs of his construing the Scriptures in the manner most favorable to Christian liberty," these are not, therefore, proofs that draw upon the poet's anti-nomian tendencies. Rather, Channing's Milton merely "teaches, that the universal church has no head but Christ, and that the power arrogated by popes, councils, and bishops, is a gross usurpation" (Channing, 58–59). This is because like all moderate Protestants, his was a vision of freedom that ignored the contradictions of the position both he and Channing shared (with the result that more radical individuals could logically object that his "new presbyter is but old priest writ large" just as their descendants could see the Unitarian manse as being as gross a usurpation as any bishop's palace).

Emerson realized this, and so revised Channing's comments on the an-tiprelatical tracts in order to avoid these contradictions (which are admittedly inherent in Milton's definition of religious liberty in any case). He admitted that his subject was a believer, and that therefore to his "antique heroism Milton added the genius of the Christian sanctity"; but he asserted as well that the poet's commitment to religious freedom had its roots in something more than the moderate Reformation's dislike of bishops—in a radically an-tinomian "indifferency of a wise mind to what is called high and low." For Emerson also wished to acknowledge the side of Milton that would abolish the priority of both past tradition and present hierarchy altogether (the Mil-ton who in certain moods would have rejected Channing's narrowly self-interested, bourgeois freedom as being itself "a gross usurpation"). Indeed, in his view, Milton was most himself when he worshiped a religious liberty tied neither to the moderate Puritan interest nor even to Christianity itself, but instead, to the unfettered right of the individual to submit to "the om-nipotence of spiritual laws" as he or she understood them. Moreover, Em-erson also makes it clear—in a manner typical of his rhetorical refiguring of dominant-class ideology throughout the lecture—that in doing so (by sub-mitting to that higher law) Milton's otherwise antiauthoritarian soul gained an authority that was decidedly patriarchal. For it is by such a submission that the autonomous, liberty-loving, great soul comes to be omnipotent in religious matters (to have an authority that can override the claims of pope, council, or Unitarian Association alike [*Early Lectures*, I, 155–56]).

The same strategy can also be seen in Emerson's revision of the next part of the *De Doctrina* review, where Channing had retold the story of how "The Defence of the People of England" had cost the poet his eyesight.[20] He

20. As Channing rather flatly put it, "before quitting the subject of Milton's devotion to lib-erty, it ought to be recorded, that he wrote his celebrated 'Defence of the People of England,' after being distinctly forewarned by his physicians, that the effect of this exertion would be the utter loss of sight" (35).

begins straightforwardly enough, declaring that it was because of the "magnanimity [which] shines in all his life" that Milton accepted "a high impulse at every risk, and deliberately" undertook "the defence of the English people, when advised by his physicians that he" did so "at the cost of his sight" (*Early Lectures,* I, 155). Yet for Emerson this tragedy really served to advance the case for his own revisionist views on authority. This is so first because Milton's self-sacrifice bespeaks a polarized obedience to "the omnipotence of higher laws" and yet an affinity with the disobedient spirit of "the agitated years" in which he lived ("when the discontents of the English Puritans were fast drawing to a head against the tyranny of the Stuarts . . . [and] questions that involve all social and personal rights were hasting to be decided by the sword, and were searched by eyes to which the love of freedom, civil and religious, lent new illumination"). Moreover, secondly, Emerson believed that in risking all to defend regicide and establish republican legitimacy, Milton had done what he himself was trying to do in this essay: to solve the moderate Puritan dilemma and reconcile the need for order with that for liberty. For "the part he took, [and] the zeal of his fellowship" in resisting tyranny were actually an act of obedience to a higher power; and so it is his balance without confliction that "makes us acquainted with the greatness of his spirit, as in tranquil times we could not have known it."

The poet's very love of hierarchy and need to submit to it, in other words, fed his antinomian, Protestant hatred of pretense; this is why "Milton, gentle, learned, delicately bred in all the elegancy of art and learning, . . . susceptible as Burke to the attractions of historical prescription, of royalty, of chivalry, of an ancient church illustrated by old martyrdoms and installed in cathedrals, . . . threw himself, the flower of elegancy, on the side of the reeking conventicle, the side of humanity, but unlearned and unadorned." For "the bishops" had made the same mistake as the consensualist clergy of Unitarian Boston: they had ceased to hold the two structures of feeling in harmonious balance and had become conflicted. " 'Instead of showing the reason of their lowly condition from divine example and command,' " they had abandoned such patriarchal justifications for their power—thereby ironically turning traitor to freedom's cause as well in seeking " 'to prove their high preeminence from [mere] human consent and authority.' " Whether Stuart bishop or Unitarian preacher, Emerson's adversaries here thus justly merit subversion and attack on *both* paradigmatically Arminian and antinomian grounds; similarly, because Milton's antiprelatical tracts did likewise in the seventeenth century (by providing the counterexample of a defense of liberty rooted in divine will and Holy Writ), their angry, antiauthoritarian author may be said to have given us "for the first time since many ages, . . . invocations of the Eternal Spirit in the commencement of his books, [which] are not poetic forms, but are thoughts, and so are still read with delight" (*Early Lectures*, I, 156–58).

Emerson's treatment of Milton and civil liberty reflects this same interest in refiguring authority so as to escape the contradictions that had long beset his class. Here too he initially imitated Channing, who had at this point defined the poet's "greatness of mind" as being best seen politically "in his fervent and constant attachment to liberty." Yet Milton's liberty was for Channing not "the liberty of ordinary politicians" but that higher freedom of inquiry which the Unitarians claimed as their own. Channing's Milton is consequently less open to radical change (and certainly less involved in the dirty business of defending liberty in a violent age) than even the historical Milton had been. He is instead an exemplary practitioner of the consensualist politics of moral suasion, voluntarism, and self-culture, one whose historic defense of regicide and whose role in Cromwell's regime deliberately receive less attention than his "attachment to a spiritual and refined freedom." For by emphasizing that side of Milton's thought, Channing could make his subject's love of liberty into a prophylactic protecting the clerical model of literary authority, a device by which one could hope to have all the pleasure and profit of political engagement without its dangers or moral consequences. This is why he declares that this "spiritual and refined" view of freedom "never forsook him in the hottest controversies, [and so] contributed greatly to protect his genius, imagination, taste, and sensibility, from the withering and polluting influences of public station, and of the rage of parties. It threw a hue of poetry over politics, and gave a sublime reference to his service of the commonwealth" (Channing, 34).[21]

Emerson in part agreed with Channing on this point, writing that although the poet was "drawn into the great controversies of the times, in them he is never lost in a party. His private opinions and private conscience always distinguish him." Similarly, he went so far as to say that "that which drew him to the [Puritan] party was his love of liberty, ideal liberty; this therefore he could not sacrifice to any party." But Emerson's idealization of Milton's defense of political freedom here takes place in the context of his revision of dominant-class ideology. And so, as earlier with religious liberty, he exaggerates the polarizing structures of feeling in New England culture in order then to reconcile them in a new rhetoric of authority. On the one hand,

21. Cited and discussed above, page 97.

therefore, he describes Milton's devotion to "ideal liberty" in ways that are sometimes clearly antinomian in spirit. He notes, for instance, that as Milton's seventeenth-century biographer "[John] Toland tells us," Milton was something of a leveler. " 'As he looked upon true and absolute freedom to be the greatest happiness of this life, whether to societies or single persons, so he thought constraint of any sort to be the utmost misery; for which reason he used to tell those about him the entire satisfaction of his mind, that he had constantly employed his strength and faculties in defence of liberty, and in direct opposition to slavery.' " Indeed, he was "truly . . . an apostle of freedom; of freedom in the house, in the state, in the church"; a believer in "freedom of speech, [and] freedom of the press."

> He pushed, as far as any in that democratic age, his ideas of *civil* liberty. He proposed to establish a republic, of which the federal power was weak and loosely defined, and the substantial power should remain with primary assemblies. He maintained, that a nation may try, judge, and slay their king, if he be a tyrant. He pushed as far his views of *ecclesiastical* liberty. He taught the doctrine of unlimited toleration. One of his tracts is writ to prove that no power on earth can compel in matters of religion. He maintained the doctrine of *literary* liberty, denouncing the censorship of the press, and insisting that a book shall come into the world as freely as a man, so only it bear the name of author or printer, and be responsible for itself like a man. He maintained the doctrine of *domestic* liberty, or the liberty of divorce, on the ground that unfit disposition of mind was a better reason for the act of divorce, than infirmity of body, which was good ground in law.

Yet as Emerson writes elsewhere in this magisterial passage, these radical attempts to refashion society in the direction of democracy and egalitarianism rested upon an "absolute" vision of the authority of the man of genius. This is why he qualifies the above statement with the assertion that the poet "in his own mind discriminated [such liberty] from savage license, because that which he desired was the liberty of the wise man, containing itself in the limits of virtue." For to Emerson, the sweeping reforms just mentioned "are all varied applications of one principle, the liberty of the wise man," who, like the author of *Paradise Lost,* will seek "absolute truth, not accommodating truth," and form "his opinions on all subjects" with a view toward the empowerment, not of the rabble, but of bourgeois intellectuals like himself: "for man as he ought to be, for a nation of Miltons" (*Early Lectures,* I, 158–59).

In other words, for all the genuine antinomianism here, Emerson's view of the poet's love of "true and absolute freedom" is itself yet another act of bourgeois idealization (and so, a self-interested attempt to put limits on that liberty). It is not, therefore, as a radical *manqué*, but as the moderate Puritan he really was, that Emerson's Milton—in direct contrast to the Milton of the Unitarians—engaged in the rough world of political revolution, literally at the risk of his life. For "throughout all his actions and opinions," as Emerson sees it, he was "a consistent spiritualist, or believer in the omnipotence of spiritual laws," one who affirmed the claims of order and hierarchy even as he denied them. And so, as in the case of his discussion of the poet and religious freedom, Emerson uses Milton to proclaim the limits of liberty: limits that stem from an ideal hierarchy of value that confirms the hegemony of "wise men" like himself. The result is a paradigmatically mixed rhetoric in which Milton proclaims "the liberty of the wise man," not the common man; one in which his "sublimest song" bursts like the decrees of Zeus or Jehovah "into heaven with its peal of melodious thunder," yet for all that, "is the voice of Milton still" (*Early Lectures*, i, 160–61).

The final pages of "John Milton" are really a continuation of this last passage, with its clever attempt at refiguring the Boston elite's ideology. For example, Emerson's need to affirm order as well as liberty explains why he cites the author of the *Novum Organum* (whom he had derided earlier in the lecture) in order to declare that "in his prose and in his metrical compositions" Milton fulfills "Lord Bacon's definition of poetry, following that of Aristotle, [that] 'Poetry, not finding the actual world exactly conformed to its idea of [the] good and fair, seeks to accommodate the shows of things to the desires of the mind, and to create an ideal world better than the world of experience.' " For though it "may be thought [by some] to abridge his praise as a poet," it is in Emerson's interest to hold that even as a reformer Milton (like Bacon) believed that a work of literature should impose order and stability upon the chaos of experience. Similarly, so interested is he in making sure that the antinomian impulses elicited by this part of his subject's career are fused with the opposite structure of feeling, that at the climax of "John Milton" Emerson even partially reverts to the didacticism of the previous generation, when he claims that in these highly political works it is Milton's "own conviction . . . which gives such authority to his strain. Its reality is its force. If out of the heart it came, to the heart it must go." Yet even in this reversal, his Milton had a consensualist purpose: for "fired 'with dearest charity to infuse the knowledge of good things into others,' [he] tasked his giant imagination, and exhausted the stores of his intellect, for an end beyond, namely, to teach" (*Early Lectures*, i, 161–62).

In much the same way, Emerson also sought to solve the ideological contradictions of his classist position when in this final part of the lecture he used the Baconian definition of poetry just cited to explain the most antiauthoritarian of Milton's writings. For him, as for any member of the Boston elite, it was only in the context of such a counterbalancing Arminianism that one could—with a gentlemanly tolerance—allow the expression of antinomian and revolutionary sentiments:

> Such certainly is the explanation of Milton's tracts. Such is the apology to be entered for the plea for freedom from divorce; an essay, which, from the first until now, has brought a degree of obloquy on his name. It was a sally of the extravagant spirit of the time, overjoyed, as in the French revolution, with the sudden victories it had gained, and eager to carry on the standard of truth to new heights. It is to be regarded as a poem on one of the griefs of man's condition, namely, unfit marriage. And as many poems have been written upon unfit society, commending solitude, yet have not been proceeded against, though their end was hostile to the state; so should this receive that charity, which an angelic soul, suffering more keenly than others from the unavoidable evils of human life, is entitled to.

Indeed, as the final paragraph of "John Milton" goes on to demonstrate, its author was every bit as much a bourgeois moderate as his teachers—only more rhetorically adroit. For he turns there to one of the standard themes in Unitarian Milton criticism and (by combining a paraphrase of Channing's comments on Samuel Johnson and Milton with the last paragraph of the *De Doctrina* review)[22] portrays his subject after the Restoration as the defeated but defiant Milton "who, in old age, in solitude, in neglect, and blind, wrote the Paradise Lost; a man whom labor or danger never deterred from whatever efforts a love of the supreme interests of man prompted." But Emerson's account of Milton in defeat freely mixes the language of antiauthoritarianism with that of idealization, thereby giving the poet both the virtues of Heaven and those of Hell. For it was in his interest as an elitist critic to leave his listeners (and, later, readers) with a rhetorical question that comes down definitely on neither side of his polarized culture, while fully expressing both its sets of claims. And so, he asks, "are we not the better; are not all men fortified by the remembrance of the bravery, the purity, the temperance, the toil,

---

[22] Cited in full above, pages 101–2 and 107, respectively.

the independence, and the angelic devotion of this man, who, in a revolutionary age, taking counsel only of himself, endeavoured, in his writings and in his life, to carry out the life of man to new heights of spiritual grace and dignity, without any abatement of its strength?" (*Early Lectures*, I, 162–63).

Emerson soon became dissatisfied with "John Milton." Even while revising it in 1838 he wrote Frederic Henry Hedge that he had just been "vamping up an old *dead* paper that more than a year since I had promised Dr. Palfrey [the editor of the *North American Review*] & with all my chemistry & chirography I cannot make it alive" (*Letters*, II, 122). One reason for this may have been that he had come to feel that his strategy of using Channing as an antagonistic model was ill-chosen, as it detracted from the clear presentation of his own position. This fact would probably have been all the more apparent to him by 1838 because of his forthright use of the poet to speak to the issue of authority in some of his other writings during the decade. In "Self-Reliance," for example, he needed no rhetorical dialogue with his consensualist predecessor to write a passage like the following:

> To believe your own thought, to believe that what is true for you in your private heart, is true for all men,—that is genius. Speak your latent conviction and it shall be the universal sense; for the inmost in due time becomes the outmost,—and our first thought is rendered back to us by the trumpets of the Last Judgement. Familiar as the voice of the mind is to each, the highest merit we ascribe to Moses, Plato, and Milton, is that they set at naught books and traditions, and spoke not what men but what they thought. . . . In every work of genius we recognize our own rejected thoughts: they come back to us with a certain alienated majesty.[23]

This famous declaration reveals a more fundamental reason why "John Milton" seemed to Emerson to be "an old *dead* paper" by the late 1830s, however. For his complicated rhetoric of paradigmatic fusion in that lecture had always been, at best, a difficult passage between the competing structures of feeling. It was an attempt to do by sheer verbal wit what his clerical

---

23. Cited from *Essays: First Series*, ed. Alfred R. Ferguson and Jean Ferguson Carr; intro., Joseph Slater. *The Collected Works of Ralph Waldo Emerson* (Cambridge, Mass.: Harvard University Press, 1979), II, 27. Other quotations from *The Collected Works of Ralph Waldo Emerson* are cited parenthetically in the text under their individual title as *Collected Works*, with volume and page numbers as indicated.

and critical ancestors had signally failed to do. Here in "Self-Reliance," Emerson shows how difficult that effort was and how easy it was to fall into contradiction on one side of the paradigmatic divide or the other. Thus, on the one hand, in this excerpt to a degree he uses the language of patriarchalism. Moses, Plato, and Milton are figures whose authority as poets is absolute. Like Calvin's God, they have only to think—*et fiat lux*— what they conceive is reality. Their "own thought . . . is true for all men" and "their latent conviction" is "universal sense," even unto the Last Trump. Yet this godly authority and kingly "majesty" are also overwhelmingly here in the service of the antinomian impulse. For from a rhetoric that (in "John Milton") tried to modulate between Arminian and antinomian claims, Emerson has shifted to a Hutchinsonian position, which more fully identifies the divine spirit with the personality of the individual. The result is the subordination of the poet's (patriarchally figured) authority to its origins in the self-generated insights of the autonomous soul—and, so, the utter evisceration of any real priority or authority outside that of the contemporaneous self. "Majesty" there still is, in "every work of genius"; but it is the majesty of a constitutional monarch, a Louis Phillipe rather than a Charles Stuart. For in the wake of such antinomianism, only the linguistic aura of divine anointing and power can remain, not the reality.

The following passage from "Literary Ethics" also illustrates this tendency to shift in one paradigmatic direction or the other (usually the antinomian one), especially because it at first seems so Arminian in its adulation for past genius and its deference to canonical priority:

> Still more do we owe to biography the fortification of our hope. If you would know the power of character, see how much you would impoverish the world, if you could take clean out of history the life of Milton, of Shakspeare, of Plato,—these three, and cause them not to be. See you not, instantly, how much less the power of man would be? I console myself in the poverty of my present thoughts, in the paucity of great men, in the malignity and dulness of the nations, by falling back on these sublime recollections, and seeing what the prolific soul could beget on actual nature;—seeing that Plato was, and Shakspeare, and Milton,—three irrefragable facts. Then I dare; I also will essay to be. (*Collected Works*, I, 102–3)

Emerson's predecessors here are positive figures who clearly inspire him. The very solidity of their achievement gives them authority and makes them reassuring presences in a tradition-creating literary canon; similarly, they clearly engage Emerson's dominant-class instinct to seek ways of affirming such Arminian qualities as continuity, order, and obedience to external authority. Yet as in the excerpt from "Self-Reliance," Emerson does not really seek to affirm these qualities per se, or even to hold them in balance with his antinomianism. Rather, they have a definitely recessive quality; and so, the climax of this meditation on Milton and the others moves in the opposite paradigmatic direction, with the rather famous declaration (in the manner of Satan in *Paradise Lost*): "Then I dare; I also will essay to be."

As this suggests, his general swerve from deference to self-assertion during the late 1830s does not mean that Emerson had escaped the contradictions of his position as a member of a bourgeois elite by becoming an antinomian. On the contrary, though he had begun to tilt more in one direction, on the whole he was still committed to the complex rhetorical balancing of "John Milton." He does as much in the following discussion of inspiration in "Intellect," where he balances the opposing structures of feeling nicely:

> To genius must always go two gifts, the thought and the publication. The first is revelation, always a miracle, which no frequency of occurrence, or incessant study can ever familiarize, but which must always leave the inquirer stupid with wonder. It is the advent of truth into the world, a form of thought now, for the first time, bursting into the universe, a child of the old eternal soul, a piece of genuine and immeasurable greatness. . . . But to make it available, it needs a vehicle or art by which it is conveyed to men. To be communicable, it must become picture or sensible object. We must learn the language of facts. (*Collected Works*, II, 198)

Paradigmatically, Emerson uses the language of patriarchy here to give the poet a superior status and prophetic authority, but then matches this with language that undermines this status by affirming the claims of freedom and equality. For his prophetic superiority is due to his receipt of a new and highly personal revelation (rather than *the* Revelation in Holy Scripture), and his apocalyptic imaginings must be communicated by being translated into "the language of facts" that all can understand.

There are many other examples in Emerson's writings in the 1830s of this rhetorical balancing using Milton. In *Nature* (1832), for instance, his definition of "the moral law" that "lies at the centre of nature and radiates to the circumference" plays off of an Augustinian definition of God that itself modulates immanence with transcendence, and hierarchy with equality (*Collected Essays*, I, 26);[24] and in "The Over-soul" a few years later the "omniscience" that "flows into the intellect" (and so "makes what we call genius") has a leveling quality:

> It is a larger imbibing of the common heart. It is not anomalous, but more like, and not less like other men. There is in all great poets, a wisdom of humanity, which is superior to any talents they exercise. The author, the wit, the partisan, the fine gentleman, does not take place of the man. Humanity shines in Homer, in Chaucer, in Spenser, in Shakspeare, in Milton. They are content with truth. They use the positive degree. . . . For, they are poets by the free course which they allow to the informing soul, which through their eyes beholds again, and blesses the things which it hath made. The soul is superior to its knowledge; wiser than any of its works. The great poet makes us feel our own wealth, and then we think less of his compositions. (*Collected Works*, II, 170–71)

Like Channing (to whom he alludes here), Emerson finds that a "humanity shines in" Milton's pages, giving him the power to bless and to reveal. Yet it is the "wisdom of humanity," not his personal revelation, that allows Milton to do so: "the great poet makes us feel our own wealth, and then [like good dissenters] we think less of his compositions."

One can find this pattern in Emerson's *Journal* during this period too. In the following entry, for instance, he describes the role of the man of letters in language that is both didactic and bardic (i.e., both ideologically consensualist and patriarchal), only then to subordinate each of these to a common origin in the egalitarian spirit of humanity: "With what satisfaction I read last night . . . some lines from Milton. In Samson Agonistes & elsewhere with what dignity he felt the office of the bard, the solemn office borne by

24. Emerson would have encountered the metaphor of God as a circle whose center is everywhere but whose circumference is nowhere in Sir Thomas Browne as well as in St. Augustine's *De Doctrina Christiana* (the work from which Milton borrowed the title for his own tract). He uses it again in *Nature* (*Collected Works*, I, 28) and it is obviously behind the title and central conceit of "Circles." Its wider philosophical implications are discussed in Vivian Hopkins, *Spires of Form: A Study of Emerson's Aesthetic Theory* (Cambridge, Mass.: Harvard University Press, 1951), 17–62; John Q. Anderson, *The Liberating Gods: Emerson on Poets and Poetry* (Coral Gables, Fla.: University of Miami Press, 1971), 34–35; and Sherman Paul, *Emerson's Angle of Vision: Man and Nature in American Experience* (Cambridge, Mass.: Harvard University Press, 1952), 71–131.

the great & grave of every age for the behoof of all men; a call which was never heard in the frivolous brains of the Moores & Hugos & Berangers of the day. . . . Humanity characterizes the highest class of genius[:] Homer, Milton, Shakspeare. We expect flashes of thought, but this is higher yet. The sorrows of Adam & Eve" (*JMN*, v, 191–92). In much the same way, in 1834, he praised "Michel Angelo Buonaroti: John Milton: Martin Luther: George Fox: Lafayette: Falkland: [and] Hampden" for their resistance to authority and love of liberty, calling them (in Milton's words) " 'men akin unto the universe,' " men whose very names are "seeds" ready to sprout in later generations. For they spoke their own truth, and stood up for their own rights; and so, any "sentiment which like Milton's comes down to new generations is that which was no sham or half-sentiment to Milton himself but the utterance of his inmost self" (*JMN*, IV, 328). Yet this list of worthies is not a slate of radicals; it is largely a list of bourgeois preachers, artists, and politicians (most of them from the antiradical factions of the Reformation and Anglo-American Puritanism). The presence of the Marquis de Lafayette (an aristocrat who favored revolution on the American model) suggests the moderate tone Emerson sought to sound here, and even George Fox seems somehow pasteurized in the company of the others (all the more so because the Quakers were solidly middle-class by Emerson's day).

Furthermore, passages from the *Journal* or the public works that do not themselves fit the pattern just outlined tend to balance one another when seen in the context of all of Emerson's production at this point. For example, sometimes, when he was in a skeptical mood, he would counsel a wise passivity before the operations of an inscrutable and arbitrary Over-soul. As he puts it in "Being and Seeming," when "a question is asked of the understanding which lies in the province of the Reason . . . the understanding foolishly tries to make an answer"; but in doing so "our constructiveness overpowers our love of truth," and so inevitably causes despair. The best course is therefore to submit as if to Calvin's God, taking inspiration from Milton in Sonnet XIX. For after all, "Why teach? Learn rather. Learn and Wait. 'They also serve who only stand and wait' " (*Early Lectures*, II, 302–3). Yet in a more buoyant mood (in a passage in "English Literature" that is an early version of the key paragraph on correspondence in the "Language" chapter of *Nature*), he used Milton to provide two contradictory glosses to what would in a few months become one of his central statements on poetic authority: "It is not words only that are emblematic: it is things which are emblematic. Every fact in outward nature answers to some state of the mind and that state of the mind can only be described by presenting that natural fact as a picture" (*Early Lectures*, I, 220). For him, this truth is equally manifested by Milton's retelling of a Greek myth that affirms meaning and order in the face of death (the way the poet "describes Proserpine gathering flowers in Enna, 'Herself a fairer flower by gloomy Dis was gathered' ") and by the poet's classic description of an aroused, revolutionary, antinomian England (the way "Milton gives manly form to the abstraction of a state: 'Methinks I see in my mind a noble and puissant nation rousing herself like a strong man after sleep and shaking her invincible locks (the laws): methinks I see her as an eagle muing her mighty youth and kindling her undazzled eyes at the full midday beam' " [*Early Lectures*, I, 222–23]).

Moreover, these glosses then lead to one of the great summaries of Emerson's views on poetic authority—a passage that (in antinomian fashion) affirms the autonomy of the true poet and the originality of his vision and then (in patriarchal fashion) trumpets his despotic power as a visible saint graced with insight into the operations of the Over-soul:

> All reflexion goes to teach us the strictly emblematic character of the material world. Especially is it the office of the poet to perceive and use these analogies. He converts the solid globe, the land, the sea, the sun, the animals into symbols of thought: he makes the outward creation subordinate and merely a convenient alphabet to express thoughts and emotions. This act or vision of the mind is called Imagination. It is that active state of the mind in which it forces things to obey the laws of thought; takes up all present objects in a despotic manner into its own image and likeness and makes the thought which occupies it the center of the world. (*Early Lectures*, I, 224)

The poet here is something of a tyrant: the "active state of . . . [his] mind . . . forces things to obey the laws of thought; takes up all present objects in a despotic manner into its own image and likeness and makes the thought which occupies it the center of the world." Like an anointed monarch, he subordinates all to his authority. Yet such chrismed despotism was bound to provoke a reaction on Emerson's part, good New Englander that he was; and so (in contradiction to this patriarchal language) his poet is also archetypally antinomian. For in exercising his authority he blasphemously parodies the Creator in the Garden when He made Adam into His own "image and likeness"; and in general, his ambition is—from an orthodox view—the same as Satan's in *Paradise Lost:* to be as God and do what the demon tried to do in Pandemonium (to create a material realm to match that of Heaven).

Thus, as in "John Milton," Emerson here employs a rhetoric that tries to satisfy both of the basic impulses in his culture. His poet is both an affirmer of the order of things and a usurper, an angel and a devil; and as such, he reflects Emerson's ideologically middling heritage and its sociocultural roots. This conflicted inheritance (as much as idealism) is also what lies behind the imagery of the following passage in the "Literature" lecture from "The Philosophy of History" series given during 1836 and 1837. For what allows the poet there to link his own "peculiar genius" with "the want of the times" is the imagination's esemplastic power to incarnate "the Unity of Nature" within his soul; and in pursuit of that goal, he must therefore take up a quintessentially bourgeois position, sandwiched between—and trying to please both—the ultimate Patriarch and the democratic mob: "The man of genius must occupy the whole space between God or pure mind, and the multitude of uneducated men. He must draw from the infinite Reason on the one side and he must penetrate into the heart and mind of the rabble on the other. From one he must draw his strength: to the other, he must owe his aim. The one yokes him to the real; the other to the apparent. At one pole is Reason; at the other, Common Sense."[25] Moreover, this conflicted (but rhetorically resolved) position is the source of the poet's authority. For "from this double polarity of the literary man" in prophetic fashion "comes on the one hand that conscious dignity which the true bard always feels,—so conspicuous in the remains of Hesiod, and the elder Greek poets, in all the Hebrew poets, in Dante, Chaucer, and Milton,—as the dispensers of truth for the behoof of all men;—a conscious dignity, I may remark, which discriminates very widely the man of genius from the brilliant and frivolous men of talent"; and yet "from their sympathy with the populace" there also (for Milton and the others) "arises that [leveling] humanity even feminine and maternal, which always characterizes the highest class of genius; of which the meeting of Hector and Andromache in Homer, the sorrows of Adam and Eve in Milton, and how many tears and smiles in Shakspear's women, may serve as famous examples" (*Early Lectures*, II, 61–63).

This pattern is also apparent in his attack on Unitarianism as a "solecism against faith" during *The Divinity School Address* crisis of 1838. For instance, several months before the actual address itself, he spoke to a group

25. This passage bespeaks Emerson's reading in Coleridge, and so has a particularly witty ending, since he replaces the expected Coleridgean opposite of "Reason" (the Understanding) with "Common Sense" (thus specifically targeting the Scottish philosophy then so influential in America).

of Harvard students about the very matters that would so shortly shock some of their elders. In doing so, he not unexpectedly revealed his own deep antinomian impulses at this time:

> 1 April. Cool or cold windy clear day. The Divinity School youths wished to talk with me concerning theism. I went rather heavy-hearted for I always find that my views chill or shock people at the first opening. But the conversation went well & I came away cheered. I told them that the preacher should be a poet smit with love of the harmonies of moral nature: and yet look at the Unitarian Association & see if its aspect is poetic. They all smiled No. A minister nowadays is plainest prose, the prose of prose. He is a Warming-pan, a Night-chair at sick-beds & rheumatic souls; and the fire of the minstrel's eye & the vivacity of his word is exchanged for intense grumbling enunciation of the Cambridge sort, & for scripture phraseology. (*JMN*, v, 471)

Emerson's contrast here between the decay and formalism of the Standing Order and the liveliness of the true poet-priest (who has been "smit with love of the harmonies of moral nature") involves a specifically Miltonic attack upon the authority of the Unitarian clergy, because in the phrase just quoted he daringly revises the invocation of the Holy Ghost at the opening of *Paradise Lost*, book III (lines 1–55). Milton had asked there that the "holy Light, offspring of Heav'n first-born" (line 1), might lighten his darkness, and cause him to be "smit with the love of sacred song" (*Paradise Lost*, III, line 29); and so, by replacing the poet's "sacred song" with "the harmonies of moral nature," which emanate from the Over-soul, Emerson does in miniature here what he would later do at large in the address itself. He denies the uniqueness and authority of biblical revelation and (in a semisecularized way) suggests that the Hutchinsonians and early Quakers were right to give the inner light of the inspired individual priority even over the Bible. Moreover, by implication this revision is also aimed at Milton himself, who in Emerson's view had perhaps too readily accepted the authority of the Christian revelation, when he should have been of the devil's party and done what Emerson does here (which is behave like a more radical reincarnation of the Milton of the antiprelatical tracts).

In much the same way, Emerson later invoked the example of the rebellious Milton and others like him several more times in his *Journal*, as the pressure of the impending crisis grew and he steeled himself to the deed. His entry for May 1 bespeaks this, since in it he lists Milton as one of a number of daring defenders of freedom whom he would emulate; but then he undercuts the authority that comes from that emulation with the following closing self-admonition, which denounces all precedent: "Be lord of a day through wisdom & justice & you can put up your history books: they can teach you nothing" (*JMN*, v, 487). Similarly, in a *Journal* entry for June 10, Emerson defined the nature of true genius in words that later appear almost unaltered in "Self-Reliance": "Great men again do not brag of their personal attributes but like Napoleon generously belong to the connexion of events. He identified himself with the new age & owned himself the passive organ of an idea." Yet such a wise passivity before the geniuses of the past and the spirit of one's age—which smacks of the Arminian need to affirm order (particularly in conjunction with so ambiguous a figure as the authoritarian usurper Bonaparte)—was not enough for Emerson in this refulgent summer. Faced as he was with the coming storm, he therefore went on in this passage to invoke the only figure whose precedent seemed applicable to his own situation, Milton's Satan:

> This is an obscure perception of the great philosophy that the Eternal is stirring at our heart, working through our hands, & predominates & will predominate in all our being. And we are now men, & must accept in the highest mind the transcendant destiny, & not pinched in a corner, not cowards fleeing before revolution, but pious aspirants to be noble clay,—plastic in the almighty effort,—we must advance & advance & advance into Chaos & the Dark. (*JMN*, vii, 11–12)

Despite this satanic self-identification, this entry (which was originally written in the first person) is a good example of Emerson's desire (even at his most antinomian) to find a way of rhetorically satisfying both of the sets of paradigmatic demands made upon him. Indeed, until the last phrase identifies just what his "almighty effort" is going to be, Emerson's prose seems to be almost conventionally religious and deferential to the Almighty (as He was traditionally understood). For he at first avers that it is "the Eternal," not the infernal, that is stirring at his heart and working through him, and so, he seems much like an evangelical enthusiast at the moment of conversion. Moreover, in a most significant choice of imagery, Emerson tells us that even at this moment of incipient revolt against the Establishment of which he had been a part, he is inspired by his "transcendant destiny" to stand up to revolution, rather than join it or flee before it like a coward. No Jacobin, he desires to be a "pious aspirant to be noble clay"; and it is precisely that hieratic (and hypostatic) wish which leads ever so cleverly to the inverting conclusion, in which he puts upon himself not the acolyte's surplice but the scorched mantle of Milton's Satan and flies through the Abyss in defiance of the Deity upon a course that to many of Emerson's contemporaries most definitely seemed to lead to "Chaos & the Dark."

This daring inversion of expectations works to fuse the language of patriarchy and that of antinomianism into a new rhetoric supportive of a transcendentally infernal poetic authority in another way as well, for Emerson also seems here for the first time to have fully exploited the opportunities presented by the contradictions of his class's moderate Puritan inheritance. This is why at this point in the *Journal* he rhetorically tries to uncover the analogies between Satan's archetypal rebellion and Puritanism's seventeenth-century defiance of ecclesiastical formalism and tyranny. By suggesting that Milton's archangelic rebel is merely a projection of Puritanism's antinomian spirit, he can preemptively deflect the charges of heresy and infidelity soon to rain down upon him; and by presenting himself as an angelic bringer of light who is merely disguised as a demon, (in the tradition of Milton) he may justify his figurative resort to arms against the slumbering deities of Unitarian Harvard (religious "liberals" who are here rather savagely cast in the role of Stuart bishops or Calvin's dogmatic God). Similarly, as the inversion at the end of this entry also suggests, Emerson meant to abolish the moralistic aesthetic distinctions of Brattle Street as well; for though even a Channing might step back from the brink of admiring Satan's amoral, rebellious creativity, Emerson in Heaven's—and Hell's—name will not. By 1838 the didacticism of the previous, consensualist generation of Bostonians had ceased to mean anything to him; and so, full of divine grace, he prepared here for the upcoming commencement by asserting—as he would in the address itself—that seen aright, such a journey as he urged upon the students before him would not bring Sin and Death into the world, let alone Divinity Hall. Rather, it would merely—in the best sense of the phrase—advance the standard of truth "some furlongs forward into Chaos."[26]

Emerson was up to the same thing several years later when he returned to *The Divinity School Address* incident poetically in "Uriel" (*RWE*, IX, 13–15). For in that poem he meant to do publicly what he had privately done in his

---

26. Although this phrase picks up on Emerson's Miltonic imagery here, it actually appears instead later (in *Representative Men*) as part of a description of Shakespeare's imagination; see below, page 152.

Journal: to replace the paradigmatic (and philosophical) dualism of his consensualist Unitarian teachers with a paradigmatic (and philosophical) mo-
nism of his own devising. His means of doing so was to create a persona for
himself ("Uriel") that would appease both of the structures of feeling in his
culture. His choice of title indicates this, since much of book III of *Paradise
Lost* centers upon a confrontation between a patriarchal, divinely graced,
light-bearing, order-affirming angel and an antinomian, demonic, rebellious, antiauthoritarian temptor. Milton's Uriel is in book III the "angel of
light" who acts as the messenger and servant of God ("the same" archangel
"whom John saw also in the sun" when he was inspired to write the last book
of the New Testament [*Paradise Lost*, III, 622–23]). As such, he is the representative of patriarchalism and the Christian revelation when he there con-
fronts the archetypal antinomian, who has disguised himself as "a stripling
Cherub" in order to find out the way to Eden. Moreover, Uriel is philosoph-
ically something of a Unitarian (and, so, a representative Arminian) too, for
"though regent of the sun, and held / The sharpest-sighted Spirit of all in
heav'n," he trusts too much in appearances; consequently, in the course of
his giving an account of the story of creation, he is fooled by Satan into revealing the secret of earth's location (*Paradise Lost*, III, 681–742). It is a mistake he only realizes later, in the next part of the poem, in that great favorite
of Unitarian Miltonists, Satan's "Address to the Sun" in book IV (at the end
of which he finally recognizes the "artificer of fraud" on "th' Assyrian
mount . . . disfigured" [*Paradise Lost*, IV, 121, 126–27]).[27]

For his part, Emerson took this opposition and collapsed it. Like Milton's
angel (and like the Arminian side of Milton himself), his Uriel is thus in part
a servant of the patriarchal God, a holy and fearless speaker of divine truth,
an upholder of morality and cosmic order. Yet (like Milton's Satan and Milton in his antinomian moods), he is also a defender of freedom and a defier
of tyranny, an autonomous spirit who

> with low tones that decide,
> And doubt and reverend use defied,
> With a look that solved the sphere,
> And stirred the devils everywhere,

27. A treatment of Emerson and Milton that is particularly relevant here (especially as it tries
to understand Emerson's reception of the author of *Paradise Lost* in terms of his theory of the
poet's role) is Charles Mignon, " 'Classic Art': Emerson's Pragmatic Criticism," in *Studies in the
American Renaissance: 1983*, ed. Joel A. Myerson (Charlottesville: University Press of Virginia,
1983), 203–21.

Gave his sentiment divine
Against the being of a line.
'Line in nature is not found;
Unit and universe are round;
In vain produced, all rays return;
Evil will bless, and ice will burn.'
                    (lines 15–24)

By fusing these representative spirits into one, Emerson not only created a rhetoric of authority capable of establishing the legitimacy of the man of letters in a conflicted bourgeois culture, he also found the means in the poem to address the specific points of dispute created by his *Divinity School Address*. For as a paradigmatic affirmer of order, Emerson's Uriel on the one hand does what Milton's Uriel does in book III of *Paradise Lost:* he gives an accurate account of the nature of things and of their creation. Yet because he is also an antinomian rebel, he plays the role of Milton's Satan here too; and so, in the process of angelically telling the truth, he also satanically denies the authority of the version of the truth then current at Unitarian Harvard, by declaring first, that Unitarianism's conventional morality, didactic aesthetics, and soteriology are false ("Evil will bless, and ice will burn"); and second, that its natural supernaturalism is really a kind of false dualism ("Line in nature is not found; / Unit and universe are round").

As this suggests, in Emerson's view it was precisely by being both angelic and demonic (both like the Milton of the invocations in *Paradise Lost* and the Milton who defended regicide) that he could reveal the complex nature of things and so solve the problem of authority that had vexed the previous six generations of his ancestors. Only by defying "doubt and reverend use" at the same time, only by solving the sphere and yet stirring the devils, only by affirming order and yet defying authority can true "laws of form, and metre just" (line 12) be found and true distinctions between "what subsisteth, and what seems" (line 14) be established (thereby making the demon-angel, who reveals such truth a model for those who would do likewise and reject even Emerson's own hard-won *auctoritas*). Not, of course, that in this poem he was saying that this was what *had* happened. For although it is generally now agreed that Andrews Norton's "The Latest Form of Infidelity" historically represented an extreme response to *The Divinity School Address*, Emerson's forebodings about the reaction of many of his peers were all too soon fulfilled. "The rash word" had indeed, it sometimes seemed to him, "boded ill to all"; and "all" had indeed seemed to slide in the minds of many "to confusion" as the result of his talk (lines 30–34). As a consequence, like Satan in the "Address to the Sun," Emerson found himself isolated and depressed in the months following the talk. In a real sense, therefore, "A sad self-knowledge, withering," did indeed fall "On the beauty of Uriel," with the result that "In heaven once eminent, the god / Withdrew, that hour, into his cloud" (lines 35–38). Yet after this period was over, in the early 1840s, at least, it still seemed (at times) to him that he had achieved his goal: that he had, as a man of letters, provided a solution to the crisis of authority facing his class, despite the personal cost. For like Milton at the Restoration, who justified "the ways of God to men" under the threat of imminent arrest; and like Uriel after his encounter with Satan in the epic, though outwardly defeated and tricked, Emerson could still declare the true order of things in verse of real power. And like Milton, who against all odds stood for liberty, and like Milton's Satan, whose "Address to the Sun" contains the classic statement of antinomian denial ("Evil, be thou my good; by thee at least / Divided empire with heav'n's King I hold / . . . and more than half perhaps will reign" [*Paradise Lost*, IV, 110–12]), he could still thunder defiance at the Almighty and His self-appointed minions. For he had found a language to do both: a "voice of cherub scorn" that "Shamed the angels' veiling wings" with its godly devotion to truth, yet one that caused "the upper sky" to blush, tinging Heaven itself with the color of Hell and making the gods shake, "they knew not why" (lines 48 and 54–55).

4

THE TRANSCENDENTALIST
MILTON

"Uriel" represents something of a high point in Emerson's use of Milton. Not only did his interest in the poet wane from about 1841 on, but the careful rhetorical balance he had achieved in that poem between his culture's structures of feeling fell apart too. At first, to be sure, he still often expressed high regard for the author of *Paradise Lost*. In the essay "Experience," in *Essays: Second Series* (1844), for instance, he listed Milton's writings (along with the Bible and the works of Homer, Dante, and Shakespeare) as one of the great monuments of Western culture (*Collected Works*, III, 37); and in 1841 he called him "a grand genius" (*JMN*, VIII, 24). A year later he stated that in contrast to the "worldly" Thomas Carlyle, Milton dwelt in a "celestial region" along with Michelangelo (*JMN*, VIII, 187); and in the same year he compared his verse favorably to that of Henry Thoreau (!), saying that his protege was not up to the level of those "men of purer fire [who] write down the catches much more faithfully & so we have the Comus and Penseroso[,] Hamlet & Lear" (*JMN*, VIII, 257). As late as 1845, in fact, he still set Milton alongside Shakespeare in the role the former had so often played in the 1830s: that of an exemplar of the Aristotelian virtue of "humanity" (*JMN*, IX, 248). Yet though Emerson had always followed the Unitarians in giving Milton second place among English writers,[1] the fact that it is Shakespeare who is his exemplary poet in *Representative Men* (1850) suggests that a dimunition of interest in Milton on his part was underway during these years. Indeed, the author of *Paradise Lost* is markedly absent in the chapter in that book on "The Poet" (perhaps Emerson's most far-reaching treatment of the

1. A good summary of Emerson's views on Shakespeare and Milton can be found in Anderson, 59–66.

Western literary tradition), being mentioned prominently only once, at the end—and then only so that Emerson might apply *to Shakespeare* the Miltonic allusion he had used with regard to himself at the time of *The Divinity School Address* crisis. Significantly, moreover, even in that case, the form of the allusion (to Satan's flight past Chaos and Old Night) clearly puts Milton on a much lower level than that which he had formerly enjoyed with Emerson:

> Other admirable men have led lives in some sort of keeping with their thought, but this man in wide contrast. Had he been less, had he reached only the common measure of great authors, of Bacon, Milton, Tasso, Cervantes, we might leave the fact in the twilight of human fate; but that this man of men, he who gave to the science of mind a new and larger subject than had ever existed, and planted the standard of humanity some furlongs forward into Chaos,—that he should not be wise for himself,—it must even go into the world's history, that the best poet led an obscure and profane life, using his genius for the public amusement. (*Collected Works*, IV, 124–25)

Two reasons for Emerson's turn away from Milton can be seen in this passage. The first is that in comparison with Shakespeare's impersonality, Milton's strong presence in his writings was no longer as valuable to Emerson as it had once been. The second (and deeper one), however, is that after "Uriel" Emerson found he could no longer use the poet and his writings as a means of rhetorically uniting the conflicting sides of his cultural heritage. Rather, now, in the incidental references to Milton that do occur, the poet becomes alternatively an Arminian or an antinomian to an Emerson whose struggle to deal with his own contradictory position and polarized loyalties was leading him back into the ideological compromises typical of his class.

The "Literature" chapter of *English Traits* (1856)[2] illustrates this second reason particularly well, since in it Emerson presents a portrait of English society that is largely a projection of his own sense—as an educated Boston gentleman—of simultaneous inclusion in, and yet exclusion from, British high culture and the social hierarchy that spawned it. Thus, Emerson's England is at once the colonial parent he wants to revere and the colonial tyrant from whom he and his countrymen have lately rebelled. Its culture is both a

2. All references to this work are from Ralph Waldo Emerson, *English Traits*, ed. Howard Mumford Jones (Cambridge, Mass.: Harvard University Press, 1966). The best critical treatment of this book is Philip L. Nicoloff, *Emerson on Race and History: An Examination of "English Traits"* (New York: Columbia University Press, 1961).

noble tradition that beckons his allegiance and a structure that would shackle him to an aristocratic past (thereby destroying his creative autonomy); and the poets it has produced are simultaneously the servants of an ideal cultural order he covets and liberators who, like himself, would be free of the priority of the past it represents.

Emerson therefore speaks for only one side of his New England heritage when he contends later in the "Literature" chapter (in a sneering, pseudo-aristocratic put-down of both the peasantry and the very middle class to which he belonged) that "the English muse loves the farmyard, the lane and market. . . . He is materialist, economical, mercantile." For it is only in one mood that he pictures the English poet as an idealizing, inspired, Arminian figure imposing order on a potentially revolutionary culture through the imagination's esemplastic power to transform the language of commerce into the authoritative dialect of Heaven; and it is only in one mood that he regards the following list of English literary worthies as allies in what is a fundamentally conservative cause:

> Chaucer's hard painting of his Canterbury pilgrims satisfies the senses. Shakspeare, Spenser and Milton, in their loftiest ascents, have this national grip and exactitude of mind. This mental materialism makes the value of the English transcendental genius; in these writers and in Herbert, Henry More, Donne and Sir Thomas Browne. The Saxon materialism and narrowness, exalted into the sphere of intellect, makes the very genius of Shakspeare and Milton. When it reaches the pure element, it treads the clouds as securely as the adamant. Even in its elevations materialistic, its poetry is common sense inspired; or iron raised to white heat. (*English Traits*, 150–51)

Similarly, it is only in a certain mood that in *Representative Men* he could affirm the order and meaning-imposing qualities of the English literary canon so as to allow men of the emerging bourgeois dominant class like himself to co-opt "Shakspeare, Homer, Dante, Chaucer" as fellow idealizers (and so, pacifiers) of the quotidian—in the process making them into men who "saw the splendour of meaning that plays over the visible world; knew that a tree had another use than for apples, and corn another than for meal, and the ball of the earth than for tillage and roads: that these things bore a second and finer harvest to the mind, being emblems of its thoughts, and conveying in all their natural history a certain mute commentary on human life" (*Collected Works*, IV, 124). As his allusion to the English mind's Satan-like, materialist capacity for treading "the clouds as securely as the adamant" suggests, there was another side to Emerson in the 1840s and 1850s: an antinomian mood that responded to England and its literary tradition in a different way. It is the mood in which he chose to play the ex-colonial dissenter and revolutionary by depicting England's literary greatness—and, so, its authority over Americans—as a thing of the past. This is why, in the "Literature" chapter of *English Traits*, he contended that since the Elizabethan age the truly authoritative, Platonic (or idealist) tradition as outlined above had gone into decline. For in his view, even the handful of exceptions to this trend (the few English poets since the seventeenth century who had spoken with insight into things unseen) had suffered from a lack of authority caused by the materialistic course of English life. Among other things, this utterly compromises England's claims over American writers like Emerson; for as he rather untidily puts it, "whoever discredits analogy and requires heaps of facts before any theories can be attempted, has no poetic power, and nothing original or beautiful will be produced by him." Historically, therefore, "Locke is as surely the influx of decomposition and of prose [in English culture], as Bacon and the Platonists of growth. [For] the Platonic is the poetic tendency; the so-called scientific is the negative and poisonous." Consequently, though " 't is quite certain that Spenser, Burns, Byron and Wordsworth will be Platonists, and that the dull men will be Lockists," the Lockists have had the upper hand for so long that they have robbed Britannia of her cultural authority over her former colonies (*English Traits*, 154–55).

Significantly, furthermore, so strong was Emerson's desire to overthrow the hegemony of England and the English literary canon, that he believed even Milton had been no counter to these disempowering historical developments. For the English in the seventeenth century had so forsaken the "insight of general laws" (that power of imposing the eternal order on the multiplicity of things, in which "Shakspeare is supreme") that they had descended irrevocably from "the lofty sides of Parnassus." Even the author of *Paradise Lost* thus came too late to speak with true patriarchal authority: at best, "Milton, who was the stair or high table-land to let down the English genius from the summits of Shakspeare, used this privilege [only] sometimes in poetry, more rarely in prose. For a long interval afterwards, it is not found" (*English Traits*, 157–58).

As this suggests, although Emerson was still trying to deal with the conflicting structures of feeling in his culture during the 1850s, he could no longer bring off the rhetorical tour de force that makes "Uriel" such an interesting document in New England literary history. Milton had become for him (as here in *English Traits*) the occasion for contradiction rather than an opportunity for synthesis: a figure who elicited his hankering after order and hierarchy in ways that did not mesh with his other, more antinomian sentiments. The proximate cause of this shift is that (like the character "Uriel") Emerson the critic had himself now fallen into history and a historical way of thinking; and so, John Milton could no longer act as a model for his efforts to affirm, and yet dissent from, the authority of English culture. For he now realized two things: first, that even by Milton's time the great historical shift had taken place that had produced both the New England dominant class and the conflicted culture over which it sought hegemony; and second, that this entailed the foreclosure of certain possibilities. In other words, he now saw not only the root of his dilemma, but also the fact that—short of converting to Rome and burying himself in the traditional subculture it afforded—there was simply no going back: the coherent, traditional (patriarchal) society that had made the authority of a Shakespeare possible was beyond his reach; and even the most brilliant rhetoric could no longer reverse the effects of postmedieval history (in which Western culture headed in an ever more satanic direction).

In such circumstances, the Milton of Emerson's later years became merely a great Englishman: a man representative of his national culture at a particular point in its history. If he was anything more, it was that he was for Emerson a rather Arnoldian figure as well: one who imperfectly united the Hebraic and Hellenic, the materialist and idealist, the Puritan and the humanist elements that made up Anglo-America's nineteenth-century cultural heritage. But as this role out of the future *Culture and Anarchy* implies, rather than providing Emerson with a means of escape from the bourgeois dilemma, Milton instead thus now exemplified the contradictions that bound them both—contradictions from which there was no longer even such possibility of release as existed in the poet's time. As Emerson put it in an 1846 *Journal* entry:

> Criticism is in its infancy. The anatomy of Genius it has not unfolded. Milton in the egg, it has not found. Milton is a good apple on that tree of England. It would be impossible by any chemistry we know to compound that apple other wise: it required all the tree; & out of thousands of apples good & bad, this specimen apple is at last procured. That is, we have a well-knit, hairy, industrious Saxon race[,] Londoners intent on their trade. . . . Out of this valid stock choose the validest boy, & in the flower of this strength open to him, the

whole Dorian & Attic beauty and the proceeding ripeness of the same in Italy. . . . Well, on the man to whose unpalled taste this delicious fountain is opened, add the fury & concentration of the Hebraic Genius, through the hereditary & already culminated Puritanism—and you have Milton, a creation impossible before or again; and all whose graces & whose majesties involve this wonderful combination;—quite in the course of things once, but not iterated. (*JMN*, ix, 440)

Or as he remarked in 1852 to the Saint George's Society of Montreal, "England is like a ship anchored in the sea, at the side of Europe, & right in the heart of the modern world." Though there still be in her "as great individuals now, as once" there were (men like Shakespeare, Milton, Bacon, and Newton: like "Scott, Byron, Coleridge, Wordsworth"), still they are men who are anchored upon the shoals of modernity—those shifting shallows which Milton first explored and amidst which Emerson too now found himself becalmed (*JMN*, x, 507–8).

This note of declination and foreclosed possibility can also be heard in Emerson's use of the poet to comment upon issues of civil and ecclesiastical freedom during the decades leading up to the Civil War. For whether he was treating John Milton as a lawgiver or as a foe of tyranny, Emerson generally emphasized either the difficulty of Miltonic moral action in the modern world or the absence of it. Immediately after the above-cited passage from his 1852 Saint George's Day speech, for instance, he quoted some lines from the Wordsworth sonnet on Milton that had earlier drawn his attention (like Channing's) to the question of liberty in the nineteenth century: " 'We must be free or die, who speak the tongue / That Shakspeare spake; the faith & manners hold / Which Milton held. . . .' " He then paired that poem's contradictory antinomian reminder of the poet's love of freedom and Arminian celebration of England's noble past with a famous passage from Milton's prose. His purpose in doing so was to characterize the bourgeois malaise of London, the metropolis of the modern world; but in the process, he expressed a point of view every bit as conflicted as Wordsworth's:

> The commercial relations of the world are so intimately drawn to London, that it seems as if every dollar in the world contributed to strengthen the English Government.
> "But, in a Protestant nation, that should have thrown off these tattered rudiments long ago, after the many strivings of God's Spirit, &

our fourscore years vexation of him in this our wilderness, since reformation began,—to urge these rotten principles, & twit us with the present age, which is to us an age of ages, wherein God is manifestly come down among us to do some remarkable good to our Church or State, is, as if a man should tax the renovating & reingendering spirit of God with innovation, & that new creature for an upstart novelty."

> *John Milton*
> *Animadversions* [Sec. v]
> *Jenks*, Vol. I, 200.
> (*JMN*, x, 509)

Emerson's aim in this passage (in which an antinomian bit of Milton buttresses an Arminian condemnation of dollar chasing worthy of the Unitarian pulpit) was to expound upon the same paradigmatically muddled theme that appears in an 1848 *Journal* entry: that though "Milton mixes with politics but from the ideal side," in the commercial nineteenth century "there are no men in England quite ideal, living in an ideal world, & working on politics & social life only from that" (*JMN*, x, 330). He felt the same was true of America too, especially as the slavery crisis began to heat up.[3] This explains why, for instance, he mentioned the poet in 1850 while delineating the intellectual and moral superiority of his own region over the South; for he believed that the key difference between the two was that New England had been more influenced by the libertarian strain in Reformation thought: "Luther's religious movement was the fountain of so much intellectual life in Europe; that is, Luther's conscience animating sympathetically the conscience of millions, the pulse passed into thought, & ultimated itself in Galileos, Keplers, Swedenborgs, Newtons, Shakspeares, Bacons, & Miltons. The morale of New England makes its intellect possible. At the South, they are really insensible to the criminality of their laws & customs. They are still semibarbarous, have got but one step beyond scalping" (*JMN*, xi, 314). Yet this list of Protestant heroes is no list of radicals; as he noted a year later (in the wake of the Compromise of 1850), for him the chief evidence that this heritage was absent in his own day was that the "gentlemen to whom the honour & dignity of the community were confided" now contrasted sadly with their Puritan ancestors:

---

3. Emerson's antislavery activities during the decade before the Civil War are summarized in Rusk, 366–69 and 388–90. His statements on the abolition of slavery in the British Empire, the Fugitive Slave Act, etc., are in *RWE*, xi, 97–281.

I look in vain for such a class among us. And that is the worst symptom in our affairs. There are persons of fortune enough and men of breeding & of elegant learning but they are the very leaders in vulgarity of sentiment. I need call no names. The fact stares us in the face. . . . It is the want perhaps of a stern & high religious training, like the iron Calvinism which steeled their fathers seventy five years ago. But though I find the names of old patriots still resident in Boston, it is only the present venerable Mr. Quincy who has renewed the hereditary honour of his name by scenting the tyranny in the gale. The others are all lapped in after dinner dreams and are as obsequious to Mr[.] Webster as he is to the gentlemen of Richmond & Charleston. . . .

It was always reckoned even in the rudest ages the distinction of the gentleman[,] the oath of honour of the knight[,] to speak the truth to men of power or to angry communities, and to uphold the poor man against the rich oppressor. Will the educated people of Boston ask themselves whether they side with the oppressor or the oppressed? Yet I know no reason why a gentleman . . . should not be true to his duties in Boston in 1850, as haughtily faithful & with as sovereign superiority to all hazards as his fathers had in 1770, or as Mr[.] Hampden or Mr[.] Eliot in London in 1650, Arundel, or More, or Milton,[.] (*JMN*, XI, 352–53)

Even though this passage largely draws upon the British Whig Milton tradition and the long-standing American identification of the Revolution with the English Civil War, Emerson's language also clearly manifests his class self-interest. One sign of this is that he couches his defense of liberty here as part of the hereditary responsibilities of knights and gentlemen (something that robs his antiauthoritarianism of any leveling social implications it might have had and implicitly affirms both the existence of the present social hierarchy and the continuance of upper-class leadership). Similarly, Emerson's freedom-loving heroes are themselves either Puritan moderates or Catholic lords and knights: figures who provide fitting precedent not for Jacobins, but for the Brahmin revolutionaries of 1776 and their antebellum descendants. As this suggests, the later Emerson was simply more contradictory (and in that, more like a Unitarian Miltonist) than the Emerson who had satanically brazened out *The Divinity School Address* crisis. He was also more discouraged than he had been. And so, he no longer believed that present-day Boston had any Mores, Hampdens, and Miltons ready to do battle against oppression (whether from Arminian or antinomian motives), nor did he himself feel capable of taking up arms as he had against the legions of Unitarian orthodoxy fifteen years previously.

Emerson struck a similar note of angry frustration a few years later at the time of the infamous enforcement of the Fugitive Slave Act in the case of Thomas Sims. Once again invoking the example of Milton and other great poets in order to contrast their authority with the increasing disempowerment of his own class, he wrote:

> Euripides & Aeschylus are again the wellknown pair of Beauty & Strength, which we had in Raphael & Angelo, in Shakspeare & Milton.
> What Aeschylus will translate our heaventempting politics into a warning ode, strophe & antistrophe? A slave, son of a member of Congress, flees from the plantation-whip to Boston, is snatched by the marshal, is rescued by the citizens; an excited population; a strong chain is stretched around the Court House. Webster telegraphs from Washington urgent orders to prosecute rigorously. Whig orators & interests intervene. Whig wisdom of waiting to be last devoured. Slave is caught, tried, marched at midnight under guard of marshals & pike & sword-bearing police to Long Wharf & embarked for Baltimore. "Thank-God-Choate" thanks God five times in one speech; Boston thanks God. (*JMN*, XIII, 64)

Moreover, during these years he used Milton prominently in other places to convey his discouragement at the course of contemporary events. In a notebook on the history of liberty he compiled at the time of Bloody Kansas (*JMN*, XIV, 373–430), for instance, he cited the poet as an authority against the institution of slavery (*JMN*, XIV, 409) and noted with approval a friend's remark—in context, hardly complimentary to their contemporaries—that "if we had such a tract written for Liberty now, as Milton wrote for unlicensed printing in 16[44], it would have more than equal effect" (*JMN*, XIV, 402). Similarly, he also praised *Areopagitica* as "an immortal pamp[h]let" (*JMN*, XIV, 202) of the very sort now lacking.

Yet in these same *Journals* Emerson often played his old conflicted tune as well. Thus, at one point he used Milton's own simultaneously Arminian and antinomian post-Restoration reference to the Stuart court as " 'Those sons of Belial flown with insolence & wine' " (*Paradise Lost*, I, 501–2) in order to attack New England's pro-slavery opponents (*JMN*, XIV, 417); and later, in the *Journal* notebook on the history of liberty, in one of his most stinging indictments of his class's failure to assert its authority during a time of crisis, he sardonically—and self-contradictorily—recorded the view that the Yankee elite's hegemony had become so eroded that they had completely acquiesced to playing a marginal, even frivolous role:

> 'Tis against the plain interest of young men to allow freedom. Young man! the poor Kansas settlers give no elegant suppers, no Saturday dinners, no private box have they at the opera.
>   If you vote to garotte them, & stand by Missouri & the Union, you can just as well praise the Kansas of a thousand years ago, namely, Marathon; talk just as glibly of Milton & the Puritans. You can edit Landor; you can, like Guizot & Sparks, write eulogies of Washington. Judges, Bank Presidents, Railroad men, men of fashion, lawyers universally all take the side of slavery. (*JMN*, xiv, 404)

As this suggests, during the 1850s Milton increasingly elicited Emerson's sense that the game was finally up, both for him and for those like him. For he had come to believe that in the face of such raw power, competing interests, violence, and civil strife, the class to which he belonged no longer had either purpose or effect in national politics. It was a development not unrelated to the failure of his personal attempt to forge a new rhetoric that would resolve the contradictions of New England culture; and so, just as he had earlier concluded that the ambiguities of the modern world had robbed Milton of his relevance for poets like himself individually (by foreclosing any possibility that a modern man of letters might attain the authority of a Shakespeare), Emerson now believed that the effects of the West's fall into modernity had corrupted New England's traditional leaders politically as well—so much so that his peers could not have followed the poet's heroic example even had they wanted to. It should come as no surprise, therefore, to learn that Milton fades out of view amidst these frustrations of Emerson's later years, until in the preface to *Parnassus* (1874) he produced one last, genteel tribute to the author of *Paradise Lost* (a tribute that with unwitting self-irony uses him to cavil at the genteel weakness of nineteenth-century literature).[4] It is an almost mannerist treatment of all the issues raised in Emerson's more robust years. Yet as such, it aptly concludes the movement of the Emersonian Milton down from its high point in "Uriel." For in the end, like his ancestors, the sometime minister of the Second Church was caught in

---

4. Ralph Waldo Emerson, ed., *Parnassus* (Boston: Houghton Mifflin, 1874), iii–xi.

the contradictions and circumstances of his class and culture—which, as with his forbears, set limits upon what mere words could do.

There is more one could say about Emerson and Milton, but it is only a very little more. The poet's influence on his successor's prose style was minimal,[5] and (with the important exception of "Uriel") there are "few Miltonic echoes in Emerson's poetry itself."[6] The same is not true of the other Transcendentalists, however. For like Emerson, they too had to deal with the contradictions and polarities their culture had inherited from its Puritan past; and like him, they too turned to Milton in order to help them do so.

Jones Very, for example, followed Emerson's lead and developed an intense undergraduate interest in Milton. Very was the son of a once prosperous Salem sea captain and was specially tutored for Harvard, where he studied for the Unitarian ministry. Though born of a common-law marriage and not unfamiliar with hard work in the years after his father's death, he was thus (at least by education) early acculturated to the bourgeois milieu of the liberal manse and the College. He received Milton much in the manner of his Harvard teachers: identifying strongly with his ambitions and personal purity and taking his career as a model for his own. His "Account [of his] 3d Term of College 1834" (which was written in the wake of his religious conversion) illustrates the extent of this identification.[7] For instance, Very notes there that on 25 April 1834 he had begun reading *Paradise Lost*. After commenting that "Bently's emendations show more skill than practical judgment" and praising Milton's classical learning, he quotes the poet's account of his "morning haunts" and reminds himself that the great puritan's "domestic habits" are especially relevant in his own case, since they "were those of a severe student." As such they reinforce his desire (expressed in the

---

5. Possible Miltonic influences on Emerson's prose style are discussed by Barbara L. Packer, *Emerson's Fall: A New Interpretation of the Major Essays* (New York: Continuum, 1982), 53–55, 80–81, 134. Porte, *Representative Man*, 161–203, discusses Emerson's retelling of the story of the Fall in "The Protest" and "Experience."

6. Pettigrew, 56. The few echoes that do occur are usually short borrowings of little significance (e.g., lines 13–15 of "The Humble-Bee," which recall Satan's flight across the Abyss in *Paradise Lost*, book ii: "Sailor of the atmosphere / Swimmer through the waves of air; / Voyager of light and noon" [*RWE*, ix, 39]). The two possible exceptions to this (besides "Uriel") are the poem "Grace," which bears some resemblance to Milton's Sonnet vii: "How soon hath Time, the subtle thief of youth" (see G. R. Elliott, "On Emerson's 'Grace' and 'Self-Reliance,' " *New England Quarterly* 2 [1929]: 93–104); and "Initial, Dæmonic, and Celestial Love" (*RWE*, ix, 103–18), which uses the material from *Paradise Lost* found in "Uriel" to similar effect.

7. Edwin Gittleman, *Jones Very: The Effective Years, 1833–1840* (New York: Columbia University Press, 1967), 1–136, describes the poet's family background, education, and youthful religious development.

previous entry) to be (like Emerson) "resolved to live temperate next week and go to bed early si posseur [*sic*]."[8] Similarly, the same year Very compiled a "Scrapbook" that recorded his readings and thoughts on the nature of the imagination and the poetic vocation.[9] As a collection, these quotations and commentary provide yet more strong evidence of the degree to which Very took Milton as a role model. Its title page, in fact, uses Milton's praise of Greek philosophy in *Paradise Regained* (IV, 321–30) to address one of Very's central concerns as an undergraduate: the traditional Christian difficulty in reconciling the authority of secular learning with religious faith;[10] and later, the collection portrays Milton as an exemplary bourgeois Renaissance humanist, particularly emphasizing his status as a divinely inspired justifier of God's ways to man.[11]

As this last example implies, John Milton was a specifically Arminian role model for the young Very. The Bowdoin Prize Exhibition he wrote during his junior year (on the theme of "The Practical Application in this Life, by Men as Social and Intellectual Beings, of the Certainty of a Future State") provides evidence of this.[12] Taken as a whole, it is as conventional (and self-interested) an example of Unitarian social thought as one could find. In particular, the presentation has the solidly Arminian purpose of proving that Christianity provides men with rational incentives for ethical behavior and "self-culture," thereby encouraging public morality and deference to the established order. Very uses the poet to illustrate these precepts and, in doing so, shows how much his Milton resembles that of Channing or the undergraduate Emerson. Indeed, at one point, in accounting for "the godlike actions of a Howard[,] a Washington[,] or a Milton" ([p. 16]), he actually comes close to plagiarizing the *De Doctrina* review. For like Channing, he distinguished between spiritual and physical genius; and like his predecessor,

8. Jones Very, "1830's Commonplace Book" (Harvard University Archives, HUD 836.90), [pp. 87–88]; hereafter cited by title in text with parenthetical square bracketed page numbers assigned.

9. This "Scrapbook" also provides useful information about Very's debt to Coleridge and the German Idealists, as well as about his early reading in Channing and Emerson.

10. Jones Very, "Scrapbook 1834" (Harvard University Archives, HUD 834.90), [title page]; hereafter cited by title in text with parenthetical square bracketed page numbers assigned according to Very's own numbering scheme.

11. One of these references to Milton is from Symmons's biography of the poet, concerning the God-given nature of learning (155), thereby demonstrating Very's direct exposure to one of the principal texts in the Whig Milton tradition (Very, "Scrapbook," [p. 74]). The entry is then followed by a series of citations on the divine origin of poetic inspiration.

12. This piece is bound as part of volume VI of the Bowdoin Prize Dissertations (Harvard University Archives, HU 89.165.121); hereafter cited with parenthetical square bracketed page numbers assigned according to Very's own numbering scheme.

he ascribed the greatness of a Milton to his moral and interior (i.e., intellectual) distinction. He followed Channing too in asserting that this quality of spirit allowed Milton to go beyond the mere martial heroism of a Caesar or a Napoleon; and (citing the same line from *Paradise Lost*) he paraphrased the *De Doctrina* review's attack on Calvinism in order to prove that men of battle, "the conquerors of the world, the brightest stars on the page of history, 'hide their diminished heads' before the brighter beams of the sun of righteousness" emanating from a divine poet like Milton or Jesus of Nazareth.[13] Rather than seeking to grasp "the sword or the sceptre, as the noblest instruments of power," a true moral hero like one of these "is animated by a nobler aim, he wishes not to subdue, to crush the spirit of man, but to elevate it to a consciousness of its own worth, to awaken in it those higher aspirations, which he feels within himself. He needs no mighty physical power to effect this—no sword, no sceptre. He seizes the soul . . . and stamps on the glowing page the copy of his own mind, his 'thoughts that wander through eternity', and sends them forth" ([pp. 18–19]).

Very maintains that there are many examples in history of this triumph of virtue, belles lettres, and moral suasion over party politics and military prowess—a contention that had often been made by Boston's consensualist elite in order to justify their threatened authority. Interestingly, in his view, the two best examples of such self-culture triumphant are the same pair of late seventeenth-century religious liberals who had also found favor with Channing and other Brahmin critics:

> As Milton in literature, so Newton in science might be instanced as the noblest illustrations of the effect produced by the certainty of a future state on the human soul. They felt it in its power, and what was its effects? They did not follow their bright paths drawn by earthly renown or thirst for gold—no, they found a satisfying enjoyment in their pursuits themselves; in humbly tracing the Eternal Mind "in these his lower works." Such minds look far beyond "this visible[,] diurnal sphere." 'Twas not the mere results of those great discoveries, which agitated the mind of Newton so much at their completion—no, 'twas the expansion of soul produced by those unseen realities . . . 'twas *this*, which raised his soul, and bore it onwards on the pinions of sublimity towards the throne of the Eternal. ([p. 22])

13. Channing, cited above, page 104. For Very's early acquaintance with the writings of Channing and Emerson, see Gittleman, 16–17, 77, and 121–30; and David Robinson, "Jones Very, the Transcendentalists, and the Unitarian Tradition," *Harvard Theological Review* 68 (1975): 103–24.

Even leaving aside Very's specific indebtedness to the *De Doctrina* review, his advocacy here of self-culture and his high-minded clerical disdain for both economic self-interest and earthly accomplishment mark this passage as being typically Unitarian. For such opinions are really expressions of the New England dominant-class desire to repress its bourgeois origins in the interest of furthering its hegemony. Moreover, this paradigmatic agendum lies behind his treatment of Milton in the three great critical essays he completed during his years of "divine possession" (1838–39). Even then, when one would think him most open to the antinomian structure of feeling (not to mention the influence of European romanticism), the Milton of "Epic Poetry," "Shakespeare," and "Hamlet" is surprisingly Arminian (in part, perhaps, because this trio took shape out of earlier material).[14]

For example, "Epic Poetry" generally expresses views borrowed from contemporary German criticism.[15] In line with much of this reading, Very holds, for instance, that a great work of art sums up the national and popular culture of its age. He asserts as well that history is progressive, proceeding from its origins in the objective culture of the Homeric age to the subjective culture of the nineteenth century; and like some in Germany (but even more, like the Unitarian clerk he was), he credits this last and highest stage of development not to humanity's emancipation from religion but to its achievement of the highest form of religion: a benificent and liberal Christianity such as that purveyed by his own denomination. Significantly, moreover (and in a manner typical of the Unitarian and Common Sense compromise with the Enlightenment), this last point then leads him to assert that literature has an essentially religious and didactic mission, one that makes it particularly well suited to the introspectiveness of the nineteenth century. For he believed that because his age had progressed to so high a level of self-culture, it was particularly open both to the power of preaching and poetry (two skills New England Arminians had long sought to cultivate) and to the ministrations of an infused soul like his own (the last being itself an instance of that third Unitarian clerical desiderata: clerkly good example).

As this summary of "Epic Poetry" suggests, Very's self-empowering "antinomianism" during his period of orphic inspiration in fact substantially proceeded out of the Arminianism of his calling, class, and education. One sign of this is that like its companion pieces, this piece is no call to arms; rather,

14. These three pieces are cited from Jones Very, *Poems and Essays, Complete and Revised Edition, With a Biographical Sketch by James Freeman Clarke and a Preface by C. A. Bartol* (Boston: Houghton Mifflin, 1886), 3–66; hereafter cited as Very, *Works*.
15. Very's debt to the Germans is discussed by Gittleman, 96–136.

at most, it embodies the paradigmatic contradictions of New England culture as they typically manifested themselves in the thought and feeling of men of Very's profession. Thus, for instance, Very accompanied his depiction of an advance from the heroic literature of antiquity to the Christian epics of Dante and Milton with no demand that the authority of the European past, which that great tradition represented, be rejected. Instead, this part of "Epic Poetry" is really just another example of one of the standard themes in Unitarian Milton criticism, the triumph of moral and intellectual genius over physical prowess, and an illustration of how that criticism so easily fell into the confliction of the class by which it was written. The following passage, for instance, which asserts the superiority—the special case of Tasso excepted—of Christian over classical epic, demonstrates the truth of the latter observation, since it simultaneously affirms both the antinomian desire for freedom and the Arminian need for a God-given moral and cosmic order:

> To escape this thraldom and reach a point from which the heroic character of their age might be seen dilated to its full height, modern poets have fled beyond the bounds of time and woke the echoes of eternity. It was only from this point that the Christian world could be moved; it is only in that region without bounds that the heroism of immortality can be shown in visible action. Milton and Dante chose this spot, on which with almost creative power they might show to mankind worlds of their own "won from the void and formless Infinite," and from which their own heroic spirits might be reflected back upon their own times in all their gigantic proportions. (Very, *Works*, 4)

As this implies, for Very the modern poet could only safely be empowered within the confines of Christianity (which affirms the ultimate patriarchal authority of the Heavenly Father). This is because like his coreligionists he believed that it was only within that context that the demonic voice of the poetic god within could emerge without upsetting the divinely ordained nature of things. Moreover, this also explains why later in the essay he asserted that in the greatest examples of modern heroic action (*Hamlet* and *Paradise Lost*) "the effect of Christianity was to make the individual mind the greatest object of regard, the centre of eternal interest . . . transferring the scene of action from the outward world to the world within." Fortunately, in his view, religion had channeled this giving to "all modern literature the dramatic tendency" so that it had had only a psychological rather than a (more potentially revolutionary) practical effect. Like Bryant and Channing, Very could therefore acquiesce in the historical rise of individualism without having to draw the logical conclusions that flow from such an openness to the antinomian structure of feeling. This is why he writes that just "as the mind of Homer led him to sing of the physical conflicts of his heroes with *visible* gods *without;* so the soul of the modern poet, feeling itself contending with motives of godlike power *within*, must express that conflict"—but only in the realm of the imagination, "in the dramatic form, in the poetry of sentiment" (Very, *Works*, 14–15).

Very's description of *Paradise Lost* in "Epic Poetry" also confirms these fundamentally contradictory paradigmatic allegiances. On the one hand, Milton is for him still a patriarchal authority figure: the sublime, divinely anointed poet-priest of Jehovah. This is because more than any other epic poet, he has engaged in a radical and wholesale idealization of reality. As Very puts it, the "highest development of the heroic character yet shown in action was that exhibited by the sublime genius of Milton," whose "mind had taken a flight above the materiality of Dante"—let alone that of Homer, Virgil, and other bards. Yet on the other hand, Very maintains that the chief evidence for this idealization is the demonic, subjectivizing, antinomian side of Milton's epic. This was why "his first intention [was] of making Paradise Lost a *tragedy*" (Very, *Works*, 18); and it is why he was "compelled . . . to make [the] choice of the *Fall of Man* as his subject," for he shared "the strong feeling we have of our own free agency, and of the almost infinite power it is capable of exercising. An intense feeling of this kind seems to have pervaded Milton's whole life, and by this he was probably directed in the choice of his theme. We find in his 'Speech for the Liberty of unlicensed Printing,' written many years before the conception of his poem, a sentence confirming this supposition" (Very, *Works*, 18–19).

Given who he was, Jones Very thus almost instinctively recognized something of himself in Milton's moderate puritan dilemma. This was because, like the poet, he too was both of the devil's party and of the sect of Heaven, and so (as in the following excerpt) could not really help but fall into similarly bourgeois confusion:

> Milton gives us the philosophy of Christian epic poets, when he says that "he who would not be frustrate of his hope to write well hereafter in laudable things, ought himself to be a true poem; that is, a composition and pattern of the best and honorablest things; not presuming to sing of high praises of heroic men or famous cities, unless he

have in himself the experience and practice of all that which is praise-worthy." What, indeed, are the writings of the great poets of our own times but epics; the description of those internal conflicts, the inter-est in which has so far superseded those of the outward world? A suf-ficient answer to the charge of egotism and selfishness to which they are exposed, is given in the words of Coleridge. "In the 'Paradise Lost' indeed in every one of his poems, it is Milton himself whom you see; his Satan, his Adam, his Raphael, almost his Eve, are all John Milton. . . . The egotism of such a man is a revelation of spirit." (Very, *Works*, 23–24)

Despite the "possession" of his "effective years" (and despite his latent Calvinism),[16] as this quotation indicates, Very was still very much a minister and poet of the Boston religion. Like his consensualist *confrères*, he sought to affirm conventional morality and belief, yet did so in ways that reveal a countervailing individualism. This is, for example, why he here defined such antinomian qualities as egotism and self-revelation in Arminian terms as "the philosophy of Christian epic poets." For unlike Emerson in "Uriel" (who was aware of his culture's polarization and was intent upon rhetorically dealing with it), Very was more like Channing in being unable to get beyond his dominant-class heritage. It is a disability that also explains why he fol-lowed the *De Doctrina* review rather than the example of his fellow Transcen-dentalist when it came to Milton's Satan.[17] For as his most striking declara-tion about the fiend in "Epic Poetry" demonstrates ("This sense of free agency is what constitutes Adam the hero of 'Paradise Lost.' . . . But that which renders Adam the hero of the poem makes Satan still more so; for Mil-ton has opened to our gaze, within his breast of flame, passions of almost infinite growth, burning with intensest rage. *There* is seen a conflict of 'those thoughts that wander through eternity,' at the sight of which we lose all sense of the material terrors of that fiery hell around him, and compared with which the physical conflicts of the archangels is a mockery" [Very, *Works*, 19–20]), Very could not decide whether to applaud or condemn Satan's de-fiance. And so, like Channing, he stepped back from enlisting in the fallen

16. On Very's Calvinist tendencies, see Yvor Winters, *In Defense of Reason* (New York: Swal-low Press and William Morrow, 1947), esp. 262–82; Warner Berthoff, "Jones Very: New En-gland Mystic," *Boston Public Library Quarterly* 2 (1950): 63–76; and James A. Levernier, "Cal-vinism and Transcendentalism in the Poetry of Jones Very," *ESQ: A Journal of the American Renaissance*, n.s., 24 (1978): 30–41.
17. Cf. the Channing passages on Satan's allurements cited above, pages 91–96.

host, preferring Unitarian muddle to anything more decisive—let alone creative, like "Uriel."

His companion piece on "Shakespeare" illustrates his habitual paradigmatic confliction as well. On the one hand, Very complains that Shakespeare's villains never exhibit "that consciousness of the unconquerable will that we find in Milton": the volcanic individualism and self-assertiveness that in the case of Satan "has indeed made us feel in the impulses of our nature a depth and strength of which before we had scarcely any conception." Yet it quickly becomes clear that Very admires Milton's fiend for more than just his rebelliousness. In addition, he admires Satan because his perfidy provides him with more occasion than do the great playwright's characters for moralizing of a traditional clerical sort. While "Shakespeare represents man as he is," and so gives his readers "the wickedness of such an one as Lady MacBeth, and even Iago," this is mere pardonable human evil, not the "gigantic iniquity" of "a dæmon more than human, for whom there remains no place of repentance, and for whom is reserved the blackness of darkness forever." Milton's protagonist is by comparison, therefore, the greater achievement, because "his is that sin unto death, for which we may not pray." We can have little sympathy with his plight, and thus, much to Milton's credit, his fate makes us concentrate on the pious, consensualist lessons we must learn from the language's archetypal authority fable: that "there is no joy in iniquity" and that " 'How awful goodness is' " and "how lovely" virtue (Very, *Works*, 44–45).

On a broader scale, "Shakespeare" also retracts the progressive view of literary history advanced in "Epic Poetry." For in contrast to the latter essay's account of the development of poetry toward ever greater self-expression and individualism, in "Shakespeare" Very holds views much more like those of Emerson in *English Traits* and *Representative Men*. He declares that it is Shakespeare (and not the poets of his own century) who marks the high point in English literary history. This is because as a writer and a man the author of *Hamlet* achieved a consensualist balance between self-assertion and self-effacement that marks the true unity of the individual will with the Spirit. His plays illustrate this balance between submission and autonomy, and demonstrate that (in Miltonic terms) Shakespeare played neither the role of Calvin's patriarchal God nor that of His Arch-foe, but instead, the middling part assigned to the Son by *Paradise Lost*'s eighteenth-century New England interpreters.

Very's Shakespeare is thus a consensualist exemplar, a poet fit for bourgeois Yankee men of letters to imitate. As with "Epic Poetry," moreover, this suggests that biographically "Shakespeare" proceeded out of a year of "divine possession" that was far from subversive. Rather than being a writer in the radical tradition, Very was actually a pretty conventional Unitarian try-ing—like others of his ilk—to negotiate the contradictions of his culture. (Indeed, one might hazard the guess that this is probably one reason why he appealed so much to Emerson, since the latter was at this point struggling to come to terms with the same conflicting structures of feeling.) Certainly Very's cultural background and socioprofessional position help explain why in "Shakespeare" he adopted an Arminian rather than an antinomian view of post-Renaissance literary history—in particular, by holding that Milton was a post-Edenic man caught in the fallenness of modernity (one circumscribed by its demonic egotism and self-consciousness). For Very, the saving balance of the Renaissance has been hopelessly lost; and so, unlike Shakespeare, the author of *Paradise Lost* could not be a consensualist Son-surrogate. Rather, he was, like us, a polarized figure: an Adam in whom "we see the struggle of the child to become the perfect man in Christ Jesus" (Very, *Works*, 46), yet a member too of that fallen order of angels which inhabits the modern world. Very's Milton thus justifies the ways of God to men, but (like Wordsworth or other nineteenth-century poets) he also lies prostrate upon the fiery lake, emitting only a reflected light akin to that of Satan. For as a proto-modern, he is a poet-priest who nonetheless will not submit to the patriarchal Father's will, and so he is one of those who cannot partake of the Beatific Vision:

> Like the fallen angel, they cannot escape the consciousness of them-selves, and the brightness of poesy, instead of blazing directly down upon their heads, causes them from the obliqueness of its rays to be ever accompanied by their own shadow. But when the war of self which these and other bards have so nobly maintained shall have ceased, and the will of the Father shall be done on earth as it is in heaven; when man shall have come to love his neighbor as himself; then shall the poet again find himself speaking with many tongues; and the expectant nations shall listen surprised to a note more sub-lime, yet accordant with the rolling numbers of the Chian minstrel, and more sweet than the wild warblings of the bard of Avon. . . . Each soul shall show in its varied action the beauty and grandeur of Nature; and shall live forever a teacher of the words it hears from the Father. (Very, *Works*, 47)

The same division of desire—between submission and rebellion—can also be seen in those few of Very's poems which bespeak a Miltonic influence. For though most of his borrowings or allusions to the author of *Paradise Lost* are brief and of little consequence,[18] the exceptions to this pattern manifest the familiar fissures within New England culture. Some of Very's poems are thus somewhat antinomian in tone. For example (as William I. Bartlett has noted), the adolescent "Pleasure" (1834) is written in blank verse and attempts to reproduce Milton's epic similies. More significantly, it borrows freely from Satan's speech to Beelzebub (*Paradise Lost*, 1, 242–70) and (slightly paraphrasing Milton) takes as its theme the demon's Promethean declaration that "the mind / Is its own home."[19] Yet even here, Very's fiend is also rather tragic in his defiance; and later, when in one of his most memorable poems, the sonnet "The Dead" (Very, *Works*, 83), he alludes to Milton's description of Satan's fallen "legions, angel forms, who lay entranced, / Thick as autumnal leaves that strow the brooks / In Vallombrosa" (*Paradise Lost*, 1, 301–3), he does so in a manner that is both Arminian and antinomian. For as was so often the case in the occasional satire of the Revolutionary and Federalist periods, in making the subversive Emersonian point that contemporary New England is spiritually corpse-cold, Very cast his enemies—and not himself—in a demonic role, thus satisfying the demands of both structures of feeling:

> I see them,—crowd on crowd they walk the earth,
> Dry leafless trees no autumn wind laid bare;
> And in their nakedness find cause for mirth,
> And all unclad would winter's rudeness dare;
> No sap doth through their clattering branches flow,
> Whence springing leaves and blossoms bright appear;
> Their hearts the living God have ceased to know
> Who gives the spring time to th' expectant year;
> They mimic life, as if from him to steal
> His glow of health to paint the livid cheek;
> They borrow words for thoughts they cannot feel,
> That with a seeming heart their tongue may speak;

18. Typical of these inconsequential brief allusions and borrowings from Milton is Very's late poem "Skepticism with Regard to the Gospels" (Very, *Works*, 271), in which lines 9–10 ("Ah, faithless age! which cannot see the light, / E'en though it does with noon-day brightness beam") seem—given the context—to evoke *Samson Agonistes*, line 80 ("O dark, dark, dark, amid the blaze of noon").

19. William I. Bartlett, *Jones Very: Emerson's "Brave Saint"* (Durham, N.C.: Duke University Press, 1942), 28 and 188–89. One might mention here that in general certain features of Very's style (e.g., his fondness for epic simile and inverted word order) are more likely the result of his classical education than of his reading in Milton.

And in their show of life more dead they live
Than those that to the earth with many tears they give.

While this Miltonic allusion[20] bespeaks Very's partial adherance to the side of the New England soul that refused to rest easy with religious establishments and forms (or with a merely intellectual and ethical spirituality), it does not make him a latter-day Gortonite. Nor, for that matter, does the rest of his poetry. On the contrary, even Very's repeated, seemingly antinomian demands in verse that his contemporaries accede to his authority on account of his unity of soul with the Holy Ghost in the end allied him with conventional morality and the Standing Order rather than reform. This was because (Harvard-trained consensualist that he was) he instinctively tried to renew rather than pull down. In his poetry as elsewhere, he therefore actually preached that there was a limit to reform and boundaries to the activities of the Spirit. As the final reference to the devil's fall (*Paradise Lost*, I, 738–51) in "The Evening Choir" shows,[21] this made Very not a defiant Satan but at best a reluctant Samson: a poet whose desire to tear down the religious fabric about him was balanced by the more moderate (but equally Yankee) need to defer to Heaven's King. This is why in the following lines Very is as hostile to the common man ("the multitude") as to the Church, and in the end takes on not only the persona of Satan but also those of Samson and Saint Paul. For he meant throughout (as in some of his other poems) to contain his antinomianism within the confines of Christian (or at least Unitarian) orthodoxy, thus preserving order, hierarchy, and his own traditional role as a poet-priest:

I would not, when my heart is bitter grown,
And my thoughts turned against the multitude,
War with their earthly temple; mar its stones;
Or, with both pillars in my grasp, shake down
The mighty ruin on their heads. With this
I war not, nor wrestle with the earthly man.
I war with the spiritual temple raised
By pride, whose top is in the heavens, though built

20. Of course, in this passage Milton himself followed his normal practice and tried to improve upon the simile's earlier appearances in such writers as Homer, Virgil, and (most famously) Dante—sources Very also knew well; see Christopher Ricks, *Milton's Grand Style* (Oxford: Oxford University Press, 1963), 123–24; and Alastair Fowler, ed., *Paradise Lost* by John Milton (London: Longman's, 1974), 62.

21. *Dial* 3 (1842): 97–98.

On the earth; whose site and hydra-headed power
Is everywhere;—with Principalities,
And them who rule the darkness of this world,
And Spirits of wickedness that highest stand.
'Gainst this and these I fight; nor I alone,
But those bright stars I see that gather round
Nightly this sacred spot. Nor will they lay
Their glittering armor by, till from heaven's height
Is cast Satan with all his host headlong!
Falling from sphere to sphere, from earth to earth
Forever;—and God's will is done.

(lines 53–71)

The later literary career of Jones Very exhibits a similar pattern whenever John Milton appears. For Very did not die at the end of his "effective years" in 1840, but lived on until 1880, staying quietly at home in Salem, writing largely unmemorable poems and hymns, and serving as a Unitarian supply minister. Nowhere in this later stage, however, did he ever again write as extensively about the poet as he did in "Epic Poetry" and "Shakespeare"; indeed, the references to Milton in Very's poems during these years of semi-seclusion (as in his occasional sermons)[22] are mostly incidental and have little significance. Yet on occasion (like Emerson) the growing crisis over slavery forced him to look anew at his Puritan heritage and the poet's place in it. At a number of points, therefore, Milton figures in his thought much in the manner of the British Whigs or Americans of the Revolutionary generation; as before, however, the potentially revolutionary elements in these invocations are more than counterbalanced by passages in which Very's Milton bespeaks the Arminianism of his class, denomination, and profession.

For instance, as early as 1833 Very composed a neoclassical political poem on the subject of abolition (entitled "Lines Written on Reading Stuart's Account of the Treatment of Slaves in Charleston")[23] in which with reformist zeal he attacked slaveowners. Yet to do so he used antisatanic language much like that later borrowed by Whittier (from *Paradise Lost* as much as from 1 Samuel) for his attack on Daniel Webster in "Ichabod!": "Alas! how fallen from that station be, / Who, blest with reason, proud in being free, / Can

22. Very's sermons are mostly collected in one large volume at the Houghton Library, Harvard University (MH Ms Am 1405.1); hereafter they are referred to by Very's own sermon numbering system with parenthetical square bracketed page numbers assigned.

23. Reprinted in Bartlett, 182–83.

from his proper sphere a being draw, / Deprive of rights, of liberty, and law"
(lines 15–18). In much the same way, the abolitionist sonnets Very composed
later during the 1840s and 1850s on one level demonstrate his conviction—
indeed, passion—as an abolitionist (Very, *Works*, 441–65); yet because in
them he stresses the necessity of obedience to the will of God, the Miltonic
material he uses is really largely Arminian in feeling. In other words, like his
earlier 1833 poem, Very's abolitionist sonnets are hardly revolutionary;
rather, he consistently takes the heavenly point of view, demonizing those
who, by introducing the original sin of slavery into the New World garden,
would tamper with his idealized vision of ordered liberty. His sonnet "On the
Nebraska Bill" is typical, since it associates the Fall with the passage of that
act of Congress in order to arouse his readers' antinomian sympathies for the
oppressed, but in such a way as to satisfy the Arminian structure of feeling
(and, so, rob his reform views of any more generally subversive force they
might have had):

> An Eden land, an Eden in the west,
> Where once the Indians roamed erect and free,
> Where now their few and weary tribes find rest,—
> Shall it be blasted, cursed by slavery?
> Our plighted faith to the red man was given
> That there should be the asylum of his race;
> Our vow to Afric's sons is writ in heaven,
> And shall we thus fair Freedom's name disgrace?
> Oh, plant not then the poisonous upas there,
> Nor heed the subtle serpent's guileful speech;
> But rather bid all races come and share,
> And Freedom's gospel to the nations teach;
> That unborn millions there may learn its name,
> And the glad tidings through the world proclaim.
>
> (Very, *Works*, 446)

These later contradictory poetic invocations of Milton and the puritan
heritage[24] find a parallel in Very's sermons, which also appealed to both polarities in Yankee culture. Several of them (e.g., Nos. 82 and 96) thus treat
Protestantism's historic resistance to tyranny, and others likewise use that

---

24. One or two other poems celebrating the puritan ancestry of the abolitionist movement can
be found in Very, *Works*, 443–44.

tradition (and Milton's place in it) to address the issue of slavery in particular. A good example of the latter is Sermon No. 60 (on Matthew 13:27,
"From whence then hath it tares?"). First delivered on 8 July 1860, it opens
with a long denunciation of the ways in which slavery has corrupted both
church and state, and declares (in the manner of a jeremiad) that the only
good thing about the South's peculiar institution is that it has brought on a
moment of moral reckoning: a time of potentially radical change when Very's
contemporaries will see that "we live in a new era of the world's history. A
time of Reformation . . . like that in which the modern nations gained Religious freedom by shaking off the priestly rule of Rome." Very then justifies
the loss and destruction that may result by assuring his congregation that in
the end the struggle will cleanse the national soul, much as did the Puritans'
crusades of old: for though "every nation has great *Moral* battles to be fought
within its own boundaries against Ignorance, Slavery, and the horrid practice
of War," the last is sometimes justified if it can eradicate these other "tares"
among the wheat ([pp. 8–9]).

　　Yet as in the case of his abolitionist verse, the more violent implications of
Very's sermon rhetoric are generally blunted by a self-interested moderation
typical of his class. This is the reason why in 1873 in Sermon No. 4 (on Psalm
119:50, "This is my comfort in my affliction, for thy word hath quickened
me") he could look back upon the death of Lincoln and the slaughter of the
Civil War and call for renewed obedience to God and a return to the moderate constitutionalism of the Founding Fathers, rather than for continued
social reform or the political empowerment of blacks.[25] For at the center of
this sermon is no Miltonic sentiment of defiance, no peremptory demand for
change. Instead, its heart is an anecdote in which Very idealizes the late President's love of the Bible and his belief in the War as a moral struggle. As this
implies, Very believed that the Civil War neither had been, nor ought to have
been, the occasion for egalitarian social change. On the contrary, he believed
that in fighting the War Lincoln had actually sought to affirm the claims of
tradition and the divine nature of America's sociopolitical order. His Lincoln
was an Arminian, one who very much regarded the Bible as "the Statesman's
Best Manual" in the sense intended by the phrase's romantic Tory originator,
Samuel Taylor Coleridge. For his Lincoln accepted that "in it, as Milton
sings, 'Is plainest taught, and easiest learnt, / What makes a nation happy,
and keeps it so; / What ruins kingdoms, and lays cities flat!' " ([pp. 5–6]);
and in believing this biblical lesson about the sovereignty of God in the affairs

　　25. Large parts of this sermon reappear in "recycled" form in Sermon No. 73 in the Houghton collection.

of men, he therefore could not help but affirm the original, consensualist ideals of the American Republic.

The true lesson of Very's sermon on Lincoln and civic religion is thus the triumphalist one that "if God's providence, and interposition were manifested in the establishment of our national Independence, nearly a century ago; they will be as surely manifest, to all coming generations, in the events which have so recently taken place." As this implies, "the freedom of the colored race from bondage" the War won was to Very but proof that it was God's will that America reestablish its original covenant with Him by recovering its ideologically moderate heritage—a heritage Very (repeating two old Unitarian clerical complaints) feared was threatened by the party politics and new wealth of the Gilded Age ([p. 7]). In his view, the general behavior of the Grant administration represented the dangerously antinomian character of an era whose disregard for law and Holy Writ contrasted sharply with the martyred Lincoln; and the white man's Reconstruction betrayal of his paternalistic responsibilities toward the ex-slaves showed a similar contempt for constitutional and consensualist tradition.

As this suggests, even when it came to the issues most likely to elicit his antinomian sympathies, Very's temptation to move in that direction was sharply checked by the Arminianism that predominated in the thoughts and feelings of his class. Indeed, the generally conflicted sympathies of his sermons might well be characterized by a Miltonic sonnet he cited in one of them, a poem perhaps less well known (though no less moving) than the famous description in book VII of *Paradise Lost* of Milton's blindness and danger at the time of the Restoration. For in the following fourteen lines the great moderate Puritan had revealed his own deep self-division in words that might well characterize Very's position as a poet-priest of the waning New England dominant class:

Cyriack, this three years' day these eyes, though clear
   To outward view of blemish or of spot,
   Bereft of light their seeing have forgot;
   Nor to their idle orbs doth sight appear
Of sun or moon or star throughout the year,
   Or man or woman. Yet I argue not
   Against Heav'n's hand or will, nor bate a jot
   Of heart or hope, but still bear up and steer
Right onward. What supports me, dost thou ask?
   The conscience, friend, to have lost them overplied

In liberty's defense, my noble task,
Of which all Europe talks from side to side.
This thought might lead me through the world's vain
    masque
Content though blind, had I no better guide.
                                    (Sonnet XXII)[26]

Like others of her generation and background, Sarah Margaret Fuller came
to know Milton and his writings at a young age. As early as May 1824 (when
she was a few days shy of her fourteenth birthday) she wrote to her austere
Unitarian congressman father to ask that he send her her copy of *Paradise
Lost;* and two years later she was reading the poet at length.[27] Fuller continued this engagement with Milton into her twenties and early thirties, at
one point, for instance, borrowing a two-volume edition of his works from
Emerson, and later (like Emerson and Very before her) identifying her own
ambitions with those of the author of the "Letter to Diodati" (Fuller, *Letters,*
I, 277, and II, 199). Yet as Phyllis Cole has rightly suggested, there is not only
less Milton in Fuller than in some of the other Transcendentalists, there is
less and less of him as time goes by. In part (as Cole says) this could be because like some of the other younger members of the movement, she found the
poet to be too egotistical;[28] but a more likely explanation is that after a certain point in her own increasingly radical development, she found the Milton
she had inherited to be too ideologically conflicted to be of use anymore.

As this suggests, Margaret Fuller was as indebted as any upper-class Yankee to the Arminian strain in the New England Milton. This can be seen
(albeit only to a degree) in his appearances in her correspondence during her
Boston and Concord years. Thus typically, on 31 October 1840, she wrote
(probably to William Henry Channing) invoking "the high mysteries that
Milton speaks of" as the stuff of the ideal intellectual life she now lived in
Concord—significantly, in a landscape of meditation that contrasts with the
socialism of Brook Farm (Fuller, *Letters,* II, 178–80); similarly, several
months later, on 24 January 1841, she wrote at length about her poetic am-

26. Quoted in Very, Sermon No. 6 (on James 1:17, "Every Good and every perfect Gift is
from above, and cometh down from the Father of the lights, or worlds; with whom is no vari-
ableness, neither shadow of turning"), [p. 8]; and cited as in the Oxford Milton. (Very's tran-
scription differs markedly in accidentals from this and other modern editions of the sonnet.)
27. *The Letters of Margaret Fuller,* ed. Robert N. Hudspeth (Ithaca, N.Y.: Cornell University
Press, 1983–), I, 139 and 154, respectively; hereafter cited parenthetically in the text as Fuller,
Letters, with volume and page numbers as indicated.
28. See Cole, 141–45.

bitions to Caroline Sturges, confiding that unlike Milton in Sonnet XIX, she could not "*stand* and wait" for the divine inspiration that eluded her and left her in a ruined, apocalyptic state (Fuller, *Letters*, II, 199). But these brief epistolary uses pale by comparison with her employment of the poet to satisfy the demands of the Arminian structure of feeling in her review of Rufus Wilmot Griswold's edition of *The Prose Works of Milton*.[29] For in that 1845 *New-York Daily Tribune* piece (which is her most extensive treatment of Milton), her desire to affirm the claims of hierarchy, conventional morality, and godly rule is manifest. She begins, for example, by first agreeing with Griswold's praise for his subject as " 'the greatest of all human beings: the noblest and the ennobler of mankind,' " and then glossing his sentiment in the following way:

> The absolute of this superlative pleases us, even if we do believe that there are four or five names on the scroll of history which may be placed beside that of Milton. We love hero-worship, where the hero is, indeed, worthy the honors of a demi-god. And, if Milton be not absolutely the greatest of human beings, it is hard to name one who combines so many features of God's own image, ideal grandeur, a life of spotless virtue, heroic endeavour and constancy, with such richness of gifts. (Fuller, *Literature and Art*, I, 36)

Similarly, Fuller was also true to the order-affirming side of her heritage in her description in the review of the effects of Milton upon those who heed his example. This is why she precedes the passage just cited with the assertion that he or she "who chooses that way which the feet of Milton never forsook, will find in him a never failing authority for the indissoluble union between permanent strength and purity"; and it is why she then expresses the wish that "many, born and bred amid the corruptions of a false world till the heart is on the verge of a desolate scepticism and the good genius preparing to fly, be led to recall him and make him at home forever by such

29. S. Margaret Fuller, "The Prose Works of Milton. With a Biographical Introduction, By R. W. Griswold," in *Papers on Literature and Art* (New York: Wiley and Putnam, 1846), I, 35–42; hereafter references to this or to other pieces found in this authorially collected "two part" (i.e., two volume) edition of Fuller's reviews will be cited parenthetically in the text as Fuller, *Literature and Art*, with page numbers as indicated. The Griswold review first appeared in the *New-York Daily Tribune* (7 October 1845), p. 1, cols. 1–2. There are also several other textually significant newspaper and bound printings of it during or just after Fuller's lifetime. (See the relevant entries in *Margaret Fuller: A Descriptive Bibliography*, comp. Joel Myerson [Pittsburgh, Pa.: University of Pittsburgh Press, 1978].)

passages as we have read . . . in the 'Apology for Smectymnuus.' " Her
Arminian side also explains why a bit later she gives two reasons for her belief
that "these Essays of Milton deserve to be sought and studied beyond any
other volumes of English prose." For the first of them—that such a study
will establish a benificent, consensualist, mentorial relationship between the
poet and his reader, to the benefit of the latter's self-culture—shows that like
her Unitarian predecessors and Transcendentalist contemporaries, she regarded Milton as an *exemplum* of the clerical model of literary authority:

> 1st. He draws us to a central point whither converge the rays of sa-
> cred and profane, ancient and modern Literature. Those who sit at
> his feet obtain every hour glimpses in all directions. The constant
> perception of principles, richness in illustrations and fullness of
> knowledge, make him the greatest Master we have in the way of giv-
> ing clues and impulses. His plan tempts even very timid students to
> hope they may thread the mighty maze of the Past. This fullness of
> knowledge only a genius masculine and divine like his could ani-
> mate. . . . [To be sure,] he was fortunate in an epoch fitted to develop
> him to his full stature—an epoch rich alike in thought, action and
> passion, in great results and still greater beginnings. There was fire
> enough to bring the immense materials he had collected into a state of
> fusion. Still his original bias infects the pupil, and this Master makes
> us thirst for Learning no less than for Life.

Fuller's second reason for attending to the poet's prose is also a paradigmatically Arminian one. For she then takes this clericist formation of the New
England dominant-class ideology and, by characterizing Milton's prose as
the organic expression of a perfect consensualist poet (one who effectively
exercised the cultural authority Fuller's class now lacked), connects it to
that idealization of art by which the region's elite had sought to reinforce
its hegemony:

> 2d. He affords the highest exercise at once to the poetic and reflec-
> tive faculties. Before us move sublime presences, the types of whole
> regions of creation: God, man, and elementary spirits in multitudi-
> nous glory are present to our consciousness. But meanwhile every de-
> tail is grasped and examined, and strong daily interests mark out for
> us a wide and plain path on the earth—a wide and plain path, but one
> in which it requires the most varied and strenuous application of our

energies to follow the rapid and vigorous course of our guide. No one can read the Essays without feeling that the glow which follows is no mere nervous exaltation, no result of electricity from another mind under which he could remain passive, but a thorough and wholesome animation of his own powers. We seek to know, to act, and to be what is possible to Man. (Fuller, *Literature and Art*, I, 37–38)

There is another side to Fuller's Milton, however, as both her earlier reference to Milton's "Apology for Smectymnuus" and her repetition (in the first of the above reasons) of the British Whig view that the poet was fortunate in his times indicates. From the start her review manifests a desire to assuage the antinomian structure of feeling every bit as strong as the Arminianism just evidenced. Her praise for Milton as a model of "never failing authority" (which leads to the reference to "Smectymnuus"), for instance, follows close on the heels of a restatement of the two positions that (according to Nelson) defined the Whig tradition: their assertion of the poet's special relevance in a world struggling for liberty and their attack upon Tory Milton criticism both for its conservatism and its expensiveness (Fuller, *Literature and Art*, I, 35–36). More importantly, Fuller's Yankee antinomian heritage also explains why she gives a third reason for holding Milton's prose in such high esteem, one that echoes the libertarian moments in Channing and Macaulay:[30]

3d. Mr. Griswold justly and wisely observes:—"Milton is more emphatically *American* than any author who has lived in the United States." He is so because in him is expressed so much of the primitive vitality of that thought from which America is born, though at present disposed to forswear her lineage in so many ways. He is the purity of Puritanism. He understood the nature of liberty, of justice— what is required for the unimpeded action of conscience—what constitutes true marriage, and the scope of manly education. He is one of the Fathers of this Age, of that new Idea which agitates the sleep of Europe, and of which America, if awake to the design of Heaven and her own duty, would become the principal exponent. But the Father is still far beyond the understanding of his child. (Fuller, *Literature and Art*, I, 38–39)

30. The Channing and Macaulay passages Fuller has in mind here are cited above, pages 96–99 and 70, respectively.

Taken in conjunction with her first two reasons, this well-known passage suggests that Margaret Fuller's vision of the poet in the Griswold review was every bit as self-contradictory as that of her Unitarian ancestors or fellow Transcendentalists. Its beginning and end certainly support this conclusion. For Fuller opens by citing one of a group of poems that had often appeared in Unitarian criticism as a manifestation of New England's polarization of feeling: the Wordsworth Milton sonnet "quoted by Mr. Griswold on his title-page" (" 'Milton! thou shouldst be living at this hour' "); and she closes the review by portraying the blind poet as a musician who played a canticle of praise to the Almighty even as he sided with the mob for freedom's sake: "Though the organist was wrapped in utter darkness, 'only mingled and streaked with an ashy brown,' still the organ pealed forth its perpetual, sublime Te Deum! Shall we, sitting in the open sun-light, dare tune our humble pipes to any other strain? Thou may'st thank Him, Milton, for, but for this misfortune, thou hadst been a benefactor to the great and strong only, but now to the multitude and suffering also thy voice comes, bidding them 'bate no jot of heart or hope,' with archangelic power and melody" (Fuller, Literature and Art, I, 35 and 42).

But perhaps the most striking sign elsewhere in the review of Fuller's almost hereditary confusion of feeling is her avoidance of a radical response to Milton on the question of gender authority (despite the fact that his "Divorce Tract" and treatment of Adam and Eve in Paradise Lost provided her with ample excuse to do so).[31] Indeed, as Phyllis Cole has ably noted,[32] both in this New-York Daily Tribune review and in Woman in the Nineteenth Century Fuller (in a somewhat different way than Channing and Emerson before her) actually defended the poet's views on this subject as representing something like a moderate, meliorist ideal. As the history of the New England Milton suggests, in doing so, she repressed both the patent confliction of his epic and the darker side of his contradictory prose attitude toward women, in order to favor a position more typical of her class. Little wonder perhaps, then, that Milton is absent from her correspondence later, after she had left Boston and America for the wider world of Europe and come to be a full

31. In addition to her own Milton's Eve (Urbana: University of Illinois Press, 1983), Diane Kelsey McColley also lists many other significant recent feminist treatments of Milton's views on gender in her chapter on "Milton and the Sexes" in Dennis Danielson, ed., The Cambridge Companion to Milton (Cambridge, Eng.: Cambridge University Press, 1989), 147–66. A good summary of the ways in which Milton's views on gender relate to his ideological position can be found in Stavely, 34–61, who (37 n. 2) lists many of the main feminist texts as well.
32. Cole, 141–42.

participant in revolution—both political and sexual—herself.[33] For Margaret Fuller, he had necessarily become a figure who reminded her of her older, divided, Bostonian self and, so, of a social role and a set of Yankee contradictions she had left behind, to enlist at Rome against both Pope and King, during what was, for her, the latest skirmish in the never-ending battle for the Good Old Cause.

Other incidental references to John Milton can be found in Fuller's writings, of course. For instance, in one piece on the "Modern British Poets" she ranked him (along with Shakespeare and Spenser) as one of the English pantheon in order to denigrate her transatlantic contemporaries (*Literature and Art*, I, 58). In another, she criticized the verse of Elizabeth Barrett [Browning] for lacking the "plastic power" to be found in Milton and Dante (*Literature and Art*, II, 24); and while praising Philip James Bailey's now forgotten *Festus*, she held that poem to the same standard as *Paradise Lost* and the *Divine Comedy* (rating Milton's epic superior both for its "splendor and power" and for its Satan).[34] Only once, however, in her posthumous—and textually, highly suspect—*Memoirs*, does she use the poet in a significant way; and then, it is to acknowledge Emerson's influence upon her in an ideologically self-contradictory manner.[35]

This last instance does provide a clue to Milton's reception by the rest of the Transcendentalists. For the appearances of the poet and his writings in their works reflect both their precarious sociocultural situation and their contradictory ideological response to that position. The *Dial* (1841–44),[36] for

---

33. The one or two references to Milton in Fuller's correspondence while in Europe (e.g., *Letters*, IV, 282) are inconsequential and personal. Remarkably, he is virtually absent from her writings during her time in Rome itself (e.g., her dispatches back to the *New-York Daily Tribune*); for discussions of that period of political revolution and sexual awakening, see (among many other treatments) Joseph Jay Deiss, *The Roman Years of Margaret Fuller* (New York: Crowell, 1969), and Paula Blanchard, *Margaret Fuller: From Transcendentalism to Revolution* (New York: Delacorte, 1978), esp. 245–330.

34. This reference to the *Festus* review is taken from the posthumous collection, *Life Without and Life Within; or, Reviews, Narratives, Essays, and Poems*, put together by her brother, Arthur B. Fuller (Boston: Brown, Taggard, and Chase, 1860), 154.

35. *Memoirs of Margaret Fuller Ossoli*, ed. James Freeman Clark, et al. (Boston: Phillips, Sampson, and Co., 1852), I, 194–95.

36. Quotations from pieces in the *Dial* are taken from a copy in the Houghton Library, Harvard University, with volume and page numbers as indicated hereafter parenthetically in the text. In ascribing authorship, as in other matters concerning this journal and those who wrote for it, I have used Joel Myerson's definitive *The American Transcendentalists and the "Dial": A History of the Magazine and Its Contributors* (Rutherford, N.J.: Farleigh Dickinson University Press, 1980).

instance, contains several pieces that treat Milton the same way Unitarian periodicals had done a decade or two earlier. One of these, Frederic Henry Hedge's "The Art of Life,—The Scholar's Calling," is by a well-born, Harvard-educated preacher who in fact straddled the two movements.[37] Not surprisingly, therefore, his use of "Lycidas" to decry "the want of courage, the want of faith" in contemporary "Church and State" (their essential "hollowness" as institutions), is hardly radical in tone; on the contrary, by employing Milton's pastoral elegy to attack "the shallowness of teachers" in nineteenth-century New England (the fact that "no man teaches with authority" anymore) he shows that his real aim was to mourn the ineffectiveness of consensualism in transforming the region (something confirmed by the fact that just after the "Lycidas" quotation, he once again cited Milton, this time in order to call for a deeper culture that would prepare America for its own Miltons and Shakespeares; for Hedge makes it clear that he hoped that such men of genius would outdo him and his dominant-class contemporaries and accomplish reforms of a specifically moderate sort [*Dial*, I, 181–82]).

Milton's other appearances in the first volume of the *Dial* also largely tend to underscore these long-standing contradictions. William Ellery Channing the Elder's wealthy, well-connected nephew, William Henry Channing, for instance, opened his multipart novel, "Ernest the Seeker," by quoting a portion of Milton's famous description in the *Areopagitica* of Isis searching for the mangled body of Osiris (*Dial*, I, 48). In its original form this passage reads as follows:

> Truth indeed came once into the world with her divine Master, and was a perfect shape most glorious to look on: but when he ascended, and his Apostles after him were laid asleep, then strait arose a wicked race of deceivers, who as that story goes of the *Ægyptian Typhon* with his conspirators, how they dealt with the good *Osiris*, took the virgin Truth, hewd her lovely form into a thousand peeces, and scatter'd them to the four winds. From that time ever since, the sad friends of

37. Frederic Henry Hedge was the son of one Harvard professor and accompanied another (future) member of its faculty (George Bancroft) on his famous 1818 trip to Germany. He graduated from both the College and the Divinity School and later served as minister to the Unitarian society in Bangor, Maine (see ibid., 156–62). Hutchison writes of him that "as a mediator between Transcendentalism and the traditional faith [i.e., Unitarianism], Hedge occupied a position which to extremists on either side seemed highly illogical. In later years, reminiscing about the Transcendental Club, he explained that, 'though I hugely enjoyed the sessions, and shared many of the ideas which ruled the conclave, and the ferment they engendered, I had no belief in ecclesiastical revolutions. . . . My historical conscience, then as since, balanced my neology, and kept me ecclesiastically conservative, though intellectually radical' " (139–40).

Truth, such as durst appear, imitating the careful search that *Isis* made for the mangl'd body of *Osiris*, went up and down gathering up limb by limb still as they could find them. We have not yet found them all, Lords and Commons, nor ever shall doe, till her Masters second comming; he shall bring together every joynt and member, and shall mould them into an immortall feature of lovelines and perfection. Suffer not these licencing prohibitions to stand at every place of opportunity forbidding and disturbing them that continue seeking, that continue to do our obsequies to the torn body of our martyr'd Saint.[38]

Yet whereas Milton obviously meant this as an antinomian warning against any attempt by church or state to define or legislate truth, in the *Dial* Channing uses it instead as prologue to a work that fictionalizes his deep (albeit ambivalent) attraction to the Church of Rome and its absolutist claims. (An attraction he shared with many in the Victorian American dominant class because the Church's ultramontanism seemed as much the solution to, as the source of, the bourgeois division of feeling from which they suffered—thus simultaneously drawing and repelling them, religiously, politically, and aesthetically).[39]

Milton's antinomian strain is transformed in later numbers of the first volume of the *Dial* as well. A peripheral, liberal Unitarian member of the Emerson circle, the Reverend T. T. Stone, for example, invoked Milton, the defender of the true Protestant faith, against prelatical tyranny and clerical hypocrisy in "Man in the Ages" (*Dial*, I, 281). Taken as a whole, this article is no radical manifesto, however; rather, it is a minor but clear instance of the bourgeois crisis of legitimation and its cultural effects. In much the same way (though perhaps more surprisingly, given his origins in rural poverty and

38. Cited from Kelley, *Complete Prose Works of John Milton*, II, 549–50. Something of William Henry Channing's social position and the interlocking nature of the elite to which he belonged can be gleaned from Myerson's comment in *Transcendentalists and the "Dial"* that when he "was born . . . it was understood that great things were expected from a child whose family ties were to the Danas, Allstons, Cabots, and Lowells; whose father was a member of the Anthology Club; and whose uncle, the Reverend William Ellery Channing, was quickly becoming the most famous preacher of the day. These external influences on his life became stronger when, only five months after his birth, his father died. In the years that followed, the family was guided by the Reverend [Mr.] Channing, who looked upon William as his favorite nephew. Young Channing went to the Boston Latin School in preparation for Harvard, which he entered in 1825 with Oliver Wendell Holmes" (115).

39. Although there are a number of fine studies of nineteenth-century American responses to Roman Catholicism, the one that places them within the broadest cultural context is William L. Vance's magisterial two-volume *America's Rome* (New Haven, Conn.: Yale University Press, 1989).

reputation for political and ecclesiastical radicalism), like W. H. Channing, Theodore Parker also used *Areopagitica*'s retelling of the myth of Isis and Osiris in a moderate rather than an antinomian way to argue irenically for the equal truth and falsehood of all philosophies ("German Literature," *Dial*, I, 326 and 330).

Later volumes of the magazine also show the same pattern. To be sure, there is always praise for Milton of an undefined sort. Bronson Alcott, for instance, lauded both Milton's verse in general and *Comus* in particular (in "Days from a Diary," *Dial*, II, 411); Margaret Fuller included him on a list of great artists who exemplify the triumph of genius over adversity ("Lives of the Great Composers, Haydn, Mozart, Handel, Bach, Beethoven," *Dial*, II, 149); and (the Harvard-trained clergyman and publisher) James Freeman Clarke discussed and extensively excerpted George Keats's edition of his brother John's comments on Milton ("George Keats" and "Remarks on John Milton, by John Keats, Written in the Fly-Leaf of *Paradise Lost*," *Dial*, III, 495–504). Yet alongside these, there is the poem "The Blind Seer" (*Dial*, II, 47–48), by Christopher Cranch (who, though originally from Alexandria, Virginia, was the son of a judge and compatriot of John Quincy Adams, a friend of Parker's at the Harvard Divinity School, and in every other way, an adopted Bostonian). The Milton surrogate of Cranch's title is at once both paradigmatically Arminian and antinomian, since (in a stanza that paraphrases *Paradise Lost*) "He travelleth where the upper springs flow on; / He heareth harmonies from angel choirs; / He seeth Uriel standing in the Sun; / He dwelleth up among the heavenly fires" (lines 13–16); yet (in the next quatrain) he has an equal love for the "common life" of ordinary folk in this world as well (lines 17–20). Similarly, Theodore Parker's much better known memorial notice of "The Life and Character of Dr. [Charles] Follen" (*Dial*, III, 343–62) also shows the same division of paradigmatic allegiance. For Parker characterized his subject at length as one of the great friends of liberty; yet his portrait of his fallen colleague is also in many ways just a restatement of the old Unitarian ideal of the literary cleric. This is, for instance, why, despite Follen's devotion to reform, he says that Milton was an exemplar of "MORAL power" and "*moral* ACTION" (idealizing and order-affirming qualities, which—in the manner of the *De Doctrina* review—Parker opposes to mere practical genius [345]). Similarly, it is also why throughout the piece he explicitly presents his subject as an exemplar of that ministerial exercise of cultural authority which for so long had been a desideratum both of New England's literary men of God and of the secular clerisy that succeeded them.

As this suggests, even if it was not a wholly conscious one, one of Parker's major motives in memorializing Follen was to write a piece about a well-known, reform-minded cleric that steered a middle way between the two polarities in the New England tradition. This was a time-honored course for a man of Parker's profession and education, whatever his specific religious or political beliefs; and as had often been the case in the previous two generations, it was a strategy that summoned forth John Milton. For it was surely not the physical similarity of their deaths alone—Follen had perished in a shipwreck in 1840—which suggested to Parker that he bring his obituary to a climax by applying Milton's apotheosis of Edward King ("Lycidas," lines 165–81) to the German immigrant pastor. Rather, it was also because this famous passage affirmed alike the saving power of Milton's patriarchal God and the cultural authority of poet-priests who serve him (whether through sermons or belles lettres); and so, Parker could use it to balance Follen's love of liberty and passion for reform with lines that are as Arminian in tone as they are complimentary to the deceased:

> Weep no more, woful shepherd, weep no more,
> For Lycidas, your sorrow is not dead,
> Sunk though he be beneath the watery floor:
> So sinks the day-star in the ocean's bed,
> And yet anon repairs his drooping head,
> And tricks his beams, and with new spangled ore
> Flames in the forehead of the morning sky.
> So Lycidas sunk low but mounted high,
> Through the dear might of him that walked the waves,
> Where other groves and other streams along,—
> With nectar pure his oozy locks he laves,
> He hears the unexpressive nuptial song.
> In the blest kingdoms meek of joy and love,
> There entertain him all the saints above
> In solemn troops and sweet societies,
> That sing and singing in their gay muse,
> And wipe the tears for ever from his eyes.
>
> (*Dial*, III, 362)[40]

---

40. These lines from "Lycidas" are cited as they appear in the *Dial*. Those familiar with the poem will note several interesting textual variants in comparison with modern editions.

Other examples of the persistence of the New England Milton among the Transcendentalists exist outside the pages of the *Dial* as well. For instance (once again, despite his social origins and openness to the opposing structure of feeling), Theodore Parker elsewhere also often betrayed an amazingly Arminian streak.[41] In these cases too, John Milton seems to have once more acted as a lightning rod for what were essentially conflicted cultural allegiances. The two *Dial* pieces just discussed, for instance, were later gathered into a collection entitled *The American Scholar*.[42] That book's first chapter (also called "The American Scholar") characterizes *Paradise Lost* and *Paradise Regained* (along with *Hamlet*) as being among the greatest works ever written (24) and describes Milton (along with Shakespeare, Homer, and Dante) as one of history's greatest poets. In doing so, however, it also reveals Parker's own partial—though surprising—allegiance to the "Unitarian-Whig orthodoxy" of his adopted city: first, because he gives vent to a typically Unitarian clerical disdain for the commercial instinct in American culture (24); and second, because he also holds Milton up as an example of the cultural authority of Europe (a hierarchical authority that he—like many another educated Bostonian—believed now lay within the grasp of America's writers). Similarly, Parker further idealized the poet in the next chapter (on Emerson)[43] and opened chapter 3 (on the recently deceased William Ellery Channing) with a classically Arminian account of the clerical calling (127–34). The Channing chapter is, moreover, in general, particularly illustrative of Parker's culturally conservative side, because while it gives full expression both to the radical element in his thought and his sense of the ministry's declining authority (134), it also conveys his strong belief in the clergy's indirect, consensualist mission of affirming self-culture through personal example, moral suasion, preaching, and belles lettres. Indeed, Parker presents Channing as the prime example of the success such a liberal ministry could still have in garnering central cultural influence—a claim of vocational effectiveness he illustrates by adducing his subject's three great review essays on Milton, Fénelon, and Napoleon (153–54).

Along with this standard consensualist material, however, there is an antinomianism in Parker's Channing chapter that is more in keeping with the

41. A good summary of Parker's life and thought can be found in Hutchison, 98–136.
42. Theodore Parker, *The American Scholar*, ed. George Willis Cooke, *The Centenary Edition of the Works of Theodore Parker* (Boston: American Unitarian Association, 1907–16). Pieces from this and other volumes in this nonconsecutively numbered edition are hereafter cited by individual article and volume title, with parenthetical page numbers as indicated.
43. Good examples of such praise for Milton in the "Ralph Waldo Emerson" chapter of ibid. can be found on 101–2 and 106.

general outlook of the author of "The Permanent and the Transient in Christianity." Any number of examples of it exist, but perhaps the most significant concerns Channing's response to the question of slavery. For though Parker approved of the fact that Channing had in general offended their mutual ("Tory") enemies by his commitment to reform (144–46), he also thought that his predecessor was at times not radical enough. In particular, he felt that his mentor had been mistaken in attacking the abolitionists as extremists. Yet it is typical of the ideological contradictions they shared that in this case Parker attacked Channing for adhering to the very same model of clerical authority that he himself had endorsed at the start of the chapter. Moreover, in order to prove that the older man had been derelict in his ministerial duty, he used Channing's own defense of Milton against the charges of asperity and extremism in the *De Doctrina* review as evidence against him (157–59)—a passage that, as has been shown, is itself polarized.

This self-contradicting expression of antinomian impatience with Channing's Brahmin moderation, furthermore, then sets the stage for the final few pages of the chapter, which—in sharp contrast to its opening—adhere exclusively to neither of the structures of feeling in New England culture. Rather, in the end the contradictions of both the Unitarian understanding of clerical authority and the ideology that spawned it seem to have been too much for Parker; and so, he veered in a highly polarized way from passages that use patriarchal language to confer the a priori authority of an Old Testament prophet or a seventeenth-century divine upon Channing, to pages that invoke the radical Protestant tradition of resistance to tyranny, in order both to characterize the great Unitarian and to ask for more reformers like him. As this suggests, though at one point in these final pages Parker did right himself and come close to giving his readers an ideologically coherent William Ellery Channing (one who is an Arminian clerical authority figure par excellence: a liberal preacher with an influence exceeding even that of Whig politicians like Daniel Webster), along the way—like many another Unitarian and Transcendentalist—he too foundered upon the shoals of the competing complexes of feeling in New England culture (164–71).

Other examples along these lines could be cited from Parker's works (particularly of Milton's elicitation of his antinomian sympathies)[44]—as could a body of examples from the writings of the female members of the

---

44. Two examples in the *Centenary Edition* of Parker's use of Milton in the context of his antinomianism are a passage in the "Macaulay's History of England" chapter of ibid. (325) and one in the "Ecclesiastical Institutions and Religious Consciousness" chapter of *The World of Matter and the Spirit of Man: Latest Discourses of Religion,* also ed. George Willis Cooke (69).

Transcendentalist group, instances (as the companion volume to this study will show) that reinforce and expand the above discussion of Milton and Margaret Fuller. However, the most extensive body of Miltonic material to be found among the Transcendentalists (save that of Emerson) belongs to the one member of the movement who outdid its founder in trying to resolve the polarization of their culture. For by following Emerson's lead and using the poet as the occasion for the creation of a "visionary compact,"[45] Henry David Thoreau also attained the unity of feeling that his mentor had achieved in "Uriel," thereby successfully ameliorating the effects of the persistent contradictions in New England's Puritan legacy.

---

45. I take this phrase from the title of Donald E. Pease, *Visionary Compacts: American Renaissance Writings in Cultural Context* (Madison: University of Wisconsin Press, 1987).

5

PISGAH AND KTAADN

Like his contemporary Theodore Parker, Henry David Thoreau was not born into the Boston elite. The son of a petit bourgeois family of Huguenot descent that had only arrived in New England in the middle of the eighteenth century, he was accustomed to neither great wealth nor high status. Yet partly on account of his relatives' (admittedly complicated) religious affiliations, and partly on account of his education, by the time he graduated from Harvard in 1837 he had been thoroughly introduced to the ethos of Unitarian Boston. As one might expect, he therefore came to know the New England Milton as well.[1]

Milton's prestige among Thoreau's Unitarian teachers thus at least partly explains why as early as his senior year he was reading a wide assortment of books by or about the poet in the Harvard College Library. Not even

1. Articles on the history of the Thoreau family are listed by Walter Harding and Michael Meyer, *The New Thoreau Handbook* (New York: New York University Press, 1980), 25–26. Harding and Meyer also list some useful treatments of Thoreau's religious upbringing and secular education before he entered Harvard (26). The most detailed study of Thoreau's undergraduate experience is Christian P. Gruber, "The Education of Henry Thoreau, Harvard 1833–1837," Ph.D. diss., Princeton University, 1953; see also Kenneth W. Cameron's *Thoreau's Harvard Years* (Hartford, Conn.: Transcendental Books, 1966) and *Emerson the Essayist* (Raleigh, N.C.: Thistle Press, 1945), II, 191–208, which reprint his class reading lists. The general intellectual life of antebellum Harvard is the subject of Howe's *The Unitarian Conscience* and Samuel Eliot Morison's *Three Centuries of Harvard: 1636–1936* (Cambridge, Mass.: Harvard University Press, 1936), 192–272. The impact of this largely conservative, Unitarian ethos on Thoreau is discussed by Sherman Paul, *The Shores of America: Thoreau's Inward Exploration* (Urbana: University of Illinois Press, 1958), 1–89; Robert D. Richardson, Jr., *Henry David Thoreau: A Life of the Mind* (Berkeley: University of California Press, 1986), 5–42; and Robert Sattelmeyer, *Thoreau's Reading: A Study in Intellectual History* (Princeton, N.J.: Princeton University Press, 1988), 3–24, who consider his pre-Harvard education as well.

counting the selections from Milton in Chalmers's anthology of English poetry,[2] this includes: Todd's edition; an unidentified collection from which Thoreau derived his "Notes on Milton"; the biographical volume in Symmons's edition; Toland's life of the poet and edition of his prose; Buck's 1753 biography and collected verse; and Johnson's *Life*.[3] Moreover, the poet's place in the Harvard curriculum probably also helps explain his further reading after graduation. For example, in addition to using the Milton material in Emerson's library, Thoreau himself owned the 1826 Boston edition of Milton's prose; a three-volume reprint of Mitford's life and edition of the poetry; and the 1808 Philadelphia edition of *Paradise Lost* (books that along with Todd and Chalmers he kept and referred to for the rest of his life).[4]

Despite this, however, unlike Emerson or Jones Very, as an undergraduate Thoreau also recoiled to a degree against the Milton of his Unitarian tutors. His two senior essays on "The Speeches of Moloch & the Rest" in *Paradise Lost* and " 'L'Allegro' & 'Il Penseroso,' "[5] for instance, both deliberately concentrated on the technical and aesthetic qualities of Milton's poetry to the neglect of the ideological issues more customary in New England at the time. " 'L'Allegro' & 'Il Penseroso' " ends by replacing the portrait of Milton drawn by the previous two generations (that of a morally earnest youth who grew into the stern puritan defender of liberty) with one of a poet who loved this sweet life and wrote verse for the sheer pleasure of it. "These poems are to be valued," Thoreau argues, "if for no other reason, on account of the as-

2. Alexander Chalmers, ed., *The Works of the English Poets, from Chaucer to Cowper,* 21 vols. (London: J. Johnson, etc., 1810), was a revision of Samuel Johnson's famous edition, to which had been prefaced his *Lives of the English Poets.* It was a standard reference work for Thoreau throughout his life; see Sattelmeyer, *Thoreau's Reading,* 149.

3. Thoreau's Harvard library charges are reproduced by Kenneth W. Cameron in *Emerson the Essayist* (see above, n. 1). Except for Toland, full biographical and bibliographical data for each title can be found in Sattelmeyer, *Thoreau's Reading,* 212 and 238.

4. The 1808 *Paradise Lost* and 1826 Boston edition of the prose are listed by Sattelmeyer, *Thoreau's Reading,* 237–38. For what is likely Mitford, see Walter Harding, "A New Checklist of the Books in Henry David Thoreau's Library," in *Studies in the American Renaissance: 1983,* ed. Joel A. Myerson (Charlottesville: University Press of Virginia, 1983), 173–74.

5. Cited from Henry David Thoreau, *Early Essays and Miscellanies,* ed. Joseph J. Moldenhauer, et al. (Princeton, N.J.: Princeton University Press, 1975), 79–83 and 73–78 respectively. Hereafter these and other works collected in this volume are cited parenthetically in the text as *Early Essays,* PE, with page numbers as indicated. Other volumes from the unnumbered Princeton Edition (PE) of *The Writings of Henry D. Thoreau* are similarly cited by short title and page number. These include *Walden,* ed. J. Lyndon Shanley (1971); *The Maine Woods,* ed. Joseph J. Moldenhauer (1972); *Reform Papers,* ed. Wendell Glick (1973); *A Week on the Concord and Merrimack Rivers,* ed. Carl Hovde, et al. (1980); *Translations,* ed. K. P. Van Anglen (1986); *Cape Cod,* ed. Joseph J. Moldenhauer (1988); and the three volumes published to date of the *Journal,* gen. ed., John C. Broderick or Robert Sattelmeyer (1981–).

sistance they afford us in forming our estimate of the *man* Milton. They place him in an entirely new, and extremely pleasing, light to the reader who was previously familiar with him as the author of the Paradise Lost alone," one in which "the immortal Milton seems for a space to have put on mortality, to have snatched a moment from the weightier cares of heaven and hell, to wander for awhile among the sons of men" rather than side with the patriarchal God or the rebellious Fiend. As such, "the tenor of these verses is in keeping with the poet's early life"—not the ideal life he pledged to live in the "Letter to Diodati" but the life he actually did live, in which "he was, as he confesses, a reader of romances, an occasional frequenter of the playhouse, and not at all averse to spending a cheerful evening, now and then, with some kindred spirits about town." Happily, therefore, "we see nothing here of the Puritan"; and so, in reading his early lyrics

> the student of Milton will ever turn with satisfaction from contemplating the stern and consistent non-conformist, and bold defender of civil and religious liberty, engaged, but not involved, in a tedious and virulent controversy,
>
> With darkness and with dangers compassed round,
>
> his dearest hopes disappointed, and himself shut out from the cheering light of day, to these fruits of his earlier and brighter years; though of the earth, yet the flights of one who was contemplating to soar "Above the Aonian mount", a heavenward and unattempted course. (*Early Essays*, PE, 77–78)

Of course, as Thoreau goes on to write in his concluding paragraph, his ostensible aim in this piece was to attack "that contemptible kind of criticism which can deliberately, and in cold blood, dissect the sublimest passage, and take pleasure in the detection of slight verbal incongruities" (the criticism of those late seventeenth- and early eighteenth-century 'improvers' of Milton who, by making *Paradise Lost* a 'correct' poem, would commit "sacrilege" and "profane" the poet's very grave [*Early Essays*, PE, 78]).[6] Yet (as the passage just quoted suggests) because this essay advanced a less ideologically engaged view of the poet as well, Thoreau was here actually also implicitly attacking the Milton he had received from his elders in the hope of escaping the contradictions that for so long had entrapped his fellow Yankees.

---

6. The Restoration and early eighteenth-century Milton critics Thoreau has in mind here are discussed by both Ricks and Griffin.

A similar motive would also appear to be behind the essay he wrote a few weeks later during January 1837 on the theme "Point out particulars in the speeches of Moloch & the rest, P.L. II, which appear to you characteristic" (*Early Essays*, PE, 79). For while admitting that by his superior rhetorical skill Milton's Satan in book II "proves himself the master spirit of the host," Thoreau robs the fallen angel of all the conventional New England associations of that sobriquet (here, almost surely taken from the *De Doctrina* review). Thus, while he believed that Satan's oratory upon the fiery lake manifested an "ambition aided by matchless cunning," a "superior subtlety," and a "spirit of revenge" that "retires before self-interest, and gives place . . . to ambition," he regarded these traits as the occasion for neither Arminian moral condemnation nor antinomian praise. Rather, he treated Milton's demon throughout as just a character in a poem, whose only significance is that he gives evidence of his creator's literary skill. The same is true of his treatment of the other speakers in the infernal conclave. For instance, although Thoreau rightly notes that Milton contrasted "the exasperated Moloch" with Satan, the former is in his view neither morally offensive nor subversively heroic; rather, for him Moloch is a morally neutral agent—an epic hero of the classical sort whose "self interest is swallowed up in [the heroically acceptable motive of] revenge." While his desire "to scale the walls of Heaven, and oppose 'infernal thunder' to the Almighty's engines" does therefore have something of romantic adventure about it (*Early Essays*, PE, 80), in the main (like Thoreau's later portraits of Belial, Mammon, and Beelzebub), it makes him an effectively drawn character rather than a clear embodiment of either of the structures of feeling in New England culture.

Other references to Milton and his works during Thoreau's undergraduate years also distance his view of the poet from that of his mentors—albeit in different ways. Earlier during his senior year (on 1 October 1836) he had, for example, submitted a theme reviewing part I of Henry Nelson Coleridge's *Introductions to The Study of the Greek Classic Poets*. Significantly, in what was one of Thoreau's first breaks from the Scottish philosophy then prevalent at Harvard, this essay opens by quoting Coleridge on one of the key distinctions made by his more famous uncle in the *Biographia Literaria:* that between the Fancy (in which " 'objects of nature or art are presented *as they are; they are* neither modified nor associated; they are, in fact, so many pretty shows passed through a magic lantern, without any connection with the being and feelings of the Speaker or the Poet impressed upon them; we look *at* them, but cannot for a moment feel *for*, or *with* them' ") and the Imagination (in which " 'the images are transfigured; their colors and shapes are modified;

one master passion pervades and quickens them; and in them all it is the wild and heart-striken Father-king that speaks alone' ''). Yet as Thoreau goes on to indicate, his purpose in quoting the younger Coleridge involved more than a desire to set up the familiar idealist polarity in which Fancy is the faculty that '' 'collects materials from the visible world, and arranges them for exhibition' '' (thereby imparting '' 'to them no touch of human interest' ''), while Imagination—in contrast to such low empiricism—'' 'takes and moulds the objects of nature at the same moment; it makes them all speak the language of man, and renders them instinct with the inspired breath of human passion' '' (*Early Essays*, PE, 50–51). Rather, Thoreau introduced this polarity only in order to collapse it into a synthesis of the sort Emerson had achieved in "Uriel."

He does this when, like his English source, he applies these two levels of mental operation to literary and cultural history. At first, he seems to find only that the Greek and Italian "appetite for visible images" (which is of the Fancy) contrasts sharply with the more noumenal sublimity of Northern European poetry. But as the following paragraph demonstrates, Thoreau also used this contrast, between the poetry of Dante (which is Southern and empiricist in tenor) and that of Milton (which is Northern and idealist in tendency), to create a rhetoric that would satisfy both of the structures of feeling in his culture. By presenting, but then negating, Coleridge's North-South antinomy—by arguing that the Mediterranean and the Northern spirits are essentially alike despite appearances to the contrary—he claims that in very different ways they are both simultaneously idealizing and tactile, both in touch with, and deferential to, the Father-God, yet wild and free.

Thus, the Southern spirit is satyrlike in its sensuality and freedom from constraint; yet its tendency to fill nature with Satyrs and Naiads shows that it balances this antiauthoritarianism with a natural respect for the divine, which it feels as an immanent presence:

One of the peculiar features of the poetry of the Greeks and Romans may be traced to the influences of a national Mythology, differing materially from that system of Polytheism which obtained among the more Northern tribes. The former inhabiting a luxurious clime, breathing a balmy and fragrant air, accustomed to the wildest profusion and riotous abundance, passing their time, mostly, in the open air, now stretched at length by the mossy fount and lulled asleep by its murmurings, now whiling away the hour in amorous lays that find an echo in the neighboring grove, the creatures of Imagination, saw in the spring which slaked their thirst some gentle nymph or Naiad. A Pan or Satyr had a hand in every sound that broke upon the stillness of the glade. Wanting a visible type, a sensible figure to which to direct his prayers and before which to offer up the firstlings of the flock or the first fruits of the harvest, the Southern hind had recourse to symbolical images. This tendency to what has been called Anthropomorphism, this appetite for visible images is a peculiar feature in the character of the Southerns at the present day, as the violent opposition to the famous Iconoclasts can testify.

Similarly, in describing the culture and poetry of the antique North, Thoreau gave them a Gothic sublimity whose mystic idealism and sense of the vertical distance between God and humanity was nonetheless palpably connected to the Anglo-Saxon spirit of liberty and its proto-Protestant hatred of forms and institutions:

> In the nations of Scandinavian or Teutonic descent a different tendency may be noticed. The scenery that surrounded them was stern and rugged, the face of nature presented little that was attractive, little to charm the eye; the towering peak, the awful sublimity of a Northern tempest, their dark and craggy dells, their boundless and almost impenetrable forests, cast a shade of awe and mystery over the beholder. Their conceptions were as subtle and unapproachable as their own mountain mists, every retired glen, every beetling crag, every dark unfathomable abyss, had its peculiar spirit; the open air was the temple of their divinity, no human structure, no tangible symbol, was compatible with their mystical conceptions of an over-ruling power. It is this neglect of the material, this fondness for the dark and mysterious, this propensity to the spiritual, that marks every page of Milton and his kindred spirits. We *see* with Dante but we *feel* with Milton. (*Early Essays*, PE, 51–52)

As this suggests, even at the age of nineteen, Thoreau was ambitiously attempting to do what most of his predecessors had never successfully done: to find a language of social accommodation that could bridge the polarities in his divided culture, thereby restoring the justification for dominant-class authority. Moreover, as the language of this paragraph also suggests, to a surprising degree he here succeeded in achieving that synthesis; for his is a subtle blend of freedom-affirming yet God-fearing rhetoric that sets him apart both from his Unitarian teachers and (with the exception of Emerson) his later Transcendentalist compatriots too. Similarly, because like them, Thoreau—albeit here only briefly—associated the polarities he dealt with with the person and writings of John Milton, his piece on Coleridge's *Greek Classic Poets* sets a precedent for the later appearances of the author in his works. For despite his desire to turn away at times from the cultural conflictions the New England Milton brought to the surface, from the start he was deeply influenced by both the received view of the poet in his region and the dominant-class need to address the crisis of authority that largely shaped it.

In an April 1836 junior-year theme on the "Advantages and disadvantages of foreign influence on American Literature," for example, he not only expressed typically Unitarian elitist-clericist disdain for the capitalism upon which bourgeois Boston's hegemony was founded (complaining that "we are a nation of speculators, stock-holders, and money-changers," not poets); he showed himself caught in the same transatlantic contradictions as Emerson in *English Traits:* on the one hand seeking to satisfy the Arminian structure of feeling by abasing himself before the cultural authority of the mother country (including that of "Milton and Shakspeare, Cowper and Johnson"); yet on the other, also wishing in good antinomian fashion to subvert that dominance (until, like "the Carthaginians," Americans come to the point where "Rome herself" will tremble "at their progress" [*Early Essays*, PE, 39–40]). Similarly, the influence of the preceding generation also explains why his youthful views on *Paradise Lost*'s sublimity were at times so unoriginally Burkean (*Early Essays*, PE, 94); and it is why even in the essay on Henry Nelson Coleridge, his powerfully synthetic characterization of Southern and Northern poetry is focused upon antiquity rather than the present. For like Emerson later on in *Representative Men*, even in 1836 Thoreau needed to investigate the origins of his culture's predicament; and like his future patron, he concluded that there had been a declination in poetic power since the Renaissance—a fall from unity of feeling at the time of Milton that for him, as for his mentor, had led to the very dilemma now facing Unitarian Boston.

Thoreau's first extended attempt to use Milton and his writings to investigate this decline into modernity came in *A Week on the Concord and Merrimack Rivers*. In that 1849 volume he followed Emerson's example in "Uriel" and took *Paradise Lost* as his creative model: first, in order to give vent to the competing structures of feeling in the New England tradition; and second, to bridge them by creating an appropriate rhetoric of paradigmatic accommodation. His means of accomplishing these goals was to turn to the romantic reinterpretation of the Fall of Man and to use it to reenvision his

journey "up country" in terms of the myth of "the American Adam."[7] That
myth (itself a nationalistic Yankee adaptation of the European Enlightenment's attempt to translate providential history and Judeo-Christian soteriology into secular terms)[8] is hardly the innocently democratic, optimistic rewriting of Genesis and *Paradise Lost* it was once thought to be. Rather, it was
one of several literary formations by which antebellum dominant-class male
authors attempted to preserve their diminishing authority;[9] as such, it was
necessarily implicated as well in the contradictions that underlie the New
England Milton.

   Henry Thoreau's account of his trip with his brother, John, to the headwaters of the Merrimack River is, as this suggests, basically an extended assertion that paradise can be regained. It is a travel narrative that maintains
that the American wilderness is the new Eden, the spot of time where humanity can be reborn into innocence. Yet as is commonly the case with such
romantic Adamic tales, Thoreau's American innocence here has been gained
through experience (specifically, the proleptic experience of John's death);
and so, it is a higher innocence than either that which humanity first lost in
the Garden or that which each individual typically loses during adolescence.
A Week proclaims instead that Americans are not hopelessly fallen, not pri-
mordially cursed like their Old World cousins to live with the mortality,
guilt, self-consciousness, history, civilization, and death that in romantic
readings of Genesis replaced Original Sin. It insists that they need not be
swept along by (what Thoreau calls) the "fall" or "lapse" of experience, the
downward current of the stream of life and history. Like the Thoreaus,
Americans can instead row upstream toward a pastoral realm in which they
are again united with nature—toward a New World Garden that, by engen-
dering an artistic wisdom to see aright, will then enable them to benefit the
human community upon returning home once more.

7. The two classic accounts of this "myth" are R.W.B. Lewis, *The American Adam: Innocence, Tragedy, and Tradition in the Nineteenth Century* (Chicago: University of Chicago Press,
1955), and F. O. Matthiessen, *American Renaissance: Art and Expression in the Age of Emerson
and Whitman* (New York: Oxford University Press, 1941), esp. 100–104 and 306–12.
8. The best introduction to this refiguration of sacred text and sacred history in late
eighteenth- and early nineteenth-century Europe remains M. H. Abrams, *Natural Supernaturalism: Tradition and Revolution in Romantic Literature* (New York: W. W. Norton, 1971).
9. Two useful recent critiques of the "myth and symbol school" that produced studies of "the
American Adam" in the immediate post-World War II era are Myra Jehlen's "Introduction:
Beyond Transcendence," to *Ideology and Classic American Literature*, ed. Sacvan Bercovitch and
Myra Jehlen (Cambridge, Eng.: Cambridge University Press, 1986), 1–18, and (from a feminist
perspective) Annette Kolodny, *The Lay of the Land: Metaphor as Experience and History in American Life and Letters* (Chapel Hill: University of North Carolina Press, 1975).

At its most resonant, therefore, *A Week on the Concord and Merrimack Rivers* is a "voyage uniting Concord with Concord by these meandering rivers" (*A Week*, PE, 303). It is a trip that metaphorically draws a circle of peace by taking the brothers back to the Garden of their origins (where, having sojourned through history and space and time, they will get behind the dead weight of all three). This is why at the beginning of their venture, "on the banks of the Concord," Thoreau announces (in a reference, from the Latin *lapsus*, or "fall," to the "lapse" of the first Adam) that his journey will follow "the same law with the system, with time, and all that is made" of that "lapse of the current [which is] an emblem of all progress" (*A Week*, PE, 12). For in general, he means to assert the paradoxical truth that by rowing against the current one may, indeed, "lapse" into progress. He means, in other words, to claim that by experiencing life deeply one can attain a new innocence, thereby turning one's self from the past to the future, from tradition to innovation, from regression to progression, from Concord, Massachusetts, to Concord, New Hampshire—and so, to a higher state of concord than that known in either place. Only then can one come to terms with the chief effects of Adam's lapse in Eden (in particular, death, both as it manifests itself in universal fashion and as it touched Thoreau personally in the demise of his brother).

In Miltonic terms, this means that *A Week* is a text written with one eye toward *Paradise Lost* and the other toward "Lycidas." Yet to put it so is to miss its deeper ideological significance. For from the perspective of Milton's reception in New England (and particularly in light of consensualist readings of *Paradise Lost* there from the middle of the eighteenth century on), this book is far from being merely a domestic version of the preoccupations of the European Enlightenment and romanticism. Similarly, from the same perspective, it is also more than just a personal search for consolation. Rather, *A Week* is nothing less than an attempt to do at length what Emerson had done in miniature in "Uriel": to use Milton's epic to create a consensualist "visionary compact" that both formally and thematically would sanction "terms of agreement from the nation's past . . . capable of bringing together the nation's citizens in the present," thus restoring "the terms constitutive of the nation's civil covenant," while still respecting the people's claims to freedom and autonomy.[10]

Yet judged on these terms, this book initially seems to be a failure, since for several hundred pages it appears to suffer from the same contradictory

10. Pease, ix–x. Although Thoreau is surprisingly absent from Pease's book, Pease's argument that many dominant-class antebellum writers were bent upon creating such consensualist "visionary compacts" seems to apply to him too.

impulses that had afflicted dominant-class writers for the previous two centuries. Thus, up through the end of the "Tuesday" chapter *A Week* is in
some ways markedly antinomian and dissenting in tone. It attacks tradition
and the established order of things in general, and Christianity in particular,
charging that they have conspired to keep man in his fallen state. As a remedy, Thoreau explicitly calls for radical change, saying in the iconoclastic
"Sunday" chapter that what nineteenth-century New England needs is a
"new Prometheus" who will replace the old "Christian fable" (*A Week*, PE,
66). It needs men who will reject forms and traditions and seek an unmedi-
ated experience of the divine in nature; men who will do as Thoreau was
doing in heading upriver, who will throw off the shackles of civilization and
the burden of generations long dead in order to seek truth in the forests. Nor
is this just a religious call; for according to Thoreau, such modern defiers of
the gods have a commission to do more than just reject the arid faith of the
Standing Order. They need to pull down the ordered fabric of civilized life
itself—particularly as it had been envisioned by generations of Yankee consensualists—for the heart of New England's problem is that it has long enshrined a habit of mind that creates Arminian communal visions like the one
the author encountered in Billerica, Massachusetts:

> The fields on either hand had a soft and cultivated English aspect, the
> village spire being seen over the copses which skirt the river, and
> sometimes an orchard straggled down to the water side. . . . It
> seemed that men led a quiet and very civil life there. The inhabitants
> were plainly cultivators of the earth, and lived under an organized po-
> litical government. The school-house stood with a meek aspect, en-
> treating a long truce to war and savage life. Every one finds by his
> own experience, as well as in history, that the era in which men cul-
> tivate the apple, and the amenities of the garden, is essentially differ-
> ent from that of the hunter and forest life, and neither can displace the
> other without loss. (*A Week*, PE, 53–54)

As Thoreau says, the problem with such consensualist heavens is that they
are postlapsarian and, so, inimical to any who (like him) value their liberty.
This is why he immediately declares that "I am convinced that my genius
dates from an older era than the agricultural" and goes on to note, rather
pointedly, that while "gardening is civil and social, . . . it wants the vigor
and freedom of the forest and the outlaw." For he believed that "there may
be an excess of cultivation as well as of any thing else, until civilization be-

comes pathetic" (*A Week*, PE, 55) and the Arminian structure of feeling becomes so satisfied that people are deprived of "the Indian's intercourse with Nature" (that savagery which "admits of the greatest independence" to both humanity and the wild).

This is certainly in his view what has happened in nineteenth-century New England. The inhabitants of his native region have settled for just such a postlapsarian, mediated experience of the divine truth of things, a cultural religion of forms that expressed itself not only in their architecture and village planning but in their dead language as well (the argot of a tradition in the last throes of the *translatio studii et imperii*):[11]

> In civilization, as in a southern latitude, man degenerates at length, and yields to the incursion of more northern tribes. . . . There are other, savager, and more primeval aspects of nature than our poets have sung. It is only white man's poetry. Homer and Ossian even can never revive in London or Boston. And yet behold how these cities are refreshed by the mere tradition, or the imperfectly transmitted fragrance and flavor of these wild fruits. If we could listen but for an instant to the chaunt of the Indian muse, we should understand why he will not exchange his savageness for civilization. Nations are not whimsical. Steel and blankets are strong temptations; but the Indian does well to continue Indian. (*A Week*, PE, 56)

Yet however antinomian in feeling the "Sunday" chapter may be, it is important to note that Thoreau's modern Prometheus is not to be found upon the barricades. Rather, as befits an inheritor of the traditions of both John Winthrop and Anne Hutchinson, his affirmation of the subversive is much moderated in the first half of *A Week*— so much so that he seems to fall into the traditional trap laid for Harvard authors by their puritan heritage. In part, this is because though he may rail against formalism and the civilized, fallen mindset of his contemporaries, his religion of nature marks a partial

11. The best treatments of *A Week* and Thoreau's commitment to a romantic primitivist view of history are Paul, *Shores of America*, esp. 191–233, and Robert F. Sayre, *Thoreau and the American Indians* (Princeton, N.J.: Princeton University Press, 1977), 28–58. Robert D. Richardson, Jr., *Myth and Literature in the American Renaissance* (Bloomington: Indiana University Press, 1978), 90–137, also gives a good general account of Thoreau's views on mythology and primitive peoples (perhaps somewhat overemphasizing the place of classical mythology in his thought). For a different interpretation of many of the matters treated here, see Gordon V. Boudreau, *The Roots of "Walden" and the Tree of Life* (Nashville, Tenn.: Vanderbilt University Press, 1990), 45–59.

withdrawal from any direct confrontation with the institutions and structures of his urbanizing, capitalist society. Even his social criticism in *A Week* as such, therefore, has much in common both with the writings of Tory English romantics like Wordsworth and Southey, and with those of his own Unitarian teachers. Similarly, even the most paradigmatically antinomian parts of the "Sunday" chapter are more than a little Arminian on account of their high-minded religiosity, disdain for the masses, and (typically Brahmin) unwillingness to be partisanly political. And finally, ironically, this disengagement is in addition also partly caused by the way Anglo-American culture's bourgeois contradictions shaped the antinomian strain in New England culture itself. For though he may wish to bring "the chaunt of the Indian muse" into the streets of Boston and London, the whole tenor of his book is not a little in keeping with the historical tendency of so many American religious radicals to withdraw from the tough business of reform (either into pietism or into perfectionist communities cut off from a fallen world).

From the "Wednesday" chapter on, furthermore, Thoreau becomes increasingly committed in this book—albeit understandably in view of his grief—to an elegiac pastoralism that is so personal as to have a decidedly narrowing effect on its scope and potential impact. Increasingly, it must be remembered that reforming society is not Thoreau's only aim; that *A Week* is in many respects primarily a memorial to his late brother; and that therefore its declaration that the burdens of the Fall can be thrown off in the "*new* Concord" has a strongly private, consolatory purpose. This is why so much of the book seems to be aimed at reversing the effects of another voyage: that of Edward King in "Lycidas." Indeed, even when Thoreau writes about setting off from the bank and sighting a lesser bittern, he calls that creature "the genius of the shore" because this "relic of a twilight ante-diluvian age which yet inhabits these bright American rivers with us Yankees . . . this melancholy and contemplative race of birds" is a species with which he can identify in light of his brother's loss. For it now seemed to him as if both he and John then "were but dwellers on the shore, like the bittern of the morning"; and so, their bird-like "pursuit" of life and nourishment upriver among "the wrecks of snails and cockles" was the appropriate central metaphor for his own even sadder search for meaning and consolation among the dead hulks of transitory nature, now that like Edward King, his sibling was gone (*A Week*, PE, 235–36 and 241).[12]

12. Part of that search for consolation in this passage was philosophical in nature, since in making the "moping" bittern's "dull, yellowish, greenish eye" akin to "my own soul [which] must be a bright invisible green" (*A Week*, PE, 235–36), Thoreau was probably alluding to the "transparent eyeball" passage in Emerson's *Nature*.

The problem is, though, that however sincere and moving it may be, this elegiac aspect of *A Week* tends to draw the reader's attention away from the potentially more far-reaching social and political implications of Thoreau's message. Furthermore, it also tends to vitiate his mythopoeic announcement of the impending reversal of the Fall (even when that announcement is understood in a nonradical way). For the inescapable fact is that just as "the genius of the shore" was unable to prevent the death by drowning of Milton's young poet, so the bittern 'pumping' by Concord's shore could not protect John Thoreau from lockjaw. Indeed, Henry Thoreau was aware of this problem even as he wrote, since like Milton he knew that the pastoral elegy was traditionally an occasion for an extended meditation upon the inevitability of mortality. And so, though he avowed that he had "not read of any Arcadian life which surpasses the actual luxury and serenity of" New England's villages and declared that "the age is golden enough" for safe voyages such as the one they had made together (a trip so vivid that—in a clear reference to Milton's symbol for Christ in "Lycidas"—it seemed to him as if his brother were still alive, like "a dolphin within cast"), nonetheless, he had to admit the truth of the old adage, *et in Arcadia ego.* For though "if men will believe it, *'sua si bona nôrint,'* there are no more quiet Tempes, or more poetic and Arcadian lives, than may be lived in these New England dwellings" (*A Week*, PE, 242–43), yet still, here too, one must front the evil and death brought into the world by Adam's fall:

> We do not avoid evil by fleeing before it, but by rising above or diving below its plane; as the worm escapes drought and frost by boring a few inches deeper. The frontiers are not east or west, north or south, but wherever a man *fronts* a fact, though that fact be his neighbor, there is an unsettled wilderness between him and Canada, between him and the setting sun, or, further still, between him and *it.* Let him build himself a log-house with the bark on where he is, *fronting* IT, and wage there an Old French war for seven or seventy years, with Indians and Rangers, or whatever else may come between him and the reality, and save his scalp if he can. (*A Week*, PE, 304)

Later, however, these contradictions are resolved when in the second half of *A Week* Thoreau manages to pull off the rhetorical reconciliation of opposites at which he aimed. He does so in the "Wednesday" and "Thursday" chapters when he climaxes his journey with just such a *"fronting* IT" as he recommends here. Like Milton (who ends "Lycidas" with a vision of Edward King's transformation into "the Genius of the shore" "through the dear might of him that walked the waves" [lines 165–85]), he does so by pledging allegiance to a myth that will both console him personally for the loss of his brother and console New England as a whole by successfully mediating between the competing structures of feeling in its culture. This double consolation occurs when Thoreau arrives at the source of the Merrimack (symbolically, a return to the headwaters of time), where in succession he revises both the patriarchalist and antinomian readings of the central action of *Paradise Lost*, in each case moving these polarized versions of Milton's conflicted epic toward an ideologically moderate resolution.

Thoreau revises the patriarchalist stratum of the poem (and its biblical original) first when he describes his discovery of a garden "between the river and Uncannunuc Mountain" that is a barely concealed version of Eden, guarded by an old farmer who (like Milton's God) is on the lookout for those who would steal a melon (from the Greek *melon*, meaning "fruit" or "apple") out of his clearing in the wilderness:

> We had got a loaf of home-made bread, and musk and water-melons for dessert. For this farmer, a clever and well-disposed man, cultivated a large patch of melons for the Hooksett and Concord markets. He hospitably entertained us the next day, exhibiting his hop-fields and kiln and melon patch, warning us to step over the tight rope which surrounded the latter at a foot from the ground, while he pointed to a little bower at one corner, where it connected with the lock of a gun ranging with the line, and where, as he informed us, he sometimes sat in pleasant nights to defend his premises against thieves. We stepped high over the line, and sympathized with our host's on the whole quite human, if not humane, interest in the success of his experiment. That night especially thieves were to be expected, from rumors in the atmosphere, and the priming was not wet. (*A Week*, PE, 290)

By saying that this "Methodist man" took a "human if not humane, interest in the success of his experiment," with its set-gun and boundaries, Thoreau is clearly alluding to a similar experiment with proscriptions and the threat of death for their violation: that of Genesis. Yet significantly, he here deliberately moderates the patriarchal demand for blind obedience present in both the biblical and Miltonic versions of the story by introducing the progressive, nineteenth-century bourgeois notion that the fruit of paradise is now grown for commercial sale and, so, may be bought by this latter-day pair of intruders (artist-voyagers who have traveled through experience back to the Garden in search of higher innocence). His aim in doing so is the classic one for men of his education and self-interest, moreover: to use *Paradise Lost* as a means for asserting his own view of authority. The encounter just cited is thus aimed on the one hand at undercutting the claims of absolutism lurking in Milton's poem by jovially turning his God into a small-time tradesman engaged in the activity most typical of middle-class Anglo-American culture: the mutual, voluntary, consenting, contractual pursuit of profit. Similarly, by making them partners to this deal, Thoreau also deprives his two intruders of such opprobrium as Adam and Eve had had in patriarchalist accounts of the events in the Garden. Just as the owner "belonged, and stayed at home there" in his patch, "and by the encouragement of distant political organizations, and by his own tenacity, held a property in his melons, and continued to plant," so his unthreatening, bourgeois manner of life provoked a similarly unthreatening, unrevolutionary response on the part of the Thoreaus. For rather than steal his apples or object to his rules and gun, they merely give him neighborly business advice ("We suggested melon seeds of new varieties and fruit of foreign flavor to be added to his stock") and claim that their purpose in being there is the eighteenth-century consensualist one of encouraging the diffusion of knowledge for the benefit of society ("We had come away up here among the hills to learn the impartial and unbribable benificence of Nature" [*A Week*, PE, 290–91]).

However, because Thoreau realized that this centrist vision of a patriarchalism defanged directly addressed only one of the two structures of feeling in his culture, he ends the passage (albeit a little unsyntactically) in a different vein: "Strawberries and melons grow as well in one man's garden as another's, and the sun lodges as kindly under his hill-side,—when we had imagined that she inclined rather to some few earnest and faithful souls whom we know." As this sentence suggests by its declaration of the social equality and yet particularity of the distribution of sunlight (traditionally, the symbol for God's grace), Thoreau was well aware that he had yet more ideological work to do. He had yet to deal with the descendants of the Puritan radicals and their potential objections to the "visionary compact" he here sought to erect. This is why the above description of the melon patch and its owner has an ironic tone throughout; and it is why a few pages later, in the "Thursday" chapter, Thoreau records a second visit to "the melon man" to buy some fruit. For this time, after the owner's son refers to the farmer as "Father" (with a capital "F") and Thoreau comments upon how honestly he and John had come by their purchase (thereby reminding the reader that this is a rewriting of *Paradise Lost*), Thoreau ushers in the story of Hannah Dustan.

As Robert Sayre has shown,[13] his aim in doing so was to make the heroine of this Indian captivity tale into an American Eve beset by satanic tempters. At one level, this portion of *A Week* therefore follows the common practice of the genre upon which it draws and autobiographically appropriates the most frequent Puritan typological interpretation of the early settlers' relations with the Indians: that of the Puritans as saints under attack in a demon-ridden wilderness.[14] However, given the symbolic place of *Paradise Lost* in New England culture, and given Thoreau's attempt in "Wednesday" to address patriarchalist readings of both that poem and its biblical source, it seems clear that he also meant to use the Mary Rowlandson story to undercut the antinomian feelings he shared with his fellow Yankees. Thus, from the beginning (when "she had seen her infant's brains dashed out against an apple-tree") to the end (when "the family of Hannah Dustan all assembled alive once more, except the infant whose brains were dashed out against the apple-tree, and there have been many who in later times have lived to say that they had eaten of the fruit of that apple-tree"), the life of this unfortunate woman is cut to an ideologically moderate pattern (*A Week*, PE, 321 and 323–24). First, Thoreau satisfies the antinomian structure of feeling by letting the Indians (who were often the embodiments of antiauthoritarianism in the New England imagination) successfully wreak their demonic havoc on this moderate puritan saint; and then, at the end (in a gloss that confirms *Paradise Lost* as his chief source for his meditation on the Fall), he veers back toward the ideological center in a passage aimed at resolving the tensions at the heart of Yankee culture:

> This seems a long while ago, and yet it happened since Milton wrote his Paradise Lost. But its antiquity is not the less great for that, for we do not regulate our historical time by the English standard, nor did the English by the Roman, nor the Roman by the Greek. "We

13. Sayre, 50–58. See also Philip F. Gura, "Thoreau's Maine Woods Indians: More Representative Men," *American Literature* 49 (1977): 366–84, which contrasts Thoreau's views on Native Americans with those of his contemporaries.

14. The best general discussion of the captivity narrative and its Puritan typological readings is given in the introduction to Alden T. Vaughan and Edward W. Clark's excellent *Puritans among the Indians: Accounts of Captivity and Redemption 1676–1724* (Cambridge, Mass.: Harvard University Press, 1981), 1–28. Annette Kolodny, *The Land Before Her: Fantasy and Experience of the American Frontiers, 1630–1860* (Chapel Hill: University of North Carolina Press, 1984), 17–34, discusses the female puritan captivity narratives, especially that of Mary Rowlandson. For a discussion of a parallel nineteenth-century example of Milton's use in a literary text that draws upon this genre, see Robert Milder, "*The Last of the Mohicans* and the New World Fall," *American Literature* 52 (1980): 407–29.

must look a long way back," says Raleigh, "to find the Romans giving laws to nations, and their consuls bringing kings and princes bound in chains to Rome in triumph; to see men go to Greece for wisdom, or Ophir for gold; . . . "—And yet, in one sense, not so far back as to find the Penacooks and Pawtuckets using bows and arrows and hatchets of stone, on the banks of the Merrimack. From this September afternoon, and from between these now cultivated shores, those times seemed more remote than the dark ages. . . .

The age of the world is great enough for our imaginations, even according to the Mosaic account, without borrowing any years from the geologist. From Adam and Eve at one leap sheer down to the deluge, and then through the ancient monarchies, through Babylon and Thebes, Brahma and Abraham, . . . down through Odin and Christ to——America. It is a wearisome while.—And yet the lives of but sixty old women, such as live under the hill, say of a century each, strung together, are sufficient to reach over the whole ground. Taking hold of hands they would span the interval from Eve to my own mother. A respectable tea-party merely,—whose gossip would be Universal History. (*A Week*, PE, 324–25)

Having just retold a tale that proclaims the primordial presence of death in New England (one that admits that throughout the history of this New World Arcady the forces of revolt and disorder had almost always had the upper hand), Thoreau here ends his consideration of Hannah Dustan with a metaphor that reduces her narrative to the respectability of a tea party. Determined to do to the antinomian understanding of Eden what he had done to patriarchalist readings of those events, he loops all the women of history into one great sororial circle, thus creating an image of community in which Hannah Dustan and Eve both escape their antinomian tempters unfallen. As such, their tea party gives the lie to the Horatian tag, *et in Arcadia ego*, because as they meet and restore moderate bourgeois social norms, they surmount the ultimate agents of social change and disorder brought into being as a result of Satan's penetration of the Garden: time and history. This is why Thoreau adds that though "the sixtieth" generation of women back from Thoreau's own mother "was Eve the mother of mankind. . . . It will not take a very great grand-daughter of hers to be in at the death of Time."

A Week on the Concord and Merrimack Rivers is, as this suggests, yet another example of the persistence of the moderate tradition in New England. Like Emerson's "Uriel," it adopts the strategy of fully realizing the polarities in its author's culture and then moderating them toward a symbolically consensualist center. Moreover, not surprisingly, like Emerson and the Unitarians, in large measure Thoreau's aim in doing so was to reaffirm the authority of the dominant-class artist (particularly the writer of belles lettres) by at once investing him with the antinomian force of the satanic visionary yet placing that power in the service of such Arminian virtues as historic continuity and stability. This is why late in *A Week*, in the wake of his two re-envisionings of the story of the Fall, he concentrates upon developing a language of paradox so that he might more authoritatively describe the nature of the poetic vocation. For (he believed) it was only through such a language that he could hope to do for the question of literary authority what he had just done for the question of authority in general.

This is the reason, for instance, that the story of the melon patch leads him to assert (like the projectors of Pandemonium) that "this world is but canvass to our imaginations" and (along with Satan and his romantic admirers) that "all things are as I am," yet also to maintain that such self-empowerment commissions us as much to ask "where is the House of Change" as to attack the claims of "the past" upon us (*A Week*, PE, 292). For in the aftermath of his trip to the headwaters of the river, he felt comfortable living as an artist with the paradoxes of his position. Similarly, his confident rhetorical movement away from contradiction toward paradox also explains why soon after relating the captivity of Hannah Dustan he can assert that "the Man of Genius, referred to mankind," is both a rebel and yet the prophetic recipient of an inspiration unavailable to the masses ("an originator" and a "demonic man," yet "an inspired" one too). For Thoreau's phrasing is so carefully textured and self-confident in its ideological moderation that it is no longer a contradiction for him to say that a Shakespeare or a Milton is one who (like an Arminian) "produces a perfect work in obedience to laws" but (like an antinomian) only does so to laws "yet unexplored" by either the powers that be or the unsaved majority. In the same way, Thoreau thinks it nothing but wisely paradoxical to declare in the same passage that his "Man of Genius" both rises above his fellows by the hand of God and yet stays equal to them. For in his first book he had found a way of rhetorically balancing the claims of hierarchy and those of equality, by using John Milton to defuse the tensions inherent in bourgeois sentiments like the following (which might serve as the motto of Unitarian Boston): that "there has been no man of pure Genius; as there has been none wholly destitute of Genius" (*A Week*, PE, 328).

Indeed, *A Week* ends on just such an authority-recovering paradoxical note when in the "Friday" chapter the Thoreau brothers float downstream, back into a world where, "as we fancied, by the faces of men, that the Fall had commenced" (*A Week*, PE, 335). For as a result of their encounters with the story of *Paradise Lost*, this is now a world dominated not by the Tree in the Garden but by " 'Elisha's apple-tree' " (Henry's symbol both for the symbiosis of continuity and change in nature and for his own newfound liminality as a writer [*A Week*, PE, 356–58]). It is a world and a way of writing in which he can now declare himself "absolved from all obligation to the past, and the council of nations," like Satan, and yet then insert a piece of his from the *Dial* in which he defers to ancient (as opposed to modern, post-Miltonic) poetry (*A Week*, PE, 359 and 366–77).[15] For he felt that at the headwaters of the Merrimack and in the history of Hannah Dustan, he had successfully escaped the confliction of previous Yankee dominant-class writers by coming to terms with the dilemma he had inherited (as much from Milton as from them). He consequently now writes not in the fallen tongue of nineteenth-century "London or Boston" but in a language invested "by the chaunt of the Indian muse" with true metaphysical wit: a dialect by which he may seek the life-giving paradox of "no higher heaven than the pure senses can furnish, a *purely* sensuous life" (*A Week*, PE, 382) such as that which he found at week's end, when, in "drawing . . . up" his boat "and fastening it to the wild apple-tree, whose stem still bore the mark which its chain had worn in the chafing of the spring freshets," he came home to the very *discordia concors* that had been his goal from the start (*A Week*, PE, 393).

Walden follows the same pattern as *A Week*, since in it Thoreau presented the Pond as yet another paradise to be regained: an Eden whose rediscovery would allow him to resolve the paradigmatic tensions in New England history (and *Paradise Lost*) in an ideologically moderate way. This is not to deny, of course, that he had other agenda in mind for his second book. One of these was, of course, the presentation of his philosophy of nature. Thus, for instance, his statement in "The Ponds" that "all our Concord waters have two colors at least, one when viewed at a distance, and another, more proper, close at hand," does have the significance usually ascribed to it. For in saying that "the first" of Walden's colors "follows the sky" and is heaven-born, reflecting the blue of the transcendent, and that the second is green and reflects the earth-born quality of sense experience, and that yet both are to be

---

15. The *Dial* piece Thoreau incorporates into *A Week* here ("Homer. Ossian. Chaucer."), presents a view of the Western literary tradition as being in a post-Miltonic decline very much like that found in Emerson's *English Traits*. It can be read in its original periodical form in *Early Essays*, PE, 154–73.

found in the Pond, which "is blue at one time and green at another, even from the same point of view . . . lying between the earth and the heavens, it partakes of the color of both" (*Walden*, PE, 176), Thoreau symbolically betrays his idiosyncratic reconciliation of empiricism and idealism.[16] Similarly, later on he had both the thirteenth chapter of Coleridge's *Biographia Literaria* and the "transparent eyeball" passage from Emerson's *Nature* in mind when he pictured Walden as an esemplastic pupil set into the landscape, one that allowed him to see into both the *i* (*ego*) of his own soul and the *I* (*Ego*) of the Over-soul: "A lake is the landscape's most beautiful and expressive feature. It is earth's eye; looking into which the beholder measures the depth of his own nature. The fluviatile trees next the shore are the slender eyelashes which fringe it, and the wooded hills and cliffs around are its overhanging brows" (*Walden*, PE, 186).[17] As Stanley Cavell and others have shown, *Walden* is one of America's great philosophical texts; and so, as in his portrayal of the Pond as the shrine at Delphi (as the *omphalos* or earth's navel: a sacred and central mirror reflecting—and yet uniting—heaven and earth) Thoreau was clearly trying in part to create an adequate symbol for the imagination's ability to front nature in both its phenomenal and noumenal dimensions:[18]

In such a day, in September or October, Walden is a perfect forest mirror, set round with stones as precious to my eye as if fewer or rarer. Nothing so fair, so pure, and at the same time so large, as a lake, perchance, lies on the surface of the earth. Sky water. It needs no fence. Nations come and go without defiling it. It is a mirror which no stone

16. The two best accounts of Thoreau's philosophical stance are Joel Porte, *Emerson and Thoreau: Transcendentalists in Conflict* (Middletown, Conn.: Wesleyan University Press, 1965), 93ff., and Stanley Cavell, *The Senses of Walden*, expanded ed. (San Francisco: North Point Press, 1981). In addition to Paul, *The Shores of America*, and Richardson, *Thoreau: A Life of the Mind*, studies useful in placing Thoreau in his philosophical context include Frederick Garber, *Thoreau's Redemptive Imagination* (New York: New York University Press, 1977); John Hildebidle, *Thoreau: A Naturalist's Liberty* (Cambridge, Mass.: Harvard University Press, 1983); James McIntosh, *Thoreau as Romantic Naturalist: His Shifting Stance Toward Nature* (Ithaca, N.Y.: Cornell University Press, 1974); Joan Burbick, *Thoreau's Alternative History: Changing Perspectives on Nature, Culture, and Language* (Philadelphia: University of Pennsylvania Press, 1987); and Henry Golemba, *Thoreau's Wild Rhetoric* (New York: New York University Press, 1990). Despite many useful insights, Sharon Cameron's *Writing Nature: Henry Thoreau's "Journal"* (New York: Oxford University Press, 1985) is methodologically flawed and seriously mistakes both the complexity of and relationship between Thoreau's published nature writings and his *Journal*.

17. Coleridge, *Collected Works*, vii, pt. 1, 295ff., and Emerson, *Collected Works*, i, 9–10.

18. Garber, 7. Cavell is the critic most interested in treating Emerson and Thoreau as philosophers. He is aware as well of Thoreau's use of Milton in writing *Walden* (e.g., see his comments, 112–16).

can crack, whose quicksilver will never wear off, whose gilding Nature continually repairs; no storms, no dust, can dim its surface ever fresh;—a mirror in which all impurity presented to it sinks, swept and dusted by the sun's hazy brush,—this the light dust-cloth,—which retains no breath that is breathed on it, but sends its own to float as clouds high above its surface, and be reflected in its bosom still. (*Walden*, PE, 188)

Indeed, much of *Walden* is devoted to advancing the philosophical position symbolized here, as well as the corollary proposition that the poet's chief task is to measure the dimensions of his or her own soul from just such a transcendental angle of vision. A whole chapter late in the narrative ("The Pond in Winter," 282–98) is famously devoted, for instance, to showing that from the ideal point of view the poet will find that his own soul (like the Oversoul) is both measurable and possessed of organic form; for like Walden Pond, it is deepest where it is widest and longest.

Yet "The Ponds" bears another interpretation as well. This is because in the chapter Thoreau also attempts to resolve the paradigmatic conflictions in New England culture through mythopoesis. Thus, a few pages after he defines Walden as the numinous esemplastic mirror of heaven and earth, he uses *Paradise Lost* to invest this patch of landscape with the same regenerative, synthesizing, paradisal qualities he had earlier assigned to the headwaters of the Merrimack:

We have one other pond just like this, White Pond, . . . but . . . I do not know a third of this pure and well-like character. Successive nations perchance have drank at, admired, and fathomed it, and passed away, and still its water is green and pellucid as ever. Not an intermitting spring! Perhaps on that spring morning when Adam and Eve were driven out of Eden Walden Pond was already in existence, and even then breaking up in a gentle spring rain accompanied with mist and a southerly wind, and covered with myriads of ducks and geese, which had not heard of the fall, when still such pure lakes sufficed them. Even then it had commenced to rise and fall, and had clarified its waters and colored them of the hue they now wear, and obtained a patent of heaven to be the only Walden Pond in the world and distiller of celestial dews. Who knows in how many unremembered nations' literatures this has been the Castalian Fountain? or what nymphs presided over it in the Golden Age? It is a gem of the first water which Concord wears in her coronet. (*Walden*, PE, 179)

Significantly, John Milton is Thoreau's vehicle for the reconciliation of the Arminian and antinomian structures of feeling here, because in mentioning "the Castalian Fountain" he alludes to the poet's extended comparison in *Paradise Lost* between the Garden of Eden and the earthly paradises of classical mythology (IV, 205–87); in that famous passage, Milton does more than merely proclaim the superiority of the biblical "heav'n on earth" (the "blissful Paradise / of God . . . by him in the east / Of Eden planted" [lines 208–10]) over the many Arcadies that litter the literary landscapes of Greece and Rome (whether they be "that fair field / Of Enna, where Prosérpine gathering flow'rs, / Herself a fairer flow'r, by gloomy Dis / Was gathered" [lines 268–71] or "th' inspired / Castalian spring" itself [line 274]). Rather, the author of *Paradise Lost* makes the comparison serve as prelude to a highly Arminian description of the prelapsarian relationship between Adam and Eve (IV, 288–355), a passage that opens with the following moderate puritan treatment of the issue of authority:

> Two of far nobler shape erect and tall,
> God-like erect, with native honor clad
> In naked majesty seemed lords of all,
> And worthy seemed, for in their looks divine
> The image of their glorious Maker shone,
> Truth, wisdom, sanctitude severe and pure,
> Severe but in true filial freedom placed;
> Whence true authority in men; though both
> Not equal, as their sex not equal seemed;
> For contemplation he and valor formed,
> For softness she and sweet attractive grace;
> He for God only, she for God in him.
> His fair large front and eye sublime declared
> Absolute rule; and hyacinthine locks
> Round from his parted forelock manly hung
> Clust'ring, but not beneath his shoulders broad:
> She as a veil down to the slender waist
> Her unadornèd golden tresses wore
> Disheveled, but in wanton ringlets waved
> As the vine curls her tendrils, which implied

Subjection, but required with gentle sway,
And by her yielded, by him best received,
Yielded with coy submission, modest pride,
And sweet reluctant amorous delay.

(lines 288–311)

As the context of Thoreau's allusion therefore suggests, his aim in "The Ponds" was to affirm the same ideologically moderate, dominant-class values of order, modified hierarchy, and limited liberty as Milton had in book IV. For like his seventeenth-century predecessor, as a New Englander reared in the values of a bourgeois elite, he felt a similar need in *Walden* to provide a balanced portrait of benevolent, loving domination and submission; and so, his allusion to this part of the epic affirms the same Pauline "love patriarchy" that informed Milton (or John Winthrop in "A Model of Christian Charity"). Moreover, this allusion also suggests that *Walden* as a whole is the story of a pastoral, implicitly consensualist realm whose wild inhabitants "had not heard of the fall": of a place unthreatened by either tyranny or disorder, where the soul's crystal clear mirror may regain its innocence untempted by Hesperian apples or vipers like those which attacked Eve and Proserpine. It is a place, in fact, in which Adam and Eve may still possibly be seen in all their Miltonic, ideologically moderate, prelapsarian glory—in which "yet perchance the first who came to this well [may] have left some trace of their footsteps." For as he says in ending his description of Concord's "first water": "I have been surprised to detect encircling the pond, even where a thick wood has just been cut down on the shore, a narrow shelf-like path in the steep hill-side, alternately rising and falling, approaching and receding from the water's edge, as old probably as the race of man here, worn by the feet of aboriginal hunters, and still from time to time unwittingly trodden by the present occupants of the land" (*Walden*, PE, 179–80).

Just as in *A Week on the Concord and Merrimack Rivers*, however, Thoreau was too wise to the ways of his culture and too aware of its historical fissures to neglect the other values and feelings New England had inherited from its past. It is no accident, therefore, that the Miltonic descriptions of Eden and of Adam and Eve in Eden to which he alludes in "The Ponds" are in *Paradise Lost* visions told from the anti-middle-class perspective of Satan, the "first grand thief" who, like a burglar, "bent to unhoard the cash / Of some rich burgher, whose substantial doors, / Cross-barred and bolted fast, fear no assault, / In at the window climbs, or o'er the tiles: / So clomb . . . into God's fold; / . . . and on the Tree of Life, / The middle tree and highest there that grew, / Sat like a cormorant" (IV, 188–96). For as portraits of Arminian harmony and yet also as the musings of the original arch-antinomian and opponent of law and order, these sections of book IV narratologically enact the opposition which is at the core of the bourgeois crisis of authority. Moreover, the very fact that Thoreau sets up Walden Pond in this chapter as a better Eden by far than that described by either Milton or Genesis is itself also an antiauthoritarian act, because it implicitly denies the priority of both the Judeo-Christian scriptures and the English literary canon. So too do his denial in the chapter of the continuing effects of Adam's Fall and his provision of a competing, romantic myth of salvation; for in all three cases, he deliberately introduces an antinomian element into what otherwise seems to be an Arminian myth of a paradise that can be regained.

Yet having said that, again (as in *A Week*), there is little contradiction in these passages, because Thoreau so carefully chooses his allusions and language that he mythically synthesizes both structures of feeling here even as he gives subtle expression to them (thereby discharging the ideological tensions that existed in his culture as well as in *Paradise Lost*). The only difference is that he achieved a "visionary compact" in his earlier book through the creation of an ideologically moderate language of paradox, whereas he does so here through allusion. Later, in the two climactic passages in *Walden*, Thoreau follows a similar strategy in order to create yet more ideologically centrist revisionings of the Fall centered around the Pond. The first of these is the section of the "Spring" chapter in which he tells how he saw the sand begin to flow and move along the sides of the railway cut (*Walden*, PE, 306–7). This motion caused him to meditate upon the processes of birth in the natural world (including human childbirth), and so—by an imaginative leap—to place himself back at the genesis of the universe itself: "The whole bank, which is from twenty to forty feet high, is sometimes overlaid with a mass of this kind of foliage, or sandy rupture. . . . What makes this sand foliage remarkable is its springing into existence thus suddenly. When I see on the one side the inert bank,—for the sun acts on one side first,—and on the other this luxuriant foliage, the creation of an hour, I am affected as if in a peculiar sense I stood in the laboratory of the Artist who made the world and me,—had come to where he was still at work, sporting on this bank, and with excess of energy strewing his fresh designs about." Thoreau then used the now discredited physio-linguistic theories of Dr. Charles Kraitsir[19] in or-

19. Kraitsir's theories and influence on Thoreau's thinking about language are treated by Gura in "Thoreau's Maine Woods Indians" and in his "Elizabeth Palmer Peabody and the Philosophy of Language," *ESQ: A Journal of the American Renaissance*, n.s., 23 (1977): 154–63, and *The Wisdom of Words: Language, Theology, and Literature in the New England Renaissance* (Mid-

der to turn these natural processes (of birth and of divine sexual union between the Father-Creator and Mother Earth) into yet another romantic narrative of the Fall and its reversal:

> I feel as if I were nearer to the vitals of the globe, for this sandy over-
> flow is something such a foliaceous mass as the vitals of the animal
> body. You find thus in the very sands an anticipation of the vegetable
> leaf. No wonder that the earth expresses itself outwardly in leaves, it
> so labors with the idea inwardly. The atoms have already learned this
> law, and are pregnant by it. The overhanging leaf sees here its proto-
> type. *Internally,* whether in the globe or animal body, it is a moist
> thick *lobe,* a word especially applicable to the liver and lungs and the
> *leaves* of fat, (λείβω, *labor, lapsus,* to flow or slip downward, a lapsing;
> λοβος, *globus,* lobe, globe; also lap, flap, and many other words,) *ex-*
> *ternally* a dry thin *leaf,* even as the *f* and *v* are a pressed and dried *b.*
> The radicals of lobe are *lb,* the soft mass of the *b* (single lobed, or B,
> double lobed,) with a liquid *l* behind it pressing it forward. In globe,
> *glb,* the gutteral *g* adds to the meaning the capacity of the throat. The
> feathers and wings of birds are still drier and thinner leaves. Thus,
> also, you pass from the lumpish grub in the earth to the airy and flut-
> tering butterfly. The very globe continually transcends and translates
> itself, and becomes winged in its orbit.

Thoreau's drift here is evident enough. He suggests that like the world in
spring or the human being in childbirth, language naturally presses onward and forward, transcending and translating its former self, under-
going a metamorphosis like that taking place before him in the sands. The
key words associated by Milton with Adam's sin (*labor, lapse, fall*) therefore
need not retain the postlapsarian meanings assigned to them in *Paradise*

---

dletown, Conn.: Wesleyan University Press, 1981), 109–44. See also John B. Wilson, "Grimm's
Law and the Brahmins," *New England Quarterly* 38 (1965): 234–39, and three articles by
Michael West: "Scatology and Eschatology: The Heroic Dimensions of Thoreau's Wordplay,"
PMLA 89 (1974): 1043–64; "Charles Kraitsir's Influence upon Thoreau's Theory of Lan-
guage," *ESQ: A Journal of the American Renaissance,* n.s., 19 (1973): 262–74; and "*Walden's*
Dirty Language: Thoreau and Walter Whiter's Geocentric Etymological Theories," *Harvard Li-*
brary Bulletin 22 (1974): 117–28. Besides the works by Gura and Cavell, two recent studies of the
history of language theory in pre–Civil War America that touch upon Thoreau are Mason I.
Lowance, Jr., *The Language of Canaan: Metaphor and Symbol in New England from the Puritans*
to the Transcendentalists (Cambridge, Mass.: Harvard University Press, 1980), 247ff., and John T.
Irwin, *American Hieroglyphics: The Symbol of the Egyptian Hieroglyphics in the American Renais-*
sance (New Haven, Conn.: Yale University Press, 1980).

Lost.[20] Rather, just as he had earlier redefined the nature of "economy" and "labor" in his chapters on "Economy" and "The Bean-Field" by digging down to their roots in the more primitive Latin and Greek (see, e.g., *Walden, PE,* 71), so too here, Adam's *lapse* or *fall* becomes the rebirth of springtime in a paradise regained; and the penalties due to Original Sin (death, and the twin labors: for man to labor by the sweat of his brow and for woman to have labor pains) lose all their sting. For both the radical roots of these words and the very motions of the human voice in making them are at Walden in harmony with the tendency of all nature to press upward toward Heaven, not down to Hell—to translate itself from its grubbish present state to the winged orbit of its origin and potential.

This triumphant passage also attempts to mediate between the claims of order and those of freedom, however. On the one hand, it announces the end of alienation and the beginning of a new reign of harmony and community in which even human language itself will be transformed back into that original tongue spoken in the loving—but hierarchical—conversations in the Garden. It claims that all of reality (including human society) is, in fact, one organic being: a "whole tree [which] itself is but one leaf, and [of which] rivers are still vaster leaves whose pulp is intervening earth, and towns and cities are the ova of insects in their axils" (*Walden, PE,* 307). Yet, on the other hand, as in "The Ponds," the very deprioritizing of Genesis and *Paradise Lost* here assuages the antinomian structure of feeling too. So also do Thoreau's denial of the continued effects of Original Sin and his claim—as one who "stood in the laboratory of the Artist who made the world and me"—of virtual creative equality with God. For collectively they overthrow centuries of Western religious dogma and replace the biblical and Miltonic accounts of this myth of divine authority with a new myth of recurrent creation, in which the human artist can—like Satan building in Pandemonium—be as God, and achieve his own romantically redefined salvation.

The railway cut incident in the "Spring" chapter thus bespeaks Thoreau's continuing desire to forge a mythic language that would allow him to bridge the polarization between Arminian and antinomian in his culture. It differs from the melon patch and Hannah Dustan sections of *A Week,* or his earlier description of the pond in *Walden,* only in that it is a rhetorical return to

20. William Ingram and Kathleen Swaim, comps., *A Concordance to Milton's English Poetry* (Oxford: Clarendon, 1972), show that in the majority of cases (in context) the poet uses the words "fall" (165), "lapse" (310), and "labor" (308) in *Paradise Lost* with the soteriological connotations to which Thoreau objects here.

Eden based upon linguistic translation (in the root sense of that word)[21] rather than paradox or allusion. Further, Thoreau had the same purpose in mind in writing his second climactic revision of the Bible and *Paradise Lost* in *Walden:* the tale of the grub and the apple-tree wood table with which he concludes the book. For despite whatever specifically New England sources it may have,[22] from its opening sentences (which refer to the end of *A Week*) to its last (blasphemous) slight at Christ, this mythic rewriting of the Resurrection (the ultimate reversal of the Fall in Milton's poem) attempts to follow an ideologically moderate course. It thus begins as his first book had ended, with the rise and fall of "the water in the river," and with the statement (also in reference to *A Week*) that Thoreau now sees "far inland the banks which the stream anciently washed, before science began to record its freshets." As this suggests, as in that earlier work, this meditation on the fluctuating yet constant, transitory yet timeless, nature of the river of life is symbolically balanced between images of dissolution and ones of permanence. Significantly, it also leads Thoreau to tie his narrative down (as he had earlier tied down his boat in *A Week*) to the apple tree, which (despite its alteration by the forces of civilization) is here too his symbol for the recovery of human innocence:

> Every one has heard the story which has gone the rounds of New England, of a strong and beautiful bug which came out of the dry leaf of an old table of apple-tree wood, which had stood in a farmer's kitchen for sixty years, first in Connecticut, and afterward in Massachusetts,—from an egg deposited in the living tree many years earlier still, as appeared by counting the annual layers beyond it; which was heard gnawing out for several weeks, hatched perchance by the heat of an urn. Who does not feel his faith in a resurrection and immortality strengthened by hearing of this? Who knows what beautiful and winged life, whose egg has been buried for ages under many concentric layers of woodenness in the dead dry life of society, deposited at first in the alburnum of the green and living tree, which has been gradually converted into the semblance of its well-seasoned

---

21. *Translation* is from the Latin *translatio*, which in turn is related to *translatus sum* (the past perfect of *transfero*). As this implies, in the original it means both "to turn one language into another" and "to move from one spiritual state to another," as in "the translation of a saint." For its significance in relation to Thoreau's interest in linguistics, his romantic primitivism, and his desire to rewrite the myth of the Fall, see *Translations*, PE, esp. 175–219.

22. Walter Harding, "The Apple-Tree Table Tale," *Boston Public Library Quarterly* 8 (1956): 213–15.

tomb,—heard perchance gnawing out now for years by the astonished family of man, as they sat round the festive board,—may unexpectedly come forth from amidst society's most trivial and handselled furniture, to enjoy its perfect summer life at last! (*Walden*, PE, 332–33)

Yet as one would expect from the fact that Thoreau plays off of the railway cut section of "Spring" here, there are strong antinomian elements in this passage. Indeed, the antiauthoritarian impulse in this quotation is predominant, since Thoreau's notion that the grub burrowing through the table and turning into a butterfly somehow survived the "layers of woodenness in the dead dry life of society" is an indictment of a postlapsarian culture too respectful of the past and its mediating myths and scriptures (one too civilized and communal, too corpse-cold and entombed, to do anything but stifle the individual as he or she tries to grow toward Heaven). This complaint, which might be found on the lips of any nineteenth-century reformer or seventeenth-century radical scandalized by "legal preachers," is then immediately followed by Thoreau's concluding paragraph, which by means of the common seventeenth-century metaphysical pun between "Son" and "sun" replaces the Christian "expectation of him whose name is Orient"[23] with attendance upon that other "son of the morning," Lucifer (thus blasphemously suggesting that salvation from the effects of Adam's "lapse" must come from a source other than that revealed in books XI and XII of *Paradise Lost*—specifically, the demonic power of autonomous, self-directed individualism): "I do not say that John or Jonathan will realize all this; but such is the character of that morrow which mere lapse of time can never make to dawn. The light which puts out our eyes is darkness to us. Only that day dawns to which we are awake. There is more day to dawn. The sun is but a morning star" (*Walden*, PE, 333).

Thoreau's whole way of proceeding here—which is to contradict Holy Writ and Milton alike—is, therefore, once more subversive and oppositional, because it redefines the content and outcome of the West's archetypal authority myth. Yet as in the "Spring" chapter, Thoreau again subtly balances these two concluding paragraphs so as to assuage the Arminian structure of feeling as well. After all, for all its gnawing, his antinomian grub merely "astonished" (rather than panicked or annihilated) the "family of man, as they sat round" that ultimate symbol of human community and ordered mutuality: "the festal board"; and England and America (i.e., "John or Jonathan")

---

23. The phrase is John Donne's, not Thoreau's.

in the end here find themselves presented not with a call to arms or the threat of violent revolution, but with a most temperate prediction that sooner or later change will come (implicitly, through individual, grublike metamorphosis or self-culture). As this suggests, despite his subversive orneriness, Thoreau did not really want to junk New England's "old table of apple-tree wood," however "trivial and handselled" that piece of "furniture" might have become. For like Theodore Parker, he was, by education and sensibility, at this stage of his life at least, an ideologically moderate member of the dominant class—despite strong inclinations to the contrary; and so, he sought here to create a finale that would carefully balance the two structures of feeling in his culture, by introducing into its central myth of birth and redemption elements (such as the communal meal, self-culture, and sociopolitical gradualism) that would blunt his otherwise subversive reading of it.

The antinomian structure of feeling, close to predominant here at the end of *Walden,* manifests itself even more strongly in Thoreau's account of his 1846 ascent of Mt. Ktaadn in *The Maine Woods.* Written at the end of his second year at the Pond, his description of that trip to the former Eastern District is, as a result, markedly more conflicted than was the case in his first two books.[24] For instance, as a landscape Thoreau's Maine is in some respects a quite antinomian place; as he says early on, "this was what you might call a bran new country; the only roads were of Nature's making, and the few houses were camps." Despite this disorderliness, however, the Arminian structure of feeling still made its claims felt there too, since ironically, it was precisely "here, then, [that] one could no longer" just play the dissenter, and "accuse institutions and society, but must front the true source of evil": the possibility (as the patriarchal Calvinists maintained) that man is utterly depraved and of the devil's party by nature (*Maine Woods,* PE, 16). Moreover, this confliction in Thoreau's description of the land over which he traveled matches his contradictory feelings toward its inhabitants, since he had the Arminian's disdain for the common folk and their destructive individualism, yet also cultivated an antinomian's hatred for civilization and its institutions. Consequently, in clearing the forest, the lumberjacks and backwoodsmen of the state earned from him both a gentleman's sneer at their rapacious acquisitiveness and a radical's curse upon their assault on the wild and free. They did so, significantly, in several paradigmatically conflicted passages that use

24. The compositional history of this part of the book and the evidence for its early date are laid out in *The Maine Woods,* PE, 357–59. (For the sake of consistency Thoreau's spelling, "Ktaadn," will be used here rather than the more usual modern form, "Katahdin.")

Paradise Lost to characterize them as the devils in Pandemonium, tearing down even as they purport to build up. Indeed, in surveying "the mission of men there" (which he says "seems to be, like so many busy demons, to drive the forest all out of the country, from every solitary beaver swamp, and mountain side, as soon as possible"), he concludes that it is both heroic and apocalyptic, since it creates progress but only by reducing the wilderness to a desolate morass of burning trees (*Maine Woods*, PE, 5 and 17).

New England's cultural conflictions also form the background of Thoreau's pledge in the "Ktaadn" section to "front the true source of evil," since he initially defined "evil" in terms of the standard romantic misprision of the Fall: that man is "evil" because he is doubly alienated from nature (on the personal level, by the separation of his spirit from his body, and on the corporate, historical level, by the divorce of civilization from its primitive origins). Here, however, the result is no myth of a paradise regained in the American forest. Rather, in contrast to the peaceful and organic order of nature, Thoreau and his companions must wander alienated through this burning wilderness, even at rest resembling Satan and his crew as they "lay vanquished, rolling in the fiery gulf," projecting "darkness visible" on the scene about them (*Paradise Lost*, I, 45–83):

> It was a savage and dreary scenery enough; so wildly rough, that they looked long to find a level and open space for the tent. We could not well camp higher, for want of fuel; and the trees here seemed so evergreen and sappy, that we almost doubted if they would acknowledge the influence of fire; but fire prevailed at last, and blazed here, too, like a good citizen of the world. . . . It was, perhaps, even a more grand and desolate place for a night's lodging than the summit would have been, being in the neighborhood of those wild trees, and of the torrent. Some more aerial and finer-spirited winds rushed and roared through the ravine all night, from time to time arousing our fire, and dispersing the embers about. It was as if we lay in the very nest of a young whirlwind. At midnight, one of my bedfellows, being startled in his dreams by the sudden blazing up to its top of a fir-tree, whose green boughs were dried by the heat, sprang up, with a cry, from his bed, thinking the world on fire, and drew the whole camp after him. (*Maine Woods*, PE, 62)

Whatever it may say about Thoreau the romantic, in light of his earlier reception of Milton this scene partway up Mt. Ktaadn also demonstrates his new sense of the irreconcilability of the two structures of feeling in New England culture. For in making camp and creating fire and eating together, he and his companions visibly affirm Arminian claims by performing several of the basic acts by which the human community forms and structures itself. But in letting that fire get out of hand and destroy the "evergreen . . . wild trees" about them, they take this "good citizen of the world" and turn it into an agent of universal destruction. Like Milton's demons (or Boston's merchants and clerics), in other words, Thoreau and his fellow campers are hopelessly conflicted men who build only to destroy, civilize only to give uncivilized offense to Heaven, and create light only to make darkness all the more prevalent; and so, *The Maine Woods* as a whole must be seen as one great flight across a boggy abyss, past Chaos and Old Night, ending in satanic alienation and dominant-class muddle rather than the reintegration and paradigmatic synthesis of "Uriel" or *A Week* or *Walden*.

To be sure, at the outset of this journey Thoreau still believed—with Milton's Satan—that "the mind and spirit remains / Invincible" (*Paradise Lost*, I, 139–40). But his trek into the inchoate morass of desolate matter that was Mt. Ktaadn soon taught him differently. For it was a place immediately reminiscent not of Eden but of an earlier part of Milton's epic: "I began to work my way, scarcely less arduous than Satan's anciently through Chaos, up the nearest, though not the highest peak. At first scrambling on all fours over the tops of ancient black spruce-trees, (*Abies nigra,*) old as the flood," then walking across bogs, rocks, undergrowth, and debris. "This was the sort of garden I made my way *over*": neither an ideologically moderate melon patch nor a prelapsarian pond, but "certainly the most treacherous and porous country I ever travelled" (a country so formless that he can only adequately describe it by invoking Milton's Satan once again: " '——nigh founder'd, on he fares, / Treading the crude consistence, half on foot, / Half flying' " [*Maine Woods*, PE, 60–61, citing *Paradise Lost*, II, 940–42]).

Little wonder, then, that at the end of this hard slog (as much through the antinomian messiness of antebellum America as into the phenomenal) Thoreau found himself in the "darkness visible" of the campfire with its persistent contradictions. For he realized that in Democratic Maine, as opposed to Federalist or Whig Massachusetts,[25] no rhetorically synthetic reconciliation of paradigmatic opposites would be possible; and so, he could therefore but play the mournful Satan or Prometheus: the role of one who wanted to get

25. Howe, *The Unitarian Conscience*, 217, argues that Maine gained statehood in part because of the Massachusetts Federalists' wish (as they neared extinction) to rid themselves of their largely Democratic-Republican Eastern District constituents.

behind the conflictions of his culture but, due to the depth of his own (and his region's) antinomianism, could not. This is why he says that the scene before him at his journey's end "reminded me of the creations of the old epic and dramatic poets," of the texts in which the classical rebels appear: "Atlas, Vulcan, the Cyclops, and Prometheus." For this was antinomian country. "The tops of mountains are among the unfinished parts of the globe, whither it is a slight insult to the gods to climb and pry into their secrets, and try their effect on our humanity. Only daring and insolent men, perchance, go there," to visit a land so devoid of countervailing, Arminian forces, that it admits of no return to the prelapsarian, prebourgeois balance of feeling he had found at the headwaters of the Merrimack or by Walden's shores. In such a landscape, he concluded, the primitive and childlike were forever lost to him, because he manifested an irredeemable fallenness just by being who and where he was. After all, he says, "simple races, [such] as savages, do not climb mountains—their tops are sacred and mysterious tracts never visited by them. Pomola is always angry with those who climb to the summit of Ktaadn"; and so, by being on the summit, a Concordian like himself could not help but be an antinomian intruder[26] (one who like Satan in *Paradise Lost* can never be reconciled with the Father—who is here no benevolent consensualist melon-grower anyway, but a patriarchal tyrant dressed up as Mother Nature).

Thoreau must instead suffer the postlapsarian fate of the alienated modern, the fate of the Demon as (Aeneas-like, a wanderer) he addresses the powers of the Abyss in Milton's epic (II, 970–74):

Such was Caucasus and the rock where Prometheus was bound. Æschylus had no doubt visited such scenery as this. It was vast, Titanic, and such as man never inhabits. Some part of the beholder, even some vital part, seems to escape through the loose grating of his ribs as he ascends. He is more lone than you can imagine. There is less of substantial thought and fair understanding in him, than in the plains where men inhabit. His reason is dispersed and shadowy, more thin and subtile like the air. Vast, Titanic, inhuman Nature has got him at disadvantage, caught him alone, and pilfers him of some of his divine faculty. She does not smile on him as in the plains. She seems to say sternly, why came ye here before your time? This ground is not prepared for you. Is it not enough that I smile in the valleys? I have

---

26. Garber, 1–128, and Hildebidle are perhaps the best accounts of Thoreau's symbolic use of clearings, the tops of mountains, and other such liminal and visionary places.

never made this soil for thy feet, this air for thy breathing, these rocks for thy neighbors. I cannot pity nor fondle thee here, but forever relentlessly drive thee hence to where I *am* kind. Why seek me where I have not called thee, and then complain because you find me but a stepmother? Shouldst thou freeze or starve, or shudder thy life away, here is no shrine, nor altar, nor any access to my ear.

> "Chaos and ancient Night, I come no spy
> With purpose to explore or to disturb
> The secrets of your realm, but * * *
> * * * * * * * as my way
> Lies through your spacious empire up to light."
> (*Maine Woods*, PE, 64–65)

Virtually the whole of Thoreau's first trip to Maine is spent in disappointing circumstances such as these. For in journeying past the state's chief city, Bangor (which, in an allusion to earth hanging pendant above the Abyss [*Paradise Lost*, II, 1052], he describes as being "like a star on the edge of night" [*Maine Woods*, 82]), he everywhere had to confront not only humanity's alienation from "primeval, untamed, and forever untameable *Nature*" but its alienation from its prebourgeois cultural unity as well. Thus, for example, even though Mt. Ktaadn itself is "a region uninhabited by man" (in which "Nature, . . . vast, and drear, and inhuman, though in the midst of cities; . . . savage and awful, though beautiful," objects to man's presence), it too has been turned into " 'Burnt Lands' " by the loggers. It therefore symbolizes the pervasive crisis of authority that haunted New England's nineteenth-century capitalist culture. For on the one hand, it is a figure for the tenuous hold the dominant class had over American society. "Like some pasture run to waste, or partially reclaimed by man," it is the property of some "brother or sister or kinsman of our race," of some "proprietor." Yet on the other hand, the mountain also symbolizes that class's fear of a world without such property rights or proprietors who will "rise up and dispute" acts of satanic trespass like the one Thoreau himself commits here. And so, Ktaadn terrorizes the author even as it demonically empowers him, because along with accessing his antinomian instincts it elicits his classist anxiety at the prospect of a society in which nature excludes civilization, and freedom, order. "This was that Earth of which we have heard, made out of Chaos and Old Night. Here was no man's garden, but the unhandselled globe. It was not lawn, nor pasture, nor mead, nor woodland, nor lea, nor arable, nor waste-land," nor any other sort of terrain falling into a category erected by the order-seeking mind of man. It was instead "the fresh and natural surface of the planet Earth, as it was made forever and ever" (a state, significantly, to which it had been restored by the demonic fire of Maine's acquisitive backwoods masses). As such, Ktaadn is a place that Harvard-educated writers like this one will not find to their liking, because it is not amenable to their ideologically moderate temper: "Man was not to be associated with it. It was Matter, vast, terrific,—not his Mother Earth that we have heard of, not for him to tread on, or be buried in,—no, it were being too familiar even to let his bones lie there—the home this of Necessity and Fate." Indeed, as befits a realm created out of that inchoate region nearer Milton's Hell than Heaven, "there was there felt the presence of a force not bound to be kind to man. It was a place for heathenism and superstitious rites,—to be inhabited by men nearer of kin to the rocks and to wild animals than we." For though it be "a specimen of what God saw fit to make this world," the end of Thoreau's voyaging is a place in which absolute freedom raises that same spectre of dissolution which had haunted the Federalist literary imagination some sixty years before at the time of Charles Brockden Brown:

> I stand in awe of my body, this matter to which I am bound has become so strange to me. I fear not spirits, ghosts, of which I am one,— *that* my body might,—but I fear bodies, I tremble to meet them. What is this Titan that has possession of me? Talk of mysteries!—Think of our life in nature,—daily to be shown matter, to come in contact with it,—rocks, trees, wind on our cheeks!   the *solid* earth!   the *actual* world!   the *common sense!*   *Contact! Contact! Who* are we?   *where* are we? (*Maine Woods*, PE, 69–71)

The climax of the first part of *The Maine Woods* is thus something else besides just a treatment of the "terrible sublime" or a meditation upon the difficulties presented by Cartesian dualism—though it assuredly is both those things.[27] For even leaving aside the fact that such philosophical concerns can

27. Among the many treatments of this episode atop Mt. Ktaadn in terms of Thoreau's philosophy and his links to international romanticism are Ronald Wesley Hoag, "The Mark on the Wilderness: Thoreau's Contact with Ktaadn," *Texas Studies in Literature and Language* 24 (1982): 23–46 (which rightly connects the scene to the ideologically conflicted Burkean sublime but misleadingly sees it as mere condemnation of the economic exploitation of nature); Garber, 66–128 (even though he draws unusually negative conclusions concerning Thoreau's general attitude toward the American landscape as a visionary locus); Jonathan Fairbanks, "Thoreau: Speaker for Wildness," *South Atlantic Quarterly* 70 (1971): 487–506; McIntosh, 179–215; Paul, *Shores of America*, 358–62; Lewis Leary, "Beyond the Brink of Fear: Thoreau's Wilderness," *Studies in the Literary Imagination* 7 (1974): 67–76; and Sayre, 159–66.

themselves be interpreted as projections of Thoreau's ideological confliction (his desire to affirm the Arminian structure of feeling through idealization, yet his even stronger pull toward the antinomian disorderliness of pure empiricism), the events atop Mt. Ktaadn represent an admission that his earlier faith in his ability to create a rhetoric of paradigmatic synthesis had been misplaced. Like Emerson, he had discovered the persistence of the devil (and all he symbolized) in New England culture—if not so obviously in Unitarian eastern Massachusetts, then at least not far from there in a place that until only recently had been part of the commonwealth.

Perhaps this is the reason that in the short decade that remained to Thoreau after the publication of *Walden* in 1854,[28] Milton declined as an influence on his works. There are, to be sure, one or two references to Satan amidst Chaos in the two later sections of *The Maine Woods* ("Chesuncook" and "The Allegash and East Branch" [PE, 84–325]), but these are incidental and seem intended to give unity to the book as a whole.[29] Similarly, there is also the late excursion, "Wild Apples," where Thoreau invoked Milton several times as part of one more reworking of the myth of the American Adam around the tree *Paradise Lost* had forever identified with that of Eden.[30] Yet as William L. Howarth has pointed out, textually this piece belongs to the early Walden period; thematically it is derivative of his earlier writings; and tonally, it is unabashedly nostalgic.[31] In his "nature writing" in the 1850s (e.g., his *Journal* or his unfinished project on "The Fall of the Leaf"), Thoreau was typically more concerned instead with exploring the relationship between the consciousness and the phenomenal than in returning to his earlier symbolic and idealizing ways.[32] Moreover, with one or two exceptions, in his political writings Thoreau's well-documented use during this decade of his Puritan heritage and the traditions of Protestant liberty to bolster the cause

28. Leo Stoller, *After Walden* (Stanford, Cal.: Stanford University Press, 1957); Garber, 179ff.; and Paul, *Shores of America*, 369ff., are the most straightforward accounts of Thoreau's later life.

29. The history of the two later sections of *The Maine Woods* is laid out in PE, 359–67.

30. K. P. Van Anglen, "A Paradise Regained: Thoreau's 'Wild Apples' and the Myth of the American Adam," *ESQ: A Journal of the American Renaissance*, n.s., 27 (1981): 28–37. As noted there (37 n. 14), the identification in the English-speaking world of the apple with the tree of the knowledge of good and evil is itself largely Miltonic, since *Paradise Lost* (IX, 585) had popularized the view of the Ursinian (Heidelberg) Catechism on this point. (See Harry F. Fletcher, *The Intellectual Development of John Milton* [Urbana: University of Illinois Press, 1956–61], II, 96.)

31. William L. Howarth, *The Book of Concord: Thoreau's Life as a Writer* (New York: Viking, 1982), 184–85.

32. In addition to Porte, Cavell, and Sharon Cameron on the *Journal*, see ibid., esp. 169–216, which also discusses the significant place of "The Fall of the Leaf" in the later stages of Thoreau's philosophical development.

of abolition involved not the invocation of John Milton but that of Christ and Cromwell—thereby providing more evidence both of the lessened role of the poet in his thought and (given the nature of those two men) of the persistence of the ideological confliction that had led to that decline in the first place.[33]

His one halfway famous reference to Milton during the 1850s, the "Humane House" passage in *Cape Cod*, illustrates his belief that he could no longer use the author of *Paradise Lost* to create a rhetoric capable of bridging the polarities of New England culture, as it is a classic statement of the inexorable battle between the Arminian and the antinomian in the region's imagination. Thoreau declares there that this "charity house" was intended by its organizers as a palpable sign of human caring and communal concern for those in need. In an environment as harsh and desolate as the Cape, it was to stand as a beacon of light to those *in extremis*, beckoning them in to the warmth of a home away from home. Yet the reality of the house is very different, for when Thoreau "looked into [it] to see how the shipwrecked mariner might fare," what he found was evidence that genteel charity was here (as it had so often been in New England history) a cover for upper-class indifference—and even hostility—toward the laboring masses:

33. There are many examples of Thoreau's use of his Puritan heritage and the traditions of Protestant liberty on behalf of abolition. For instance, in 1845 he unfavorably compared the response of a Concord Lyceum audience to Wendell Phillips to the antinomian spirit of the Pilgrims (*Reform Papers*, PE, 61), and in "Resistance to Civil Government" and "Slavery in Massachusetts" he several times invoked New England's radicalism at the time of the American Revolution in order to shame his contemporaries (e.g., *Reform Papers*, PE, 67 and 95). Yet his allusions to, or quotations from, Milton in this regard are almost nonexistent, the main exceptions being a brief demonization of conformists in "Resistance to Civil Government" and a more explicit reference in "Slavery in Massachusetts" that pejoratively compares Milton's Satan with those who helped return the fugitive bondsman Anthony Burns to the South (*Reform Papers*, PE, 66 and 106–7 respectively). Perhaps the main reason for the poet's absence is that as the debate over abolition heated up, Thoreau felt the need at once for a more sacrificial and yet a more militant hero—hence his many references to Christ and Cromwell in "A Plea for Captain John Brown" (*Reform Papers*, PE, 112–38).

It should be mentioned at this point that Thoreau's citations of, or references to, Milton in his *Journal*—never numerous (aside from those which occur in those parts of that work which are drafts for the mythopoeic published narratives already discussed)—become even scarcer as one enters the 1850s. Moreover, those that do occur follow the pattern of increasing antinomianism and yet confliction found in his books. (For instance, in two seemingly antiauthoritarian entries made between the end of July 1850 and mid-January 1851 he completely reversed himself by encompassing the contradictory attitudes toward Milton as a great British poet found in Emerson's *English Traits*. First, he declared that his subject was an exemplar of the natural in poetry and so is one who should be revered as a man of poetic authority; yet then he stated that like all members of the English canon, Milton "breathes no quite fresh & in this sense wild strain" and so must be eschewed by Americans lest they bow to tradition [*Journal 3: 1848–1851*, PE, 97 and 179 respectively].)

Far away in some desolate hollow by the sea-side, just within the bank, stands a lonely building on piles driven into the sand, with a slight nail put through the staple, which a freezing man can bend, with some straw, perchance, on the floor on which he may lie, or which he may burn in the fire-place to keep him alive. Perhaps this hut has never been required to shelter a shipwrecked man, and the benevolent person who promised to inspect it annually, to see that the straw and matches are here, and that the boards will keep off the wind, has grown remiss and thinks that storms and shipwrecks are over; and this very night a perishing crew may pry open its door with their numbed fingers and leave half their number dead here by morning. When I thought what must be the condition of the families which alone would ever occupy or had occupied them, what must have been the tragedy of the winter evenings spent by human beings around their hearths, these houses, though they were meant for human dwellings, did not look cheerful to me. They appeared but a stage to the grave. The gulls flew around and screamed over them; the roar of the ocean in storms, and the lapse of its waves in calms, alone resounds through them, all dark and empty within, year in year out, except, perchance, on one memorable night. Houses of entertainment for shipwrecked men! What kind of sailor's homes were they? (*Cape Cod*, PE, 57–58)

Furthermore, upon closer inspection, this postlapsarian monument to the New England need to assuage the Arminian structure of feeling by building "a city on a hill" that would include even the marginalized and disempowered is no less parsimonious or self-interested than Winthrop's original had been in "A Model of Christian Charity." For as Thoreau goes on to say, like his symbol here for the Standing Order, the steepleless meetinghouse in Eastham, it was intended by the dominant class as a sign of the graciousness of the love patriarchy they had long sought to erect in Massachusetts. But when looked at with an Emersonian "eye" (that same "pupil" which was grounded in the landscape of Concord by Walden Pond), the house is a desolate parody of their hegemonic designs upon society:

This "charity house," . . . this "humane house," . . . had neither window nor sliding shutter, nor clap-boards, nor paint. As we have said, there was a rusty nail put through the staple. However, as we wished to get an idea of a humane house, and we hoped that we should never have a better opportunity, we put our eyes, by turns, to a knot-hole in the door, and, after long looking, without seeing, into the dark—not knowing how many shipwrecked men's bones we might see at last, looking with the eye of faith, knowing that, though to him that knocketh it may not always be opened, yet to him that looketh long enough through a knot-hole the inside shall be visible,—for we had some practice at looking inward,—by steadily keeping our other ball covered from the light meanwhile, putting the outward world behind us, ocean and land, and the beach—till the pupil became enlarged and collected the rays of light that were wandering in the dark, (for the pupil shall be enlarged by looking; there never was so dark a night but a faithful and patient eye, however small, might at last prevail over it,)—after all this, I say, things began to take shape to our vision,—if we may use this expression where there was nothing but emptiness,—and we obtained the long wished for insight.

Indeed, from a Transcendentalist angle of vision, the corpse-cold formalism of dominant-class charity is all emptiness and darkness:

Though we thought at first that it was a hopeless case, after several minutes' steady exercise of the divine faculty, our prospects began decidedly to brighten, and we were ready to exclaim with the blind bard of "Paradise Lost and Regained,"—

"Hail! Holy Light, offspring of Heaven, first born.
Or of the eternal coeternal beam
May I express thee unblamed?"

A little longer, and a chimney rushed red on our sight. In short, when our vision had grown familiar with the darkness, we discovered that there were some stones and some loose wads of wool on the floor, and an empty fire-place at the further end; but it *was not* supplied with matches, or straw, or hay, that we could see, nor "accommodated with a bench." Indeed, it was the wreck of all cosmical beauty there within. (*Cape Cod*, PE, 59–60)

Instead of the love and grace that two centuries of ministers and magistrates had claimed to be peculiarly their own, instead of that Spirit Whom Milton addressed in the invocation in *Paradise Lost* partially quoted here (III, 1–55), in this allegedly charitable foundation Thoreau finds a "darkness visible" without even such elements for fire as would make it effectively demonic. As he goes on to say, "turning our backs on the outward world," looking "through the knot-hole into the humane house, into the very bowels of mercy; . . . for bread we found a stone. . . . how cold is charity! how inhumane humanity!" Far from providing an endorsement to dominant-class claims, his moment of vision in this chapter thus bespeaks the eternal opposition between Arminianism and the skeptical, antiauthoritarian spirit in Yankee culture, as well as the inefficacy of all attempts (whether Puritan or consensualist) to compromise between the two. For though the angelic and the demonic *are* combined here (in the heaven of a mission house black and selfish as Hell), that combination is meant to underscore the region's historic polarizations rather than ameliorate them. Only Thoreau himself (who in this passage is both a blind poet-prophet like Milton and yet also, like Satan, a quoter of Scripture to his own purpose) manages to fuse the two structures of feeling. For he alone, like a good Christian, turns his back on the world and looks here "with the eye of faith"; and yet he alone also mockingly corrects the New Testament on the nature of the reward given "to him that knocketh."

However, even this personal synthesis of feeling is obviously cold comfort for Thoreau now. For it has little effect on the society around him, and there is no sense of transformation or hope here, as there had been at the end of his Miltonic meditations in *Walden* and *A Week*. Like the author of *Paradise Lost* in his great invocation to the Holy Ghost at the start of book III, Thoreau had "sung of Chaos and eternal Night, / Taught by the Heav'nly Muse to venture down / The dark descent"; but lacking the Christian assurance of his predecessor or even his own former faith (as one "smit with the love of sacred song") in the poet's ability to transform his culture rhetorically, he now found it too "hard and rare," in such circumstances as faced men of his class in nineteenth-century New England, to be able "up to reascend" to those heavenly heights which once he thought he had inhabited (lines 18–21, and 29). And so, too elect here for his neighbors—himself his own church and his own state—he falls back into a secular version of the ultimate logical conclusion of Luther's revolt: that individualistic particularism upon which Milton himself in the end had staked his salvation.

EPILOGUE:
FRESH WOODS AND
PASTURES NEW

As this suggests, what Henry Thoreau had discovered by the shores of the Atlantic was that he too was largely trapped by the contradictions of his culture. To be sure, till the end he still felt the old antinomian urge to follow Emerson at his most radical (something that is proved by the obvious record of his involvement with abolitionism in the years preceding the Civil War). Yet he now realized that even the Emerson who had advised the graduating class of the Harvard Divinity College to be "yourself a newborn bard of the Holy Ghost" had defined such inspired poet-priests as ones who let "the breath of new life be breathed . . . through the forms already existing." For so strong were the bourgeois interests out of which the region's high culture had developed that even in *The Divinity School Address* Emerson could not help but frame his most potentially individualistic and revolutionary sentiments in terms of personal self-culture and its potential for reviving the Standing Order (reducing his satanism to the meliorist optimism of the belief that "if once you are alive, you shall find" that society's institutions "shall become plastic and new. The remedy to their deformity is, first, soul, and second, soul, and evermore, soul. A whole popedom of forms, one pulsation of virtue can uplift and vivify" [*Collected Works*, 1, 90 and 92]). By the time he wrote *Cape Cod* Thoreau understood this about his mentor and, despite his greater determination to satisfy the antinomian structure of feeling, saw its implications for his own work. He saw how easy it was in New England for such sentiments to become implicated in their opposite, and how difficult it was to find a rhetoric that would bridge the divide between the desire for liberty and the claims of order without falling into the contradictions of the "Humane House." For though he rejected the false consciousness of previous generations of Yankee intellectuals, he could not annul the concrete historical and structural conditions that had given rise to their conflicted ideology. As a consequence, he too found himself in the end stymied and all too aware of the ways in which literature (and literary reception) function "politically" in the broadest sense.

Of course, Thoreau was not the last New Englander, let alone the last American author (particularly of his educational and ideological background) to face this dilemma or come to this set of realizations. These conflicting structures of feeling lay at the heart of Anglo-American culture and especially shaped the institutional and cultural forms through which the dominant classes in both countries tried to establish their hegemony. Late eighteenth-century and antebellum bourgeois novelists such as Brockden Brown, Cooper, Stowe, Hawthorne, and Melville, and poets and critics like Whittier, Lowell, and Longfellow therefore all had to confront the same forces and issues as the Transcendentalists and their predecessors (as from very different perspectives did Whitman and a number of subversive female and African-American authors too). Because of this, John Milton also figures in the works of all these writers, primarily as a presence who focused their thoughts and feelings on issues of authority and legitimation. For like the regicide who nonetheless justified God's ways to man, they too lived with the tension that informs the end of "Lycidas" (in which Milton had bowed to the past by moving traditionally from pastoral to epic, yet looked to the future by moving westward, toward the setting sun and America, "to fresh woods, and pastures new"). The story of the New England Milton consequently leads to that of the Milton who helped shape the American Renaissance, as well as the writings of those who dissented from its ideology and aims: the conflicted Milton of Melville and the democratically synthetic Milton of Whitman as well as the Milton whose subversive hand can be seen in the works of Frederick Douglass or William Wells Brown. It is a story that ranges geographically beyond the confines of Unitarianism's eastern Massachusetts enclave, and socioculturally beyond the neat world of Beacon Hill and Harvard, thus placing all that has been said heretofore on this subject in its most capacious perspective: that of John Milton and the coming of the Civil War.

BIBLIOGRAPHY

Abrams, M. H. *Natural Supernaturalism: Tradition and Revolution in Romantic Literature.* New York: W. W. Norton, 1971.

Adams, John Quincy. *Lectures on Rhetoric and Oratory, Delivered to the Classes of Senior and Junior Sophisters in Harvard University.* 2 vols. Cambridge, Mass.: Hilliard and Metcalf, 1810.

Adler, Jacob H. "A Milton-Bryant Parallel." *New England Quarterly* 25 (1951): 377–80.

Alcott, Bronson. "Days from a Diary." *Dial* 2 (1842): 409–37.

Allen, Gay Wilson. *Waldo Emerson: A Biography.* New York: Viking, 1981.

Anderson, John Q. *The Liberating Gods: Emerson on Poets and Poetry.* Coral Gables, Fla.: University of Miami Press, 1971.

The Anthology Society: Journal of the Society Which Conducts "The Monthly Anthology and Boston Review," October 3, 1805 to July 2, 1811. Edited and introduced by M. A. DeWolfe Howe. Boston: The Boston Athenaeum, 1910.

Bailyn, Bernard. *The Ideological Origins of the American Revolution.* Cambridge, Mass.: Harvard University Press, 1967.

————, ed. *Pamphlets of the American Revolution.* 1 vol. to date. Cambridge, Mass.: Harvard University Press, 1965–.

Barish, Evelyn. *Emerson: The Roots of Prophecy.* Princeton, N.J.: Princeton University Press, 1989.

Bartlett, William I. *Jones Very: Emerson's "Brave Saint."* Durham, N.C.: Duke University Press, 1942.

Baym, Nina. *Novels, Readers, and Reviewers: Responses to Fiction in Antebellum America.* Ithaca, N.Y.: Cornell University Press, 1984.

Beasley, Frederick. *A Vindication of the Fundamental Principles of Truth and Order, in the Church of Christ, From the Allegations of the Rev. William E. Channing, D.D.* Trenton, N.J.: Justice, 1830.

Bell, Michael Davitt. *The Development of American Romance: The Sacrifice of Relation.* Chicago: University of Chicago Press, 1980.

Bercovitch, Sacvan. *The American Jeremiad.* Madison: University of Wisconsin Press, 1978.

————. *The Puritan Origins of the American Self.* New Haven, Conn.: Yale University Press, 1975.

Berthoff, Warner. "Jones Very: New England Mystic." *Boston Public Library Quarterly* 2 (1950): 63–76.

Blanchard, Paula. *Margaret Fuller: From Transcendentalism to Revolution.* New York: Delacorte, 1978.

Boudreau, Gordon V. *The Roots of "Walden" and the Tree of Life.* Nashville, Tenn.: Vanderbilt University Press, 1990.

Boyer, Paul, and Stephen Nissenbaum. *Salem Possessed: The Social Origins of Witchcraft.* Cambridge, Mass.: Harvard University Press, 1974.

Breitweiser, Mitchell R. *Cotton Mather and Benjamin Franklin: the Price of Representative Personality.* Cambridge, Eng.: Cambridge University Press, 1984.

Bridenbaugh, Carl. *Mitre and Sceptre: Transatlantic Faiths, Ideas, Personalities, and Politics, 1689–1775.* New York: Oxford University Press, 1962.

Brisman, Leslie. *Milton's Poetry of Choice and Its Romantic Heirs.* Ithaca, N.Y.: Cornell University Press, 1973.

Brown, Arthur W. *Always Young for Liberty: A Biography of Willliam Ellery Channing.* Syracuse, N.Y.: Syracuse University Press, 1956.

Bryant, William Cullen. *The Prose Writings of William Cullen Bryant.* Edited by Parke Godwin. 2 vols. New York: D. Appleton, 1884.

Buckminster, Joseph Stevens. "The Dangers and Duties of Men of Letters." Phi Beta Kappa address, Harvard University, 31 August 1809. *The Monthly Anthology and Boston Review* 7 (1809): 145–58.

Buell, Lawrence. *Literary Transcendentalism: Style and Vision in the American Renaissance.* Ithaca, N.Y.: Cornell University Press, 1973.

———. *New England Literary Culture: From Revolution through Renaissance.* Cambridge, Eng.: Cambridge University Press, 1986.

Burbick, Joan. *Thoreau's Alternative History: Changing Perspectives on Nature, Culture, and Language.* Philadelphia: University of Pennsylvania Press, 1987.

Caldwell, Patricia. *The Puritan Conversion Narrative: The Beginnings of American Expression.* Cambridge, Eng.: Cambridge University Press, 1983.

Cameron, Kenneth W. *Thoreau's Harvard Years: Materials Introductory to New Explorations, Record of Fact and Background.* 2 vols. Hartford, Conn.: Transcendental Books, 1966.

———, comp. *Emerson the Essayist: An Outline of His Philosophical Development Through 1836 with Special Emphasis on the Sources and Interpretation of "Nature."* 2 vols. Raleigh, N.C.: The Thistle Press, 1945.

———, comp. *Ralph Waldo Emerson's Reading: A Corrected Edition.* Hartford, Conn.: Transcendental Books, 1962.

Cameron, Sharon. *Writing Nature: Henry Thoreau's "Journal."* New York: Oxford University Press, 1985.

Cavell, Stanley. *The Senses of Walden.* Expanded ed. San Francisco: North Point Press, 1981.

Chalmers, Alexander, ed. *The Works of the English Poets, from Chaucer to Cowper; including the series edited with prefaces, biographical and critical, by Dr. Samuel Johnson: and the most approved translations. The additional lives, by Alexander Chalmers.* . . . 21 vols. London: J. Johnson etc., 1810.

Channing, Edward T. *Lectures Read to the Seniors in Harvard College.* Boston: Ticknor and Fields, 1856.

Channing, William Ellery. *The Character and Writings of John Milton. Memorable Sermons.* No. 17. Boston: American Unitarian Association, n.d.

———. "Milton." Review of *A Treatise on Christian Doctrine, compiled from the Holy Scriptures alone,* by John Milton, trans. Charles R. Sumner. *The Christian Examiner and Theological Review* 3 (1826): 29–77.

————. *The Works of William Ellery Channing, D.D.* 6 vols. Boston: James Monroe, 1848.

Channing, William Henry. "Ernest the Seeker." *Dial* 1 (1840): 48–58 and 233–42.

Charvat, William. *The Origins of American Critical Thought (1810–1835).* Philadelphia: University of Pennsylvania Press, 1936.

Clarke, James Freeman. "George Keats." *Dial* 3 (1843): 495–500.

————, comp. "Remarks on John Milton, by John Keats, Written in the Fly-Leaf of *Paradise Lost.*" *Dial* 3 (1843): 500–504.

Cohen, Charles L. *God's Caress: The Psychology of Puritan Religious Experience.* New York: Oxford University Press, 1986.

Colacurcio, Michael J. *The Province of Piety: Moral History in Hawthorne's Early Tales.* Cambridge, Mass.: Harvard University Press, 1984.

Cole, Phyllis. "The Purity of Puritanism: Transcendentalist Readings of Milton." *Studies in Romanticism* 17 (1978): 129–48.

Coleridge, Samuel Taylor. *The Collected Works of Samuel Taylor Coleridge.* Gen. ed., Kathleen Coburn. 11 vols. to date. Princeton, N.J.: Princeton University Press, 1969–.

Conn, Walter. *Christian Conversion: A Developmental Interpretation of Autonomy and Surrender.* New York: Paulist Press, 1986.

Cranch, Christopher. "The Blind Seer." *Dial* 2 (1841): 47–48.

Cressy, David. *Coming Over: Migration and Communication between England and New England in the Seventeenth Century.* New York: Cambridge University Press, 1987.

Cushing, William. *Index to "The Christian Examiner." Volumes I–LXXXVII. 1824–1869.* Boston: William Cushing, 1879.

————. *Index to "The North American Review." Volumes I–CXXV. 1815–1877.* Cambridge, Mass.: John Wilson and Son, 1878.

Davidson, Cathy N. *Revolution and the Word: The Rise of the Novel in America.* New York: Oxford University Press, 1986.

Davidson, Philip. *Propaganda and the American Revolution, 1763–1783.* Chapel Hill: University of North Carolina Press, 1941.

Davis, Richard Beale. "The Early American Lawyer and the Profession of Letters." *Huntington Library Quarterly* 12 (1949): 191–206.

Deiss, Joseph Jay. *The Roman Years of Margaret Fuller.* New York: Crowell, 1969.

Delbanco, Andrew. *William Ellery Channing: An Essay on the Liberal Spirit in America.* Cambridge, Mass.: Harvard University Press, 1981.

Demos, John Putnam. *Entertaining Satan: Witchcraft and the Culture of Early New England.* Oxford: Oxford University Press, 1982.

Douglas, Ann. *The Feminization of American Culture.* New York: Knopf, 1977.

Dulles, Avery, S. J. *The Catholicity of the Church and the Structure of Catholicism.* Oxford: Clarendon, 1985.

————. *Models of the Church.* Garden City, N.Y.: Doubleday, 1974.

Dunn, Richard S. *Puritans and Yankees: The Winthrop Dynasty of New England, 1630–1717.* Princeton, N.J.: Princeton University Press, 1962.

Dwight, Timothy. *Travels in New England and New York.* Edited by Barbara M. Solomon and Patricia M. King. 4 vols. Cambridge, Mass.: Harvard University Press, 1969.

Edgell, David P. *William Ellery Channing: An Intellectual Portrait.* Boston: Beacon, 1955.

Elliott, Emory. *Power and the Pulpit in Puritan New England.* Princeton, N.J.: Princeton University Press, 1975.

―――― . *Revolutionary Writers: Literature and Authority in the New Republic 1725–1810*. New York: Oxford University Press, 1982.

Elliott, G. R. "On Emerson's 'Grace' and 'Self-Reliance.' " *New England Quarterly* 2 (1929): 93–104.

Ellison, Julie. *Emerson's Romantic Style*. Princeton, N.J.: Princeton University Press, 1984.

Emerson, Ralph Waldo. *The Collected Works of Ralph Waldo Emerson*. Edited by Alfred R. Ferguson, et al. 4 vols. to date. Cambridge, Mass.: Harvard University Press, 1971–.

―――― . *The Complete Works of Ralph Waldo Emerson*. Edited by Edward Waldo Emerson. 12 vols. Boston: Houghton Mifflin, 1903–4.

―――― . *The Early Lectures of Ralph Waldo Emerson*. Edited by Stephen E. Whicher, et al. 3 vols. Cambridge, Mass.: Harvard University Press, 1959–71.

―――― . *English Traits*. Edited by Howard Mumford Jones. Cambridge, Mass.: Harvard University Press, 1966.

―――― . "John Milton." [Essay]. MH bMs. Am 1704.10 (196). The John Gorham Palfrey Papers. Houghton Library, Harvard University.

―――― . *The Journals and Miscellaneous Notebooks of Ralph Waldo Emerson*. Edited by William H. Gilman, et al. 16 vols. Cambridge, Mass.: Harvard University Press, 1960–82.

―――― . "Lectures on Biography: I. Introduction. Tests of Great Men. . . ." [Notes]. MH bMs. Am 1280.194 (7). The John Gorham Palfrey Papers. Houghton Library, Harvard University.

―――― . *The Letters of Ralph Waldo Emerson*. Edited by Ralph L. Rusk. 6 vols. New York: Columbia University Press, 1939.

―――― , ed. *Parnassus*. Boston: Houghton Mifflin, 1874.

Engell, James. *The Creative Imagination: Enlightenment to Romanticism*. Cambridge, Mass.: Harvard University Press, 1981.

Everett, A. H. "Early Literature of Modern Europe." Review of *Tableau Historique de la Littérature Française*, by M. J. de Chenier; and *Historia de la Literatura Española*, by F. Bouterwek, trans. J. G. de la Cortina and N. Hugalde y Mollenido. *The North American Review* 38 (1834): 158–77.

Fairbanks, Jonathan. "Thoreau: Speaker for Wildness." *South Atlantic Quarterly* 70 (1971): 487–506.

Ferguson, Robert A. *Law and Letters in American Culture*. Cambridge, Mass.: Harvard University Press, 1984.

Fiedelson, Charles, Jr. *Symbolism and American Literature*. Chicago: University of Chicago Press, 1953.

Fiering, Norman. *Jonathan Edwards' Moral Thought and Its British Context*. Chapel Hill: University of North Carolina Press, 1981.

Fish, Stanley E. *Surprised by Sin: The Reader in "Paradise Lost."* Berkeley: University of California Press, 1967.

Fletcher, Harry F. *The Intellectual Development of John Milton*. 2 vols. Urbana: University of Illinois Press, 1956–61.

Fliegelman, Jay. *Prodigals and Pilgrims: The American Revolution against Patriarchal Authority, 1750–1800*. Cambridge, Eng.: Cambridge University Press, 1982.

Fuller, S. Margaret. *The Letters of Margaret Fuller*. Edited by Robert N. Hudspeth. 5 vols. to date. Ithaca, N.Y.: Cornell University Press, 1983–.

―――― . *Life Without and Life Within; or, Reviews, Narratives, Essays, and Poems*. Edited by Arthur B. Fuller. Boston: Brown, Taggard, and Chase, 1860.

———. "Lives of the Great Composers, Haydn, Mozart, Handel, Bach, Beethoven." *Dial* 2 (1841): 148–203.
———. *Memoirs of Margaret Fuller Ossoli.* Edited by James Freeman Clark, et al. 2 vols. Boston: Phillips, Sampson, and Co., 1852.
———. *Papers on Literature and Art.* 2 vols. New York: Wiley and Putnam, 1846.
———. "The Prose Works of Milton. With a Biographical Introduction, By R. W. Griswold." Review. *New-York Daily Tribune,* 7 October 1845, p. 1, cols. 1–2.
Garber, Frederick. *Thoreau's Redemptive Imagination.* New York: New York University Press, 1977.
Gardiner, J.S.J. "Milton's Moral and Political Conduct." *The Monthly Anthology and Boston Review* 6 (1809): 87–88.
Gilmore, Michael T. *American Romanticism and the Marketplace.* Chicago: University of Chicago Press, 1985.
Gittleman, Edwin. *Jones Very: The Effective Years, 1833–1840.* New York: Columbia University Press, 1967.
Golemba, Henry. *Thoreau's Wild Rhetoric.* New York: New York University Press, 1990.
Gray, John C. "Dante." Review of *La Divina Commedia di Dante Alighieri,* and *The Vision, or Hell, Purgatory and Paradise of Dante Alighieri,* trans. H. F. Carey. *The North American Review* 8 (1819): 322–46.
Green, Judith Kent. "A Tentative Transcendentalist in the Ohio Valley: Samuel Osgood and the *Western Messenger.*" In *Studies in the American Renaissance: 1984,* edited by Joel A. Myerson, 79–92. Charlottesville: University Press of Virginia, 1984.
Greenwood, F.W.P. "Milton's English Prose Works." Review of *A Selection from the English Prose Works of John Milton. The North American Review* 25 (1827): 73–89.
Gregory, Ruth W. "American Criticism of Milton, 1800–1938." Ph.D. diss., University of Wisconsin, 1938.
Griffin, Dustin. *Regaining Paradise: Milton and the Eighteenth Century.* Cambridge, Eng.: Cambridge University Press, 1986.
Gruber, Christian P. "The Education of Henry Thoreau, Harvard 1833–1837." Ph.D. diss., Princeton University, 1953.
Gura, Philip F. "Elizabeth Palmer Peabody and the Philosophy of Language." *ESQ: A Journal of the American Renaissance,* n.s., 23 (1977): 154–63.
———. *A Glimpse of Sion's Glory: Puritan Radicalism in New England, 1620–1660.* Middletown, Conn.: Wesleyan University Press, 1984.
———. "Thoreau's Maine Woods Indians: More Representative Men." *American Literature* 49 (1977): 366–84.
———. *The Wisdom of Words: Language, Theology, and Literature in the New England Renaissance.* Middletown, Conn.: Wesleyan University Press, 1981.
Hall, David D. *The Faithful Shepherd: A History of the New England Ministry in the Seventeenth Century.* Chapel Hill: University of North Carolina Press, 1972.
———. *Worlds of Wonder, Days of Judgment: Popular Religious Belief in Early New England.* New York: Knopf, 1989.
Harding, Walter. "The Apple-Tree Table Tale." *Boston Public Library Quarterly* 8 (1956): 213–15.
———. "A New Checklist of the Books in Henry David Thoreau's Library." In *Studies in the American Renaissance: 1983,* edited by Joel A. Myerson, 151–86. Charlottesville: University Press of Virginia, 1983.
———, comp. *Emerson's Library.* Charlottesville: University Press of Virginia, 1967.

Harding, Walter, and Michael Meyer. *The New Thoreau Handbook.* New York: New York University Press, 1980.

Hatch, Nathan O. *The Sacred Cause of Liberty: Republican Thought and the Millennium in Revolutionary New England.* New Haven, Conn.: Yale University Press, 1977.

Havens, R. D. *The Influence of Milton on English Poetry.* Cambridge, Mass.: Harvard University Press, 1922.

Hazlitt, William. *The Complete Works of William Hazlitt.* Edited by P. P. Howe, after A. R. Waller and Arnold Glover. 21 vols. London: J. M. Dent, 1930–34.

Hedge, Frederic Henry. "The Art of Life,—The Scholar's Calling." *Dial* 1 (1840): 175–82.

Heimert, Alan. *Religion and the American Mind from the Great Awakening to the Revolution.* Cambridge, Mass.: Harvard University Press, 1966.

Heimert, Alan, and Perry Miller, comps. *The Greak Awakening: Documents Illustrating the Crisis and Its Consequences.* Indianapolis, Ind.: Bobbs-Merrill, 1967.

Herron, Carolivia. "Milton and Afro-American Literature." In *Re-membering Milton: Essays on the Texts and Traditions,* edited by Mary Nyquist and Margaret W. Ferguson, 278–300. London: Methuen, 1988.

Hildebidle, John. *Thoreau: A Naturalist's Liberty.* Cambridge, Mass.: Harvard University Press, 1983.

Hill, Christopher. *Change and Continuity in Seventeenth-Century England.* Cambridge, Mass.: Harvard University Press, 1975.

——— . *Puritanism and Revolution: Studies in Interpretation of the English Revolution of the Seventeenth Century.* London: Secker and Warburg, 1958.

——— . *Society and Puritanism in Pre-Revolutionary England.* New York: Schocken, 1964.

——— . *The World Turned Upside Down: Radical Ideas during the English Revolution.* London: Maurice Temple Smith, 1972.

Hoag, Ronald Wesley. "The Mark on the Wilderness: Thoreau's Contact with Ktaadn." *Texas Studies in Literature and Language* 24 (1982): 23–46.

Hopkins, Vivian. *Spires of Form: A Study of Emerson's Aesthetic Theory.* Cambridge, Mass.: Harvard University Press, 1951.

Howarth, William L. *The Book of Concord: Thoreau's Life as a Writer.* New York: Viking, 1982.

Howe, Daniel Walker. *The Political Culture of the American Whigs.* Chicago: University of Chicago Press, 1979.

——— . *The Unitarian Conscience: Harvard Moral Philosophy, 1805–1861.* Cambridge, Mass.: Harvard University Press, 1970.

Hutchison, William R. *The Transcendentalist Ministers: Church Reform in the New England Renaissance.* New Haven, Conn.: Yale University Press, 1959.

Ingram, William, and Kathleen Swaim, comps. *A Concordance to Milton's English Poetry.* Oxford: Clarendon, 1972.

Irwin, John T. *American Hieroglyphics: The Symbol of the Egyptian Hieroglyphics in the American Renaissance.* New Haven, Conn.: Yale University Press, 1980.

Ivimey, Joseph. *John Milton: His Life and Times, Religious and Political Opinions: with an appendix, containing animadversions upon Dr. Johnson's Life of Milton, etc., etc.* New York: D. Appleton, 1833.

Jack, Ian. *Augustan Satire: Intention and Idiom in English Poetry, 1660–1750.* 1942. Corr. ed. Oxford: Oxford University Press, 1971.

Jehlen, Myra. "Introduction: Beyond Transcendence." In *Ideology and Classic American Literature*, edited by Sacvan Bercovitch and Myra Jehlen, 1–18. Cambridge, Eng.: Cambridge University Press, 1986.

Jones, James W. *The Shattered Synthesis: New England Puritanism before the Great Awakening*. New Haven, Conn.: Yale University Press, 1973.

Jorgenson, Chester E. "Emerson's Paradise under the Shadow of Swords." *Philological Quarterly* 11 (1932): 274–92.

Kolodny, Annette. *The Land Before Her: Fantasy and Experience of the American Frontiers, 1630–1860*. Chapel Hill: University of North Carolina Press, 1984.

——— . *The Lay of the Land: Metaphor as Experience and History in American Life and Letters*. Chapel Hill: University of North Carolina Press, 1975.

Leary, Lewis. "Beyond the Brink of Fear: Thoreau's Wilderness." *Studies in the Literary Imagination* 7 (1974): 67–76.

Levernier, James A. "Calvinism and Transcendentalism in the Poetry of Jones Very." *ESQ: A Journal of the American Renaissance*, n.s., 24 (1978): 30–41.

Levin, David. *Cotton Mather: The Young Life of the Lord's Remembrancer, 1663–1703*. Cambridge, Mass.: Harvard University Press, 1978.

Lewis, R.W.B. *The American Adam: Innocence, Tragedy, and Tradition in the Nineteenth Century*. Chicago: University of Chicago Press, 1955.

Lockridge, Kenneth. *A New England Town, The First Hundred Years: Dedham, Massachusetts, 1636–1736*. New York: W. W. Norton, 1970.

Lonsdale, Roger, ed. *The Poems of Gray, Collins, and Goldsmith*. London: Longmans, Green, and Co., 1969.

Lowance, Mason I., Jr. *The Language of Canaan: Metaphor and Symbol in New England from the Puritans to the Transcendentalists*. Cambridge, Mass.: Harvard University Press, 1980.

Lynn, Kenneth S. *A Divided People*. Westport, Conn.: Greenwood Press, 1977.

Macaulay, Thomas Babington, 1st Baron. *The Works of Lord Macaulay*. London: Longmans, Green, 1898.

McColley, Diane Kelsey. *Milton's Eve*. Urbana: University of Illinois Press, 1983.

——— . "Milton and the Sexes." In *The Cambridge Companion to Milton*, edited by Dennis Danielson, 147–66. Cambridge, Eng.: Cambridge University Press, 1989.

McIntosh, James. *Thoreau as Romantic Naturalist: His Shifting Stance Toward Nature*. Ithaca, N.Y.: Cornell University Press, 1974.

McKinsey, Elizabeth R. *Niagara Falls: Icon of the American Sublime*. New York: Cambridge University Press, 1985.

——— . *The Western Experiment: New England Transcendentalists in the Ohio Valley*. Cambridge, Mass.: Harvard University Press, 1973.

McWilliams, John P., Jr. *Hawthorne, Melville, and the American Character: A Looking-glass Business*. Cambridge, Eng.: Cambridge University Press, 1984.

——— . *Political Justice in a Republic: James Fenimore Cooper's America*. Berkeley: University of California Press, 1972.

Martin, Terence. *The Instructed Vision: Scottish Common Sense Philosophy and the Origins of American Fiction*. Bloomington: Indiana University Press, 1961.

Martyn, W. Carlos. *Life and Times of John Milton*. New York: American Tract Society, 1866.

Matthiessen, F. O. *American Renaissance: Art and Expression in the Age of Emerson and Whitman*. New York: Oxford University Press, 1941.

May, Henry F. *The Enlightenment in America*. Oxford: Oxford University Press, 1976.

Middlekauff, Robert. *The Mathers: Three Generations of Puritan Intellectuals, 1596–1728.* New York: Oxford University Press, 1971.

Mignon, Charles W. " 'Classic Art': Emerson's Pragmatic Criticism." In *Studies in the American Renaissance: 1983,* edited by Joel A. Myerson, 203–21. Charlottesville: University Press of Virginia, 1983.

Milder, Robert. "*The Last of the Mohicans* and the New World Fall." *American Literature* 52 (1980): 407–29.

Miller, Perry. *Errand into the Wilderness.* Cambridge, Mass.: Harvard University Press, 1956.

————. *The Life of the Mind in America: From the Revolution to the Civil War.* New York: Harcourt, Brace, and World, 1965.

————. *Nature's Nation.* Cambridge, Mass.: Harvard University Press, 1967.

————. *The New England Mind: From Colony to Province.* Cambridge, Mass.: Harvard University Press, 1953.

————. *The New England Mind: The Seventeenth Century.* New York: MacMillan, 1939.

————, ed. *The Legal Mind in America from Independence to the Civil War.* Garden City, N.Y.: Doubleday, 1962.

Milton, John. *Complete Prose Works of John Milton.* Gen. ed., Don M. Wolfe. 8 vols. New Haven, Conn.: Yale University Press, 1953–82.

————. *Milton: Poetical Works.* Edited by Douglas Bush. Oxford: Oxford University Press, 1966.

————. *Paradise Lost.* Edited by Alastair Fowler. London: Longman, 1974.

————. *The Poetical Works of John Milton. . . . With principal notes of various commentators. To which are added illustrations, with some account of the life of Milton. By the Rev. Henry John Todd. . . .* 6 vols. London: Bye and Low for J. Johnson, [etc.], 1801.

————. *The Prose Works of John Milton, with a Biographical Introduction.* Edited by Rufus W. Griswold. 2 vols. Philadelphia: H. Hooker, 1845.

————. *The Prose Works of John Milton, with a Life of the Author, interspersed with translations and critical remarks, by Charles Symmons. . . .* 7 vols. London: T. Binsley for J. Johnson, [etc.], 1806.

————. *A Selection from the English Prose Works of John Milton.* Edited by Francis Jenks. 2 vols. Boston: Bowles and Dearborn, 1826.

Monk, Samuel. *The Sublime: A Study of Critical Theories in Eighteenth Century England.* 1935. Reprint. Ann Arbor: University of Michigan Press, 1960.

Morgan, Edmund S. *Visible Saints: The History of a Puritan Idea.* Ithaca, N.Y.: Cornell University Press, 1963.

Morison, Samuel Eliot. *Three Centuries of Harvard: 1636–1936.* Cambridge, Mass.: Harvard University Press, 1936.

Myerson, Joel A. *The New England Transcendentalists and the "Dial": A History of the Magazine and Its Contributors.* Rutherford, N.J.: Farleigh Dickinson University Press, 1980.

————, comp. *Margaret Fuller: A Descriptive Bibliography.* Pittsburgh, Pa.: University of Pittsburgh Press, 1978.

Nelson, James G. *The Sublime Puritan: Milton and the Victorians.* Madison: University of Wisconsin Press, 1963.

Nicoloff, Philip L. *Emerson on Race and History: An Examination of "English Traits."* New York: Columbia University Press, 1961.

Novak, Barbara. *Nature and Culture: American Landscape and Painting, 1825–1875.* New York: Oxford University Press, 1980.

Osgood, Samuel. "Milton in Our Day." Review of *The Poetical Works of John Milton with a Life of the Author. With Preliminary Dissertations, etc.*, ed. Charles Dexter Cleveland, and *The Prose Works of John Milton. The Christian Examiner and Religious Miscellany* 57 (1854): 323–40.

Packer, Barbara L. *Emerson's Fall: A New Interpretation of the Major Essays.* New York: Continuum, 1982.

Parker, Theodore. *The Centenary Edition of the Works of Theodore Parker.* Edited by George Willis Cooke, et al. 15 vols. Boston: American Unitarian Association, 1907–16.

———. "German Literature." *Dial* 1 (1841): 315–39.

———. "The Life and Character of Dr. Follen." *Dial* 3 (1843): 343–62.

Parkman, Francis. "Knowles's *Memoir of Roger Williams.*" Review of *Memoir of Roger Williams, the Founder of the State of Rhode Island*, by James D. Knowles. *The Christian Examiner and Theological Review* 16 (1834): 72–97.

Parks, Edd Winfield, comp. *Ante-Bellum Southern Literary Critics.* Athens: University of Georgia Press, 1962.

Paul, Sherman. *Emerson's Angle of Vision: Man and Nature in American Experience.* Cambridge, Mass.: Harvard University Press, 1952.

———. *The Shores of America: Thoreau's Inward Exploration.* Urbana: University of Illinois Press, 1958.

Pease, Donald E. *Visionary Compacts: American Renaissance Writings in Cultural Context.* Madison: University of Wisconsin Press, 1987.

Pettigrew, Richard Campbell. "Emerson and Milton." *American Literature* 3 (1931): 45–59.

Pommer, Henry F. *Milton and Melville.* Pittsburgh, Pa.: University of Pittsburgh Press, 1950.

Porte, Joel. *Emerson and Thoreau: Transcendentalists in Conflict.* Middletown, Conn.: Wesleyan University Press, 1965.

———. *Representative Man: Ralph Waldo Emerson in His Time.* New York: Oxford University Press, 1979.

Powell, Earl A. "Luminism and the American Sublime." In *American Light: The Luminist Movement, 1850–1875*, edited by John Wilmerding, 69–94. Washington, D.C.: National Gallery of Art, 1980.

Reinhold, Meyer. *Classica Americana: The Greek and Roman Heritage in the United States.* Detroit: Wayne State University Press, 1984.

Reynolds, David S. *Beneath the American Renaissance: The Subversive Imagination in the Age of Emerson and Melville.* New York: Knopf, 1988.

Reynolds, Larry J. *European Revolutions and the American Literary Renaissance.* New Haven, Conn.: Yale University Press, 1988.

Richardson, Robert D., Jr. *Henry David Thoreau: A Life of the Mind.* Berkeley: University of California Press, 1986.

———. *Myth and Literature in the American Renaissance.* Bloomington: Indiana University Press, 1978.

Ricks, Christopher. *Milton's Grand Style.* Oxford: Oxford University Press, 1963.

Roberts, J. Russell. "Emerson's Debt to the Seventeenth Century." *American Literature* 21 (1949): 298–310.

Robinson, David. *Apostle of Culture: Emerson as Preacher and Lecturer.* Philadelphia: University of Pennsylvania Press, 1982.

———. "Jones Very, the Transcendentalists, and the Unitarian Tradition." *Harvard Theological Review* 68 (1975): 103–24.

Rusk, Ralph L. *The Life of Ralph Waldo Emerson.* New York: Scribner's, 1949.

Sattelmeyer, Robert. *Thoreau's Reading: A Study in Intellectual History.* Princeton, N.J.: Princeton University Press, 1988.

Sayre, Robert F. *Thoreau and the American Indians.* Princeton, N.J.: Princeton University Press, 1977.

Schochet, Gordon J. *Patriarchalism in Political Thought: The Authoritarian Family and Political Speculation and Attitudes Especially in Seventeenth-Century England.* New York: Basic Books, 1975.

"Scraps from a Correspondent." *The Monthly Anthology and Boston Review* 1 (1803): 59–62.

Sensabaugh, George F. *Milton in Early America.* Princeton, N.J.: Princeton University Press, 1964.

Shaw, W. S. "Silva, No. 29." *The Monthly Anthology and Boston Review* 4 (1807): 368–73.

Shawcross, John T. *John Milton and Influence: Presence in Literature, History, and Culture.* Pittsburgh, Pa.: Duquesne University Press, 1991.

Silverman, Kenneth. *A Cultural History of the American Revolution: Painting, Music, Literature, and the Theatre in the Colonies and the United States from the Treaty of Paris to the Inauguration of George Washington, 1763–1789.* New York: Crowell, 1976.

———. *The Life and Times of Cotton Mather.* New York: Harper and Row, 1984.

Simpson, Lewis P., ed. *The Federalist Literary Mind: Selections from the "Monthly Anthology and Boston Review," 1803–1811, Including Documents Relating to the Boston Athenaeum.* Baton Rouge: Louisiana State University Press, 1962.

Smith, Barbara Herrnstein. "Contingencies of Value." In *Canons,* edited by Robert von Hallberg, 5–39. Chicago: University of Chicago Press, 1984.

Spiller, Robert E. "A Case for W. E. Channing." *The New England Quarterly* 3 (1930): 55–81.

Stavely, Keith W. F. *Puritan Legacies: "Paradise Lost" and the New England Tradition, 1630–1890.* Ithaca, N.Y.: Cornell University Press, 1987.

———. "'The World All before Them': Milton and the Rising Glory of America." In *Studies in Eighteenth-Century Culture,* edited by Leslie Ellen Brown and Patricia B. Craddock, 20:147–64. East Lansing, Mich.: Colleagues Press, 1990.

Stoller, Leo. *After Walden.* Stanford, Cal.: Stanford University Press, 1957.

Stone, T. T. "Man in the Ages." *Dial* 1 (1841): 273–89.

Stout, Harry S. *The New England Soul: Preaching and Religious Culture in Colonial New England.* New York: Oxford University Press, 1986.

Tanner, Laura E., and James N. Krasner. "Exposing the 'Sacred Juggle': Revolutionary Rhetoric in Robert Rogers' *Ponteach.*" *Early American Literature* 24 (1989): 4–18.

Tanselle, G. Thomas. *Royall Tyler.* Cambridge, Mass.: Harvard University Press, 1967.

Tawney, R. H. *Religion and the Rise of Capitalism: A Historical Study.* 1926. Reprint. Gloucester, Mass.: Peter Smith, 1962.

Thoreau, Henry David. *Cape Cod.* Edited by Joseph J. Moldenhauer. *The Writings of Henry D. Thoreau.* Princeton, N.J.: Princeton University Press, 1988.

———. *Early Essays and Miscellanies.* Edited by Joseph J. Moldenhauer, et al. *The Writings of Henry D. Thoreau.* Princeton, N.J.: Princeton University Press, 1975.

———. *Journal.* Gen. ed., John C. Broderick or Robert Sattelmeyer. 3 vols. to date. *The Writings of Henry D. Thoreau.* Princeton, N.J.: Princeton University Press, 1981–.

————. *The Maine Woods.* Edited by Joseph J. Moldenhauer. *The Writings of Henry D. Thoreau.* Princeton, N.J.: Princeton University Press, 1972.

————. *Reform Papers.* Edited by Wendell Glick. *The Writings of Henry D. Thoreau.* Princeton, N.J.: Princeton University Press, 1973.

————. *Translations.* Edited by K. P. Van Anglen. *The Writings of Henry D. Thoreau.* Princeton, N.J.: Princeton University Press, 1986.

————. *Walden.* Ed. J. Lyndon Shanley. *The Writings of Henry D. Thoreau.* Princeton, N.J.: Princeton University Press, 1971.

————. *A Week on the Concord and Merrimack Rivers.* Edited by Carl Hovde, et al. *The Writings of Henry D. Thoreau.* Princeton, N.J.: Princeton University Press, 1980.

Thorpe, James. "The Decline of the Miltonic Tradition." Ph.D. diss., Harvard University, 1941.

"Thoughts on Milton." *United States Literary Gazette* 4 (1826): 278–90.

Tompkins, Jane. *Sensational Designs: The Cultural Work of American Fiction, 1790–1860.* New York: Oxford University Press, 1985.

Van Anglen, K. P. "A Paradise Regained: Thoreau's 'Wild Apples' and the Myth of the American Adam." *ESQ: A Journal of the American Renaissance,* n.s., 27 (1981): 28–37.

Vance, William L. *America's Rome.* 2 vols. New Haven, Conn.: Yale University Press, 1989.

Vaughan, Alden T., and Edward W. Clark, eds. *Puritans among the Indians: Accounts of Captivity and Redemption 1676–1724.* Cambridge, Mass.: Harvard University Press, 1981.

Very, Jones. "1830's Commonplace Book." HUD 836.90. Harvard University Archives.

————. "The Evening Choir." *Dial* 3 (1842): 97–98.

————. "105 Sermons." MH Ms Am 1405.1. Houghton Library, Harvard University.

————. *Poems and Essays, Complete and Revised Edition, With a Biographical Sketch by James Freeman Clarke and a Preface by C. A. Bartol.* Boston: Houghton Mifflin, 1886.

————. "The Practical Application in this Life, by Men as Social and Intellectual Beings, of the Certainty of a Future State." In vol. VI of "The Bowdoin Prize Exhibitions." HU 89.165.121. Harvard University Archives.

————. "Scrapbook 1834." HUD 834.90. Harvard University Archives.

von Frank, Albert J. *The Sacred Game: Provincialism and Frontier Consciousness in American Literature: 1630–1860.* Cambridge, Eng.: Cambridge University Press, 1985.

Warren, Charles A. *A History of the American Bar.* 1911. Reprint. New York: Howard Fertig, 1966.

Weber, Donald. *Rhetoric and History in Revolutionary New England.* New York: Oxford University Press, 1988.

Weber, Max. *The Protestant Ethic and the Spirit of Capitalism.* Translated by Talcott Parsons. 1904–5. English trans. New York: Charles Scribner's Sons, 1930.

Weigel, John A. "The Milton Tradition in the First Half of the Nineteenth Century." Ph.D. diss., Western Reserve University, 1939.

Weinbrot, Howard D. *Augustan Caesar in "Augustan" England: the Decline of a Classical Norm.* Princeton, N.J.: Princeton University Press, 1978.

Weisbuch, Robert. *Atlantic Double-Cross: American Literature and British Influence in the Age of Emerson.* Chicago: University of Chicago Press, 1986.

Weiskel, Thomas. *The Romantic Sublime: Studies in the Structure and Psychology of Transcendence.* Baltimore: Johns Hopkins University Press, 1976.

West, Michael. "Charles Kraitsir's Influence upon Thoreau's Theory of Language," *ESQ: A Journal of the American Renaissance,* n.s., 19 (1973): 262–74.

———. "Scatology and Eschatology: The Heroic Dimensions of Thoreau's Wordplay." *PMLA* 89 (1974): 1043–64.

———. "*Walden*'s Dirty Language: Thoreau and Walter Whiter's Geocentric Etymological Theories." *Harvard Library Bulletin* 22 (1974): 117–28.

Whicher, Stephen E. *Freedom and Fate: An Inner Life of Ralph Waldo Emerson.* Philadelphia: University of Pennsylvania Press, 1953.

Willard, Sidney. "Milton on Christian Doctrine." Review of *A Treatise on Christian Doctrine, compiled from the Holy Scriptures alone,* by John Milton, trans. Charles R. Sumner. *The North American Review* 22 (1826): 364–73.

Williams, Raymond. *Marxism and Literature.* Oxford: Oxford University Press, 1977.

Wills, Gary. *Cincinnatus: George Washington and the Enlightenment.* Garden City, N.Y.: Doubleday, 1984.

———. *Inventing America: Jefferson's Declaration of Independence.* Garden City, N.Y.: Doubleday, 1978.

Wilson, John B. "Grimm's Law and the Brahmins." *New England Quarterly* 38 (1965): 234–39.

Winters, Yvor. *In Defense of Reason.* New York: Swallow Press and William Morrow, 1947.

Witherspoon, John. *Lectures on Moral Philosophy and Eloquence.* Philadelphia: William W. Woodward, 1810.

Wittreich, J. A., Jr., ed. *The Romantics on Milton: Formal Essays and Critical Asides.* Cleveland, Ohio: Case Western Reserve University Press, 1970.

Wolf, Bryan Jay. *Romantic Re-Vision: Culture and Consciousness in Nineteenth-Century American Painting and Literature.* Chicago: University of Chicago Press, 1982.

Wood, Gordon S. *The Creation of the American Republic, 1776–1787.* Chapel Hill: University of North Carolina Press, 1969.

———. "Rhetoric and Reality in the American Revolution." *William and Mary Quarterly,* ser. 3, 23 (1966): 3–32.

———. *The Rising Glory of America, 1760–1820.* New York: George Braziller, 1971.

Wordsworth, William. *Poetical Works.* Edited by Thomas Hutchinson. Revised by Ernest de Selincourt. Oxford: Oxford University Press, 1936.

Wright, Conrad. *The Beginnings of Unitarianism in America.* Boston: Starr King Press, 1955.

———. *The Liberal Christians: Essays on American Unitarian History.* Boston: Beacon, 1970.

Wynkoop, William M. *Three Children of the Universe: Emerson's View of Shakespeare, Bacon, and Milton.* The Hague: Mouton, 1966.

Youngs, J. William T., Jr. *God's Messengers: Religious Leadership in Colonial New England, 1700–1750.* Baltimore: Johns Hopkins University Press, 1976.

Zimmerman, Lester F. "Some Aspects of Milton's American Reputation to 1900." Ph.D. diss., University of Wisconsin, 1950.

INDEX

Hawthorne, Nathaniel, 57, 57n19, 76, 230; "The Grey Champion," 76; reception of Milton, vii, 230
Hazlitt, William, 88; "On Shakspeare and Milton," 95, 95n17–18, 96
Hedge, Frederic Henry, 75, 137, 182, 182n37; "The Art of Life—The Scholar's Calling," 182. *See also* Transcendental Club
hegemony, ix–xi
Herbert, George, 153
heroism, 66–68, 162–68
Hesiod, 143
Hesperides, 211
historicism, new, ix–xii
Holmes, Oliver Wendell, 183n38
Holyoke, Edward, 34
Homer, 39n75, 140, 143, 151, 153, 164–66, 171n20, 186, 199
Hood, Edwin Paxton, 69
Hooksett, New Hampshire, 202
Hopkins, Samuel, 26–27
Horace, 201, 205; *Ars Poetica*, 111
Howard of Effingham, Charles, Lord [1st Earl of Nottingham], 162
Hugo, Victor, 141
Hume, David, 29, 62, 128
Hutcheson, Francis, 26, 88
Hutchinson, Anne, 4, 16, 16n33, 138, 144, 199. *See also* Antinomian crisis
Hutchinson, Thomas, 32, 51
hypostatic union, 24, 44, 146

Iago, 168
idealism, philosophical, 91n15, 154–55, 162n9, 208, 222–23, 225–27
ideology, ix–xi, xin8, xiii, 15
imagination. *See* mind, philosophy of
immigration, Irish, 78
Incarnation, the, 24, 42–44
Independence, American. *See* Revolution, American
Independence, Declaration of, 30
Indians, American, 199–201, 204–5, 207, 211
Indian captivity narrative, 204. *See also* individual authors
influence, literary, viii
inspiration. *See* mind, philosophy of
Isis and Osiris myth, 182–84

Ivimey, Joseph, 69, 74; *John Milton: His Life and Times*, 110, 110n5, 118n13

jacobinism, American, 37–40, 49, 51, 66n36, 68, 146, 158
Jefferson, Thomas, 41, 51–52; reception of Milton, 52, 53n12
Jenks, Francis, *A Selection from the English Prose Works of John Milton*, 110, 117n11
jeremiad, 30, 174
John the Evangelist, Saint, *Book of Revelation*, 147
Johnson, Samuel, 44, 45n4, 101, 128, 136, 195; *Life of Milton*, 70, 101–3, 109; *Lives of the English Poets*, 190n2
Judaism, 117

Kames, Henry Home, Lord, 62, 88
Kepler, Johannes, 157
"kinds, the literary," 49n9
King, Edward, 200–201. *See also* Milton, John, "Lycidas"
King Philip's War, 6
Kraitsir, Charles, 212–13
Ktaadn, Mount, 217–23

Lafayette, Marie Joseph, Marquis de, 141
Lake poets, 57, 88, 89n13. *See also* individual authors
Landor, Walter Savage, 160
language, philosophy of, 37–38, 141–42, 199–201, 207, 212–16
latitudinarianism, 13
Laud, Archbishop William, 8, 116
Laudianism, 16, 117. *See also* Anglicanism
law, as a career, 12n26, 35, 35n69
Legaré, Hugh Swinton, 71n46
Levelers, 2, 14, 76
liberty, 29–40, 43, 45–46, 70–71, 97, 101, 179, 194, 199, 223–24, 224n33; civil, 29, 71–79, 97–103, 123–24, 132–37, 156–61; religious, 29, 46, 73–79, 97–108, 116–17, 130–37, 145–49, 156–61, 174, 183–84
Lincoln, Abraham, 174
Lincolnshire, 3
Linn, John Blair, 41
literary relations, Anglo-American, 57, 57n20
literature: as a means of influence, 34–35, 35n69, 36–39, 39n75, 40; popular, 57,